Using the *Teach Yourself in 24 Hours* Series

Welcome to the *Teach Yourself in 24 Hours* series! You're probably thinking, "What, they want me to stay up all night and learn this stuff?" Well, no, not exactly. This series introduces a new way to teach you about exciting new products: 24 one-hour lessons, designed to keep your interest and keep you learning. Because the learning process is broken into small units, you will not be overwhelmed by the complexity of some of the new technologies that are emerging in today's market. Each hourly lesson has a number of special items, some old, some new, to help you along.

Minutes

The first 10 minutes of each hour lists the topics and skills that you will learn about by the time you finish the hour. You will know exactly what the hour will bring with no surprises.

Minutes

Twenty minutes into the lesson, you will have been introduced to many of the newest features of the software application. In the constantly evolving computer arena, knowing everything a program can do will aid you enormously now and in the future.

Minutes

Before 30 minutes have passed, you will have learned at least one useful task. Many of these tasks take advantage of the newest features of the application. These tasks use a hands-on approach, telling you exactly which menus and commands you need to use to accomplish the goal. This approach is found in each lesson of the *24 Hours* series.

40 Minutes

You will see after 40 minutes that many of the tools you have come to expect from the *Teach Yourself* series are found in the *24 Hours* series as well. Notes and Tips offer special tricks of the trade to make your work faster and more productive. Warnings help you avoid those nasty time-consuming errors.

50 Minutes

By the time you're 50 minutes in, you'll probably run across terms you haven't seen before. Never before has technology thrown so many new words and acronyms into the language, and the New Terms elements found in this series will carefully explain each and every one of them.

60 Minutes

At the end of the hour, you may still have questions that need answered. You know the kind—questions on skills or tasks that come up every day for you, but that weren't directly addressed during the lesson. That's where the Q&A section can help. By answering the most frequently asked questions about the topics discussed in the hour, Q&A not only answers your specific question, it provides a succinct review of all that you have learned in the hour.

How to Use This Book

This book offers 24 separate hours devoted to specific topics. You should read them in order, picking the time frame you prefer best—one hour a day, a few hours each week, or one continuous 24-hour caffeine-quaffing, set-that-carpal-tunnel-nerve-ablaze frenzy.

Special Highlighted Elements

JUST A MINUTE

If something needs a little extra attention, the 24-hour clock stops for a bit, and that something is described here.

COFFEE BREAK

When there's a bit of information that has absolutely no bearing on the task at hand, you can take a short break from more serious matters and find out about it in these sections.

Q&A, Quiz, and Activities

Each hour ends with a brief Q&A section covering some questions you might want to ask. After that, there's a three-question quiz you can take and a few suggested activities for you to expand your knowledge of the material covered.

This Book's Web Site

Thanks to the World Wide Web, it's possible to supplement the material offered in the book with a Web site. Author Rogers Cadenhead maintains one at the following address:

http://www.prefect.com/java24

You also can contact the author at any time by sending e-mail to rogers@prefect.com. Feel free to drop him a line with any questions, comments, criticisms, or error reports, and be sure to let him know if you share his opinion that the Texas Rangers need a left-handed power hitter who can reach the short porch in right field.

Teach
Yourself
JAVA™ 1.1
PROGRAMMING

in 24 Hours

Teach Yourself
JAVA™ 1.1
PROGRAMMING
in 24 Hours

Rogers Cadenhead

201 West 103rd Street
Indianapolis, Indiana 46290

International Standard Book Number: 1-57521-270-6

Library of Congress Catalog Card Number: 96-72266

2000   99   98   97   4   3   2   1

Interpretation of the printing code: the rightmost double-digit number is the year of the book's printing; the rightmost single-digit, the number of the book's printing. For example, a printing code of 97-1 shows that the first printing of the book occurred in 1997.

Composed in AGaramond and MCPdigital by Macmillan Computer Publishing

Printed in the United States of America

Publisher and President   Richard K. Swadley
Publishing Manager   Mark Taber
Acquisitions Manager   Beverly M. Eppink
Director of Editorial Services   Cindy Morrow
Director of Marketing   Kelli S. Spencer
Assistant Marketing Managers   Kristina Perry, Rachel Wolfe

Acquisitions Editor
David B. Mayhew

Development Editor
Scott D. Meyers

Software Development Specialist
Bob Correll

Production and Copy Editor
Heather Stith

Indexer
Erika Millen

Technical Reviewer
Brad Seifert

Editorial Coordinator
Katie Wise

Technical Edit Coordinator
Lorraine Schaffer

Resource Coordinator
Deborah Frisby

Editorial Assistants
Carol Ackerman
Andi Richter
Rhonda Tinch-Mize

Cover Designer
Tim Amrhein

Book Designer
Gary Adair

Copy Writer
David Reichwein

Production Team Supervisors
Brad Chinn
Charlotte Clapp

Production
Michael Dietsch
Mike Henry
Mark Matthews
Gene Redding

Overview

Contents

Dedication

To my siblings, Chad "Co-Chillin Bug" Cadenhead and Kelly "Home Sweet Home Girl" Cadenhead, from their older brother "Pa-T Melt." It's a shame we're the only ones who address each other by our secret rap names.

Rogers

Acknowledgments

To the folks at Sams.net—especially David Mayhew, Mark Taber, Deborah Frisby, Scott Meyers, Heather Stith, Bob Correll, Brad Seifert, and Lorraine Schaffer. Their work made a great contribution to the book, and I have deep admiration for them (to the extent that such feelings do not create an uncomfortable workplace under the federal guidelines regarding sexual harassment).

To my agent, Brian Gill, who talked me out of quitting two hours early and renaming this book *Teach Yourself Java 1.1 Programming in Two Contiguous 11-Hour Time Periods*.

To my wife, M.C., and my son, Max. You make me feel like the protagonist of a Frank Capra movie after all the obstacles have been overcome, the end credits are about to roll, and several of our first-generation immigrant neighbors are expressing their happiness through song.

About the Author

Rogers Cadenhead (rogers@prefect.com) is a writer, computer programmer, and Web developer whose inner child is a knuckleball pitcher with the worst walk-to-strikeout ratio in the American League. He previously co-authored *Teach Yourself SunSoft Java WorkShop in 21 Days* for Sams.net and contributed to *Java Unleashed 2nd Edition*, *Laura Lemay's Web Workshop: ActiveX and VBScript*, and *Developing Intranet Applications with Java*. He also writes a question-and-answer trivia column for the *Fort Worth Star-Telegram* and *New York Times News Syndicate*. He lives in North Texas and occasionally harbors members of the Dallas Cowboys when they need to dodge a subpoena. Visit his home page at http://www.prefect.com/rogers.

Tell Us What You Think!

As a reader, you are the most important critic and commentator of our books. We value your opinion and want to know what we're doing right, what we could do better, what areas you'd like to see us publish in, and any other words of wisdom you're willing to pass our way. You can help us make strong books that meet your needs and give you the computer guidance you require.

Do you have access to CompuServe or the World Wide Web? Then check out our CompuServe forum by typing GO SAMS at any prompt. If you prefer the World Wide Web, check out our site at http://www.mcp.com.

JUST A MINUTE

> If you have a technical question about this book, call the technical support line at 317-581-3833.

As the publishing manager of the group that created this book, I welcome your comments. You can fax, e-mail, or write me directly to let me know what you did or didn't like about this book—as well as what we can do to make our books stronger. Here's the information:

FAX: 317-581-4669

E-mail: newtech_mgr@sams.samspublishing.com

Mail: Mark Taber
          Publishing Manager
          Sams.net Publishing
          201 W. 103rd Street
          Indianapolis, IN 46290

Introduction

Computer programming is not as hard as people think.

It might not be a good idea to give up one of this book's secrets so quickly, especially when you might be reading this section at a bookstore. You could memorize this knowledge and put *Teach Yourself Java 1.1 Programming in 24 Hours* back on the shelf.

However, you'll figure out how easy programming can be as you spend a few hours with this book. Anyone can learn how to write computer programs—even if they can't program a VCR—and the Java language is a great way to do it. This book is aimed at non-programmers, new programmers who hated learning it, and experienced programmers who want to quickly get up to speed with Java. It uses Java 1.1, so you'll be learning the most up-to-date way to create programs with the language.

Java is the most exciting programming language that has been released in a decade because of the things it makes possible. You can add animation to a World Wide Web page, write games and useful utilities, create programs that sport a graphical user interface, and design software that makes the most of the Internet.

This book teaches Java programming from the grounds up. It introduces the concepts in English instead of jargon, with plenty of step-by-step examples of working programs you can create. Spend some time with this book—24 hours, say—and you'll be writing your own Java programs, confident in your ability to use the language and learn more about it. You also will have experience with skills that are becoming increasingly important, such as network computing, graphical user interface design, and object-oriented programming.

These terms might not mean much to you now. In fact, they're probably just the kind of things that make programming seem like a secret ritual known only to a small group of humans with a language of their own and a unique approach to wellness. However, if you can use a computer to create an attractive resume, balance your checkbook, or create a home page, you can write computer programs by reading *Teach Yourself Java 1.1 Programming in 24 Hours*.

JUST A MINUTE

> If you do put this book down at the store without buying it, please reshelve it with the front cover facing outward on an endcap with access to a lot of the store's foot traffic.

PART

I

Getting Started

Hour

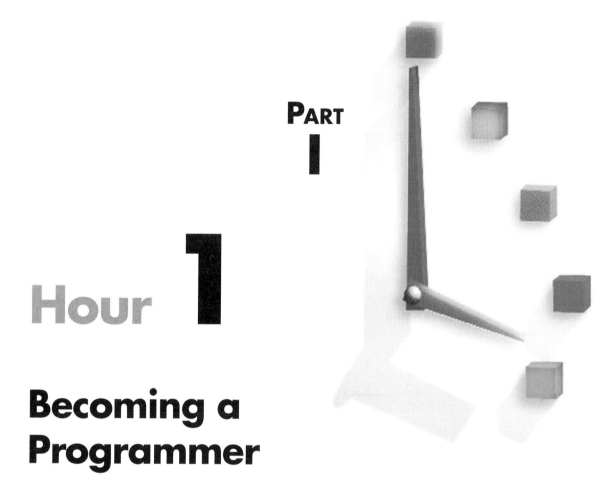

Hour 1

Becoming a Programmer

Computer programming is insanely difficult. It requires a four-year degree in computer science, thousands of dollars in computer hardware and software, a keen analytical intellect, the patience of Job, and a strong liking for caffeinated drinks. If you're a programming novice, this is probably what you've heard about computer programming. Aside from the part about caffeine, all of the rumors are greatly exaggerated.

Programming is a lot easier than most people think. There are several reasons why you might believe otherwise:

☐ Computer programmers have been telling people for years that programming is hard. This belief makes it easier for us to find high-paying jobs (or so I've heard) and gives us more leeway to goof off during business hours.

☐ Computer programming manuals are often written in a language that only a Scrabble player could appreciate. Strange acronyms like OOP, RAD, COM, and MUMPS are used frequently along with newly invented jargon like instantiation, bytecode, and makefile.

☐ Many computer programming languages have been available only with software packages costing $200 or more, which is a lot of cabbage.

Because of the growth of the Internet and other factors, this is a great time to learn programming. Useful programming tools are being made available at low cost (or no cost), often as downloads from World Wide Web sites. The goal of this book is to teach programming to the person who has never tried to program before or the person who tried programming but hated it with an intense passion. The English language will be used as much as possible instead of jargon and obscure acronyms, and all new programming terms will be thoroughly explained as they are introduced.

If I've succeeded, you will finish *Teach Yourself Java 1.1 Programming in 24 Hours* with enough programming skill to be a danger to yourself and others. You'll be able to write programs, dive into other programming books with more confidence, and learn programming languages more easily. You also will have developed skills with Java, the most exciting programming language to be introduced in a decade.

The first hour of this book provides some introductory material about programming and gives you instructions on how to set up your computer so you can write Java programs. The following topics will be covered:

☐ Choosing which programming language to learn first

☐ What Java is

☐ Using programs to boss your computer around

☐ How programs work

☐ How program errors called bugs are fixed

☐ Acquiring the free Java Developer's Kit

☐ Installing the Kit

☐ Getting ready to write programs

Choosing a Language

As you might have surmised at this point, computer programming is not as hard as it's cracked up to be. If you're comfortable enough with a computer to create a nice-looking resume, balance a checkbook with software such as Intuit Quicken, or create your own home page on the Web, you can write programs.

The key to learning how to program is to start with the right language. The programming language that you choose to use often depends on the tasks you want the computer to accomplish. Each language has things that it is well-suited for and things that are difficult, or perhaps impossible, to do with the language. For example, many people use some form of the BASIC language when they are learning how to program because BASIC is good for learning how to write programs.

JUST A MINUTE

> The BASIC language was invented in the '60s to be easy for students and beginners to learn (the B in BASIC stands for *Beginner's*). The downside to using some form of BASIC is that it's easy to fall into some sloppy programming habits with the language. Those habits can make it much more difficult to write complex programs and improve them later on.

Microsoft Visual Basic combines the ease of BASIC with some powerful features to aid in the design of Windows software. (VBScript, which is short for Visual Basic Script, offers the simplicity of BASIC for small programs that run in conjunction with World Wide Web pages.) Visual Basic has been used to write thousands of sophisticated programs for commercial, business, and personal use. However, Visual Basic programs can be slower than Windows programs written in other languages such as Borland C++. This difference is especially noticeable in programs that use a lot of graphics—games, screen savers, and the like. Because of that, game programmers and other multimedia developers don't use Visual Basic to create graphical programs such as Doom.

This book uses the Java programming language. Though Java is more difficult to learn than a language such as Visual Basic, it is a good starting place for several reasons. One of the biggest advantages of learning Java is that you can use it on the World Wide Web. If you're an experienced Web surfer, you have seen numerous Java programs in action. They can be used to create animated graphics, present text in new ways, play games, and help in other interactive efforts.

Another important advantage is that Java requires an organized approach in order for programs to work. The language is very particular about the way that programs must be written, and it balks if programmers do not follow all of its rules. When you start writing Java programs, you might not see the language's choosy behavior as an advantage. You'll write a program and will have several errors to fix before the program will be finished. Some of your fixes might not be correct, and they will have to be redone. If you don't structure a program correctly as you are writing it, other errors will result. In the coming hours, you'll learn about these rules and the pitfalls to avoid. The positive side of this extra effort is that your programs will be more reliable, useful, and error-free.

Java was invented by Sun Microsystems developer James Gosling as a better way to create computer programs. Gosling was unhappy with the way that the C++ programming language was working on a project he was doing, so he created a new language that did the job better. It's a matter of contentious debate whether Java is superior to other programming languages, of course, but the amount of attention paid to the language today shows that it has a large number of adherents. Book publishers obviously dig it—more than 89 books have been published about the language since its introduction. (This is my second book about Java. *Teach Yourself SunSoft Java WorkShop in 21 Days* was the first, and I will write more of them until prohibited from doing so by municipal, state, or federal law.) Regardless of whether Java is the best language, it definitely is a great language to learn today. There are numerous resources for Java programmers on the Web, Java job openings are increasing, and the language has become a major part of the Internet's future. You'll get a chance to try out Java during Hour 2, "Writing Your First Program."

Learning Java or any other programming language makes it much easier to learn other languages. Many languages are similar to each other, so you won't be starting from scratch when you dive into a new one. For instance, many C++ programmers find it fairly easy to learn Java because Java borrows a lot of its structure and ideas from C++. Many programmers are comfortable using several different languages and learn new ones as needed.

Just a Minute

C++ has been mentioned several times in this hour, and you might be tripping over the term wondering what it means and, more importantly, how it's pronounced. C++ is pronounced *C-plus-plus*, and it's a programming language that was developed by Bjarne Stroustrop and others at Bell Laboratories. C++ is an enhancement of the C programming language, hence the *plus-plus* part of the name. Why not just C+, then? The *plus-plus* part is a computer programming joke you'll understand later on.

Telling the Computer What to Do

A computer program, also called *software*, is a way to tell a computer what to do. Everything that the computer does, from booting up to shutting down, is done by a program. Windows 95 is a program. Ms. Pac-Man is a program. The dir command used in MS-DOS to display file names also is a program. Even the Michaelangelo virus is a program.

If you're a science fiction fan, you're probably familiar with the concept of household robots. If not, you might be familiar with the concept of henpecked spouses. In either case, someone

gives very specific instructions telling the robot or spouse what to do, something like the following:

> Dear Theobald,
>
> Please take care of these errands for me while I'm out lobbying members of Congress:
>
> Item 1: Vacuum the living room.
>
> Item 2: Go to the store.
>
> Item 3: Pick up butter, lozenges, and as many SnackWells Devil's Food Cakes as you can carry.
>
> Item 4: Return home.
>
> Love,
>
> Snookie Lumps

If you tell a loved one or artificially intelligent robot what to do, there's a certain amount of leeway in how your requests are fulfilled. If lozenges aren't available, cough medicine might be brought to you instead. Also, the trip to the store can be accomplished through a variety of routes. Computers don't do leeway. They follow instructions literally. The programs that you write will be followed precisely, one statement at a time.

The following is one of the simplest examples of a computer program, written in BASIC. Take a look at it, but don't worry yet about what each line is supposed to mean:

```
1 PRINT "Shall we play a game?"
2 INPUT A$
```

Translated into English, this program is equivalent to giving a computer the following to-do list:

> Dear personal computer,
>
> Item 1: Display the question, "Shall we play a game?"
>
> Item 2: Give the user a chance to answer the question.
>
> Love,
>
> Snookie Lumps

Each of the lines in the computer program is a *statement*. A computer handles each statement in a program in a specific order, in the same way that a cook follows a recipe or Theobald the robot followed the orders of Snookie Lumps when he vacuumed and shopped at the market. In BASIC, the line numbers are used to put the statements in the correct order. Other languages, such as Java, do not use line numbers, favoring different ways to tell the computer how to run a program.

Figure 1.1 shows the sample BASIC program running on the Bywater BASIC interpreter, which is available for free in several shareware file repositories on the World Wide Web and can run on any DOS or UNIX platform. Bywater BASIC is among many free BASIC interpreters that can be found on the Internet for Microsoft Windows, Apple Macintosh, UNIX, and Linux systems.

Figure 1.1.

An example of a BASIC program running on the Bywater BASIC shell and interpreter developed by Ted A. Campbell.

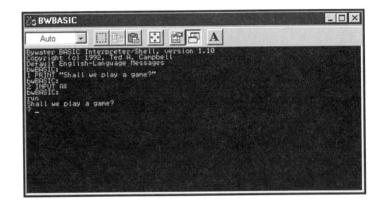

JUST A MINUTE

The quote "Shall we play a game?" is from the 1983 movie *WarGames*, in which a young computer programmer (Matthew Broderick) saves mankind after nearly causing global thermonuclear war. You'll learn how to do that in the next book of this series, *Teach Yourself to Create International Incidents with Java in 24 Hours*.

Because of the way programs operate, it's hard to blame the computer when something goes wrong while your program runs. After all, the computer was just doing exactly what you told it to do. Unless your hardware is on the fritz or a pesky virus is attacking your system, both rare occurrences, the blame for program errors lies with the programmer. That's the bad news. The good news is that you can't do any permanent harm to your computer with the programming errors you make. No one was harmed during the making of this book, and no computers will be injured as you learn how to program with Java.

How Programs Work

Most computer programs are written in the same way that you write a letter—by typing each statement into a word processor. Some programming tools come with their own word processor, and others can be used with any text-editing software. You can use the Java Developer's Kit, which you will learn about later in this hour, with any of your favorite editors.

When you have finished writing a computer program, you save the file just as you would save any other document to disk. Computer programs often have their own file extension to indicate what type of file they are. Java programs have the extension .java; an example of a Java program file name is Calculator.java.

JUST A MINUTE

> If you use a fancy word processing program that has features such as boldfaced text, different font sizes, and other stylistic touches, do not use those features while writing a computer program. Programs should be prepared as text files with no special formatting. For example, when using Microsoft Word to write a program, save the file in Text Only mode instead of saving it as a Word document. Notepad, a word processor that comes with Windows, saves all files as unformatted text.

To run a program, you need some help. The kind of help that's needed depends on the programming language you're using. Some languages require an *interpreter* to run their programs. The interpreter is a program that interprets each line of a computer program and tells the computer what to do. Most versions of BASIC are interpreted languages. The advantage of interpreted languages is that they are faster to test. When you are writing a BASIC program, you can try it out immediately, spot any errors, fix them, and try again. The primary disadvantage is that interpreted languages run more slowly than other programs.

Other programming languages require a *compiler*. The compiler takes a computer program and translates it into a form that the computer can understand. It also does what it can to make the program run as efficiently as possible. The compiled program can be run directly, without the need for an interpreter. Compiled programs run more quickly than interpreted programs, but they take more time to test. You have to write your program and compile it before trying it out. If you find an error and fix it, you must compile the program again to verify that the error is gone.

Java is unusual because it requires a compiler and an interpreter. You'll learn more about this later as you write Java programs.

How Programs Don't Work

Many new programmers become discouraged when they start to test their programs. Errors appear everywhere. Some of these are *syntax errors*, which are identified by the computer as it looks at the program and becomes confused by what you wrote. Other errors are *logic errors*, which are only noticed by the programmer as the program is being tested, if they are noticed at all. Logic errors sneak by the computer unnoticed, but they will cause it to do something unintended.

As you start to write your own programs, expect to encounter errors. They're a natural part of the process. Programming errors are called *bugs*, a term that dates back a century or more to describe errors in technical devices. The process of fixing errors has its own term also—*debugging*. Whether you want to or not, you'll get a lot of debugging experience as you learn how to write computer programs.

Next Stop: Java

Before you can start writing Java programs, you need to acquire and set up some kind of Java programming software. Although several different products are available for the development of Java programs, including many terrific ones that make programming much easier, the starting place for most new Java programmers is the Java Developer's Kit. All of the examples in this book use the Kit, and you are encouraged to forsake all other Java programming tools as you go through the remaining 23 hours of tutelage. The material will make more sense to programmers using the Kit, and using the Kit builds experience that will be beneficial no matter which development software you use later on.

The Java Developer's Kit (also referred to as the JDK) is in version 1.1 as of this writing. It is a set of tools that enable you to write and test Java programs. Users of Microsoft Windows systems may be dismayed to learn that the Kit is not graphical. You run programs from a command line (the familiar `C:\>` prompt on Windows systems) instead of using a mouse and a point-and-click environment. Figure 1.2 shows the Kit in use in an MS-DOS window on a Windows 95 system. The Java program `PlayGame.java` is compiled, and then it is run.

CAUTION

> The examples of this book were prepared on a Microsoft Windows system, and some references in the text are specific to Windows users. However, all of the material is intended for users of the Java Developer's Kit on any of the platforms it is currently available for, and all of the tutorials will work regardless of the system you're using.

At the time of this writing, the Java Developer's Kit is available directly from JavaSoft for the following systems:

☐ Microsoft Windows NT or Windows 95 systems

☐ SPARC Solaris systems with version 2.3 or later

☐ Intel x86 Solaris systems

According to JavaSoft, the Apple Macintosh version of the Kit also should be available by the time this book is published.

Figure 1.2.

A program being compiled and run with the Java Developer's Kit version 1.1.

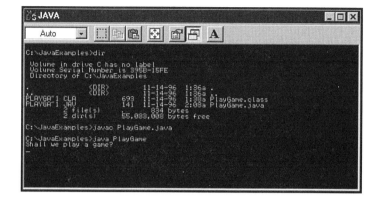

The Windows 95/NT version of the Kit is provided in two versions. One version is listed as an EXE file, which means that you can install it by clicking on the file's icon when you download it. This version is the easiest to set up.

The World Wide Web page to download versions of the Kit is the following:

```
http://www.javasoft.com/products/JDK/1.1/
```

Although JavaSoft has not announced plans to make version 1.1 of the Kit available for other systems, other companies can create their own implementations of Java development tools. Details about these tools will be listed in the Frequently Asked Questions section of the JavaSoft site. Visit the following Web page:

```
http://www.javasoft.com/nav/read/faqindex.html
```

If your system can handle the Java Developer's Kit, download it from the Web and save it on your system in a newly created directory called jdk11 or something similar. The file is several megabytes in size, so you'll have time during the download to make coffee, knit an afghan, or gnaw your foot off to escape any bear traps it might be caught in.

TIME SAVER

Although the JavaSoft Web site always will have the most current edition of Java Developer's Kit 1.1, you can find the a version of the Kit on the CD-ROM that accompanies this book. Go to the Java subdirectory of the CD and choose the folder for your system: Win95NT, SparcSol, or IntelSol. This version of the Kit will work with all sample programs in the book. Copy this installation file from the CD to your hard drive.

Workshop: Installing the JDK

After the Java Developer's Kit has been downloaded or copied to your hard drive, you can install the software. The Windows 95 or Windows NT version provides the easiest means of setting up the Kit because you can start the installation process by double-clicking on the downloaded file's name or icon. This action will install the Kit in a subdirectory of the current directory, so make sure the file is in the place you want before beginning the installation. If you put the downloaded file into the `jdk11` directory, a subdirectory called `java` will be created with the Java Developer's Kit and related files.

Other versions of the Kit are packed as an archive file that has been compressed to reduce its size. These versions will have a file extension such as `.zip`, `.z`, or `.tar` in the name. To use these, you must use decompressing software such as WinZip, `untar`, `gzip`, or PKZip.

JUST A MINUTE

> If you don't own any software that can handle archive files, you can find programs for all common archive types on the Web. Windows, DOS, and OS/2 users can find some of these programs at the Coast to Coast Web site (`http://www.coast.net/SimTel/`). The CNET Web site at `http://www.shareware.com` offers access to file collections for all popular operating systems. Both of these sites are searchable, so you can type text such as **unzip** or **untar** and find several programs that handle these archive formats.

The Kit comes with any special installation instructions that are needed and also includes a Web page that links directly to help pages on Sun's Java site. If you need more help on the installation of the Java Developer's Kit, visit the following page:

`http://www.javasoft.com/products/JDK/1.1/`

Several different programs come with the Kit; the main ones you will use are the following:

- The compiler, `javac`, takes a Java program's file and translates it into a form that the computer knows how to run.
- The interpreter, `java`, runs programs that are created by the compiler.
- The Java Web browsing tool, `appletviewer`, enables you to run Java programs that are designed to run on the Web.

Two of these programs are being used in Figure 1.2. Look at the `C:\JavaExamples>` command prompts to see `javac` and `java` commands being typed in to compile and run the `PlayGame` program.

1

JUST A MINUTE

Windows systems require two additions to the `AUTOEXEC.BAT` file in order to use the Java Developer's Kit. You have to tell your system where to find the Kit's programs and where to find a file called `classes.zip`.

If you installed the kit in the `c:\jdk11\java` directory, add the following to your `PATH` statement in the `AUTOEXEC.BAT` file:

`c:\jdk11\java\bin`

Also, add a line to `AUTOEXEC.BAT` after the `PATH` line:

`SET CLASSPATH=.;c:\jdk11\java\lib\classes.zip`

When you're done, your `AUTOEXEC.BAT` file should include something like the following:

```
PATH=c:\windows;c:\windows\command;c:\jdk11\java\bin
SET CLASSPATH=.;c:\jdk11\java\lib\classes.zip
```

Official Documentation

In addition to the Developer's Kit, JavaSoft offers documentation for the Java language in Web page format. You don't need this information to use this book because each topic is discussed fully as it is introduced, but these pages will come in handy when you write your own programs.

You can download the entire documentation, but it might be more convenient to browse it as needed from JavaSoft's Web site. The most up-to-date Java documentation is available from the following address:

```
http://www.javasoft.com/products/JDK/1.1/docs/index.html
```

Summary

During this hour, you were introduced to the concept of programming a computer—giving it a set of instructions that tell it what to do. You also downloaded and installed the Java Developer's Kit that will be used as you write sample programs throughout the book.

If you are still confused about programs, programming languages, or Java in general, that's understandable at this point. Everything will make more sense to you in the next hour, "Writing Your First Program," which takes a slow trip through the process of creating a Java program.

Q&A

Q **What does the Internet have to do with making it easier to learn programming?**

A Because of the dramatic growth of the World Wide Web, companies such as Microsoft, Netscape, and Sun Microsystems are trying to attract as many programmers as possible to their languages and related technology. To do this, they are offering many programming tools for free over the Web, such as the Java Developer's Kit and the beta release of the Microsoft Visual Basic 5 Control Creation Edition. They are offering others, such as SunSoft Java WorkShop for free 30- or 90-day trial periods. There also are numerous free products distributed over the Internet for programmers. To find out where these products are, visit Yahoo! at `http://www.yahoo.com` and search for a language you're interested in. It's much cheaper today to learn programming than it was five years ago.

Q **What is it about BASIC that makes it easier to fall into bad habits while writing programs in it?**

A One thing you'll learn as you start writing Java programs is that you have to be organized. If you don't structure your program in the correct way, it won't work. BASIC doesn't have this kind of requirement. You can write in a disorganized manner and still get the program to work successfully. Later on, however, you'll have a much harder time figuring out the program if you try to fix a bug or add an improvement.

Q **BASIC? C++? Java? What are the names of these languages supposed to mean?**

A Like many programming languages, BASIC is an acronym that describes what it is: Beginner's All Symbolic Instruction Code. C++ is a programming language that was created to be an improvement on the C language, which itself was an improvement of the B programming language. Java goes against the tradition of naming a language with an acronym or other meaningful term. It's just the name that Java's developers liked the best when brainstorming for possible monikers—beating out WebRunner, Silk, Ruby, and others.

Q **There are 89 books about Java programming?**

A Actually, as of this writing, there are 89 Java-related books now available in English, and another 171 are being prepared for publication. These figures come from a World Wide Web site by Steve Pietrowicz that lists all of the known books and upcoming ones. Visit the following page for details:

`http://lightyear.ncsa.uiuc.edu/~srp/java/javabooks.html`

1

Q Why are interpreted languages slower than compiled ones?

A For the same reason that a person interpreting a live speech is a lot slower than a translator interpreting the printed speech later on. The live interpreter has to think about each statement that's being made as it happens, while the other interpreter can work on the speech as a whole and take some shortcuts to speed up the process. Compiled languages can be much faster than interpreted languages because they can do things to make the program more efficient.

Q Is C++ harder to learn than Java?

A It's a matter of personal opinion, but Java does seem more approachable for beginners than C++. C++ and its predecessor, C, are widely regarded as "programmer's languages," meaning that they were designed for the needs of experienced programmers. There are a lot of features in C and C++ that make them faster—and more powerful—during program creation, but these features often come at the expense of understandability. Java takes a more simplified approach to programming than C++ and is probably a better place to start.

Quiz

Test your knowledge of the material covered in this chapter by answering the following questions.

Questions

1. Which of the following is *not* a reason that people think computer programming is painfully difficult?

    (a) Programmers spread that rumor to improve their employment prospects.

    (b) Jargon and acronyms are all over the place.

    (c) Mind-control waves are sent out by the CIA promoting this belief.

2. What kind of tool runs a computer program by figuring out one line at a time?

    (a) A slow tool

    (b) An interpreter

    (c) A compiler

3. Why did James Gosling hole up in his office and create Java?

    (a) He was unhappy with the language he was using on a project.

    (b) His rock band wasn't getting any gigs.

    (c) When you can't download any image files at work, the World Wide Web is pretty dull.

Answers

1. c. Of course, the CIA could have forced me to say this.

2. b. Compilers figure out the instructions beforehand so the program can run faster.

3. a. The Web was still a little-known idea when Gosling wrote Java.

Activities

If you'd like to better acquaint yourself with Java before you create your first program, do the following activity:

- Visit the JavaSoft site at http://java.sun.com and read some of the introductory articles that are presented in the What is Java? section.

Hour 2

Writing Your First Program

As you learned during Hour 1, "Becoming a Programmer," a computer program is a set of instructions that tell a computer what to do. These instructions are prepared in the same way instructions could be given to a person: You type them into a word processor. However, that's where the similarity ends. Instructions given to a computer must be written using a programming language. Dozens of computer programming languages have been created; you might have heard of some of them, such as BASIC or Pascal.

During this hour, you will create your first Java program by entering it using any word processor you like. When that's done, you will save the program, compile it, and test it out. The following topics will be covered during this hour:

- ☐ Entering a program into a word processor
- ☐ Naming a Java program with the `class` statement
- ☐ Organizing a program with bracket marks
- ☐ Storing information in a variable

☐ Changing the value of a variable

☐ Displaying the information stored in a variable

☐ Saving a program

☐ Compiling a program

☐ Running a program

☐ Fixing errors

☐ Modifying a program

What You Need to Write Programs

As explained in Hour 1, you should have installed the current version of the Java Developer's Kit on your system. The kit contains tools that enable you to compile and test Java programs. You also need a word processor to write programs.

With most programming languages, computer programs are written by entering text into a word processor (also called a *text editor*). Some programming languages, such as Visual C++ from Microsoft, come with their own word processor. SunSoft Java WorkShop, an advanced programming tool from Java's developers, also comes with its own editor.

Java programs are simple text files without any special features such as centered text, boldface text, or other enhancements. They can be written with any word processing program that can create text files. Microsoft Windows systems have several word processors you can use, including Notepad, WordPad, and the DOS program `edit`. Apple Macintosh users can create programs with Simple Text or other editors such as BBEdit Lite. Any of these programs will work fine.

TIME SAVER

Some word-processing programs are available on the CD-ROM that accompanies this book, including BBEdit Lite.

You also can use more sophisticated word processors, such as Microsoft Word, if you remember to save the programs as text. This option has different names depending on the program you are using. In Word, the file should be saved as a file of type Text Only. Other programs call these files DOS text, ASCII text, or something similar.

2

CAUTION

If you're in doubt as to whether a word processor can save files as text files, you can always use one of the simple programs that comes with your operating system. Windows users can use Notepad to create Java programs because text files created with Notepad are always saved as text-only files.

After you have decided which word processor you will use to write Java programs, go ahead and load it so you can start writing a program.

Windows 95 users must take one extra step before saving any Java-related files to disk: The .java file extension must be associated with the selected word processor. To do this, you need to create a new .java file and load it into the word processor you'll be using during this book.

To create the file, open up any file folder on your system and press the right-click button on your mouse. A pop-up menu will appear that will enable you to choose the New ¦ Text Document option. Choose this option and a file named New Text Document.txt will appear. Change the name of this file to Anything.java and confirm that you really want to choose the new name.

If you have never written Java programs on your computer, the .java file extension should not be associated with any programs yet. Double-click the Anything.java file with the left mouse button and a dialog box will appear, enabling you to choose a program for opening the .java file. Choose your preferred word processor, first making sure to click the option Always use this program to open this file.

Creating the `BigDebt` Program

One of the things that computers are best at is math, a task that most humans are happy to pass off to someone else (or something else, in this case). For your first Java program, you will use the computer to determine a depressing fact about the financial condition of the United States. Your program will be called `BigDebt`. The program figures out how much the national debt increases in an average minute. In order to determine this amount, the computer will be told how much the debt increases in an average day.

COFFEE BREAK

The national debt is the amount the United States government has borrowed to compensate for budget deficits over the years. It was approaching $5.25 trillion at last count, which equals $19,700 in indebtedness for each resident of the United States.

The following table shows the debt since 1960:

1960:	$290.2 billion
1965:	$320.9 billion
1970:	$389.2 billion
1975:	$576.6 billion
1980:	$930.2 billion
1985:	$1.946 trillion
1990:	$3.365 trillion
1995:	$4.989 trillion

Ed Hall maintains a Web page with the current national debt, updated continuously. It's available at the following location:

```
http://www.brillig.com/debt_clock/
```

Beginning the Program

Using your word processor, begin your Java programming career by entering each line from Listing 2.1. Don't enter the line number and colon at the beginning of each line—these are used in this book so that specific line numbers can be referred to.

Listing 2.1. The BigDebt program.

```
1: class BigDebt {
2:     public static void main (String[] arguments) {
3:         // My first Java program goes here
4:     }
5: }
```

Make sure to capitalize everything exactly as shown, and use your Tab key or space bar to insert the blank spaces in front of some lines. When you're done, save the file with the file name BigDebt.java. Figure 2.1 shows the full text of Listing 2.1 entered using the Zeus for Windows word processor and saved as BigDebt.java.

You have created the bare-bones form of a Java program. You will create several programs that start off exactly like this one, except for the word BigDebt on Line 1. This word represents the name of your program and changes with each program that you write. Line 3 also should make sense—it's a sentence in actual English. The rest is completely new, however, and each part is introduced in the following sections.

2

Figure 2.1.

Entering BigDebt.java
using the Zeus for
Windows word-
processing program.

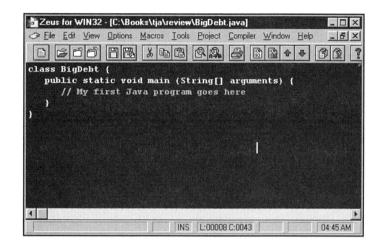

The `class` Statement

The first line of the program is the following:

```
class BigDebt {
```

Translated into English, this line means, "Computer, give my Java program the name `BigDebt`."

As you might recall from Hour 1, each instruction that you give a computer is called a *statement*. The `class` statement is the way you give your computer program a name. It also is used to determine other things about the program, as you will see later. The significance of the term `class` is that Java programs also are called *classes*.

In this example, the program name `BigDebt` matches the file name you gave your document, `BigDebt.java`. Java programs must have a name that matches the first part of their file names, and these names always must be capitalized in the same way. If the name doesn't match, you will get an error when you try to compile the program.

What the `main` Statement Does

The next line of the program is the following:

```
public static void main (String[] arguments) {
```

This line tells the computer, "The main part of the program begins here." Java programs are organized into different sections, so there needs to be a way to identify the part of a program that will be handled first. All of the programs that you will write during the next several hours use `main` as the starting point.

Those Squiggly Bracket Marks

In the `BigDebt.java` program, every line except Line 3 contains a squiggly bracket of some kind—either an { or an }. These brackets are a way to group parts of your program (in the same way that parentheses are used in this sentence to group words). Everything between the opening bracket, {, and the closing bracket, }, is part of the same group.

These groupings are called *blocks*. In Listing 2.1, the opening bracket on Line 1 is associated with the closing bracket on Line 5, which makes your entire program a block. You will always use brackets in this way to show the beginning and end of your programs.

Blocks can be located inside other blocks (just as parentheses are used here (and a second set is used here)). The `BigDebt.java` program has brackets on Line 2 and Line 4 that establish another block. This block begins with the `main` statement. Everything inside the `main` statement block is a command for the computer to handle when the program is run.

The following statement is the only thing located inside the block:

```
// My first Java program goes here
```

This line is a placeholder. The `//` at the beginning of the line tells the computer to ignore this line—it is put in the program solely for the benefit of humans who are looking at the program's text. Lines that serve this purpose are called *comments*.

Right now, you have written a complete Java program. It can be compiled, but if you run it, nothing will happen. The reason for this is that you have not told the computer to do anything yet. The `main` statement block contains only a line of comments, which is ignored. If the `BigDebt.java` program is going to provide sobering details about the United States Treasury, you will have to add some commands inside the opening and closing brackets of the `main` statement block.

Storing Information in the debt Variable

The national debt is increasing at a present rate of $59 million per day. To put this number into perspective, overpaid sports athletes could donate their salaries to the United States Treasury and barely make a dent in it. Chicago White Sox slugger Albert Belle's five-year, $50 million deal stops the debt from increasing for about 20 hours.

Aside from the publishers of computer books, most of us don't make the same kind of money as pro athletes. If we want to slow down the growing debt ourselves, a place to start is by breaking it down into minutes. Your Java program will figure this out for you.

The first step is to tell the computer what you were just told: The national debt goes up $59 million per day. Load the `BigDebt.java` file into your word processor if it's not still loaded, and replace Line 3 with the following:

2

```
int debt = 59000000;
```

This statement tells the computer to store the value 59,000,000 into a variable called debt. *Variables* are special storage places where a computer program can store information. The value of variables can be changed.

Variables can be used to hold several different types of information, such as integers, floating-point numbers, lines of text, and characters of text. In a Java program, you must tell the computer what type of information a variable will hold. In this program, debt is an integer. Putting int in the statement int debt = 59000000; sets up the variable to hold integer values.

JUST A MINUTE

> The int variable type can store values from -2.1 billion to 2.1 billion in Java programs. There are other variable types for different types of numbers and other types of information.

When you entered this statement into the computer program, a semi-colon should have been included at the end of the line. Semi-colons are used at the end of each command in your Java programs. They're like periods at the end of a sentence; the computer uses them to determine when one command ends and the next command begins.

Changing the Information Stored in debt

As it stands, the program you have written does one thing: It uses the debt variable to hold the value 59,000,000—a day's worth of growing debt. However, you want to determine the amount of debt per minute, not per day. To determine this amount, you need to tell the computer to change the value that has been stored in the debt variable. There are 1,440 minutes in each day, so tell the computer to divide the value in debt by 1,440.

Insert a blank line after the int debt = 59000000; statement. In the blank line, enter the following:

```
debt = debt / 1440;
```

If you haven't been able to suppress all memories of new math, this statement probably looks like an algebra problem to you. It gives the computer the following assignment: "Set the debt variable equal to its current value divided by 1,440."

You now have a program that does what you wanted it to do. It determines the amount the national debt grows in an average minute. However, if you ran the program at this point, it wouldn't display anything. The two commands you have given the computer in the BigDebt program occur behind the scenes. To show the computer's result, you have to display the contents of the debt variable.

Displaying the Contents of `debt`

Insert another blank line in the `BigDebt` program after the `debt = debt / 1440;` statement.
Use that space to enter the following statement:

```
System.out.println("A minute's worth of debt is $" + debt);
```

This statement tells the computer to display the text `A minute's worth of debt is $` followed
by the value stored in the `debt` variable. The `System.out.println` command means "display
a line on the system output device." In this case, the system output device is your computer
monitor. Everything within the parentheses is displayed.

Saving the Finished Product

Your program should now resemble Listing 2.2. Make any corrections that are needed and
save the file as `BigDebt.java`. Keep in mind that all Java programs are created as text files and
are saved with the `.java` file extension.

Listing 2.2. The finished version of the `BigDebt` program.

```
1: class BigDebt {
2:     public static void main (String[] arguments) {
3:         int debt = 59000000;
4:         debt = debt / 1440;
5:         System.out.println("A minute's worth of debt is $" + debt);
6:     }
7: }
```

When the computer runs this program, it will run each of the statements in the `main` statement
block on lines 3 through 5. Listing 2.3 shows what the program would look like if it were
written in the English language instead of Java.

Listing 2.3. A line-by-line breakdown of the `BigDebt` program.

```
1: The BigDebt program begins here:
2:     The main part of the program begins here:
3:         Store the value 59000000 in an integer variable called debt
4:         Set debt equal to its current value divided by 1440
5:         Display "A minute's worth of debt is $" and the new value of debt
6:     The main part of the program ends here.
7: The BigDebt program ends here.
```

Compiling the Program into a Class File

Before you can try out the program, it must be compiled. The term *compile* might be unfamiliar to you now, but you will become quite familiar with it in the coming hours. When you compile a program, you take the instructions you have given the computer and convert them into a form the computer can better understand. You also make the program run as efficiently as possible. Java programs must be compiled before you can run them. With the Java Developer's Kit, programs are compiled with the `javac` tool.

To compile the `BigDebt` program, go to the directory on your system where the `BigDebt.java` file is located, and type the following command:

```
javac BigDebt.java
```

When the program compiles successfully, a new file called `BigDebt.class` is created in the same directory as `BigDebt.java`. (If you have any error messages, refer to the following section, "Fixing Errors.") The `.class` extension was chosen because all Java programs also are called classes. A Java program can be made up of several classes that work together, but in a simple program such as `BigDebt` only one class is needed.

COFFEE BREAK

> Do you have a relative, spouse, or other loved one who only says something when things go wrong? (Me neither.) The `javac` tool only speaks up when there's an error to complain about. If you compile a program successfully without any errors, nothing happens in response.

Fixing Errors

If errors exist in your program when you compile it, the `javac` tool displays a message explaining each error and the lines they occurred on. Figure 2.2 shows an attempt to compile a program that has errors, and the error messages that are displayed as a result.

Error messages displayed by the `javac` tool include the following information:

- ☐ The name of the Java program
- ☐ The number of the line where the error was found
- ☐ The type of error
- ☐ The line where the error was found

Figure 2.2.

Compiling a version of the BigDebt *program that has errors.*

```
C:\Books\tja\Examples>javac BigDebt.java
BigDebt.java:4: Invalid type expression.
                debt = debt / 1440
                       ^
BigDebt.java:5: Invalid declaration.
                System.out.println("A minute's worth of debt is $" + debt);
                              ^
2 errors

C:\Books\tja\Examples>_
```

As you learned during the past hour, errors in programs are called bugs. Finding those errors and squashing them is called *debugging*. The following is an example of an error message from Figure 2.2:

```
BigDebt.java:4: Invalid type expression.
                debt = debt / 1440
```

In this example, the 4 that follows the file name BigDebt.java indicates that the error is on Line 4. The actual error message, Invalid type expression in this case, can often be confusing to new programmers. In some cases, the message can be confusing to any programmer. When the error message doesn't make sense to you, take a look at the line where the error occurred.

For instance, can you determine what's wrong with the following statement?

```
debt = debt / 1440
```

The problem is that there's no semi-colon at the end of the statement, which is required in Java programs.

If you get error messages when compiling the BigDebt program, double-check that your program matches Listing 2.2, and correct any differences you find. Make sure that everything is capitalized correctly, and all punctuation (such as {, }, and ;) is included. Often, a close look at the statement included with the error message is enough to reveal the error, or errors, that need to be fixed.

Running the Program

The Java Developer's Kit provides a Java interpreter so that you can try the program you have created. The interpreter makes the computer follow the instructions you gave it when you wrote the program. To see whether the BigDebt program does what you want, go to the directory that contains the BigDebt.class file, and type the following:

2

```
java BigDebt
```

When the program runs, it should state the following:

```
A minute's worth of debt is $40972
```

The computer has provided the answer you wanted! With this information, you now know that if you want to donate your salary to slow one minute's growth of the national debt, you need to make more than $40 grand per year. You also have to avoid paying any taxes.

CAUTION

Neither the author nor Sams.net Publishing makes any guarantees express or implied that the Internal Revenue Service will accept the excuse that you spent all your money on the national debt.

Workshop: Modifying the Program

The BigDebt program calculated the amount the national debt increases in a minute. If you'd like to make a dent in the debt but can't spare $40,000, you might want to see how much a second's worth of debt would cost you.

Load the file BigDebt.java into your word processor again. You need to change the following statement:

```
debt = debt / 1440;
```

This line divided the value in the debt variable by 1,440 because there are 1,440 minutes in a day. Change the line in the BigDebt program so that it divides the debt variable by 86,400, the amount of seconds in a day.

CAUTION

When you change the line of code, don't include a comma in the number (as in 86,400).If you do, you will get an error message when you compile the program. Commas may make it easier for people to read the numbers in your code, but the compiler doesn't appreciate the gesture.

You also need to change the following line:

```
System.out.println("A minute's worth of debt is $" + debt);
```

Now that you're calculating a second's worth of debt, you need to replace the word minute with second. Make the change and save the file BigDebt.java. Your version of BigDebt.java should match Listing 2.4.

Listing 2.4. The modified version of the `BigDebt` program.

```
1: class BigDebt {
2:     public static void main (String arguments[]) {
3:         int debt = 59000000;
4:         debt = debt / 86400;
5:         System.out.println("A second's worth of debt is $" + debt);
6:     }
7: }
```

Compile the file with the same command that you used previously:

```
javac BigDebt.java
```

When you run the program, you should get the following output:

```
A second's worth of debt is $682
```

Summary

During this hour, you got your first chance to create a Java program. You learned that to create a Java program you need to complete these three basic steps:

1. Write the program with a word processor.
2. Compile the program.
3. Tell the interpreter to run the program.

Along the way, you were introduced to some basic computer programming concepts such as compilers, interpreters, blocks, statements, and variables. These things will become more clear to you in successive hours. As long as you got the program to work during this hour, you're ready to proceed.

Q&A

Q Is SunSoft Java WorkShop another programming language like Java, or is it something else?

A Java WorkShop is a way to write Java programs in a graphical, point-and-click environment. It was produced by a division of Sun Microsystems, the developer of Java, as an improvement upon the Java Developer's Kit. Other products in the market offer similar features, such as Symantec Café, Microsoft J++, and RogueWave JFactory. For more information on these products, see Appendix B, "Java Programming Tools."

Q **I have several word processing programs on my system. Which should I use to write Java programs?**

A Any of them will suffice, as long as it can save files as text without any special formatting. A word processor that shows the line number your cursor is located on is especially useful. (Microsoft Word, for example, shows the line number at the bottom edge of the window along with the column number.) Because the `javac` compiler lists line numbers with its error messages, the line-numbering feature helps you debug a program more quickly.

Q **How important is it to put the right number of blank spaces on a line in a Java program?**

A Spacing is strictly for the benefit of people looking at a computer program. You could have written the `BigDebt` program without using blank spaces or the Tab key to indent lines, and it would compile successfully. Although the number of spaces in front of the lines isn't important, you should use spacing in your Java programs. Spacing indicates how a program is organized and which programming block a statement belongs to. When you start writing more sophisticated programs, you'll find it much more difficult to do without spacing.

Q **A Java program has been described as a class, and it also has been described as a group of classes. Which is it?**

A Both. The simple Java programs that you create during the next few hours will create a single file with the extension `.class`. You can run these programs with the `java` interpreter. Java programs also can consist of a set of classes that work together. In fact, even simple programs like `BigDebt` use other Java classes behind the scenes. This topic will be fully explored during Hour 10, "Creating Your First Object."

Q **If semi-colons are needed at the end of each statement, why does the comment line `// My first Java program goes here` not end with a semi-colon?**

A Comments are completely ignored by the compiler. If you put `//` on a line in your program, this tells the Java compiler to ignore everything to the right of the `//` on that line. The following example shows a comment on the same line as a statement:

```
debt = debt / 86400; // divide debt by the number of seconds
```

In this example, the compiler will handle the statement `debt = debt / 86400;` and ignore the comments afterward.

Q **What is a character?**

A A *character* is a single letter, number, punctuation mark, or other symbol. Examples are *T*, *5*, and *%*. Characters are stored in variables as text.

Q I get an `Invalid argument` error message when I use the `javac` tool to compile the `BigDebt` program. What can I do to correct this?

A You are probably leaving off the `.java` extension and typing the following command:

```
javac BigDebt
```

Make sure that you are in the same directory as the file `BigDebt.java`, and type the following command to compile the program:

```
javac BigDebt.java
```

Q I couldn't find any errors in the line where the compiler noted an error. What can I do?

A The line number displayed with the error message isn't always the place where an error needs to be fixed in your program. Examine the statements that are directly above the error message to see whether you can spot any typos or other bugs. The error usually is within the same programming block.

Quiz

Test your knowledge of the material covered in this chapter by answering the following questions.

Questions

1. When you compile a Java program, what are you doing?
   - (a) Saving it to disk
   - (b) Converting it into a form the computer can better understand
   - (c) Adding it to your program collection

2. What is a variable?
   - (a) Something that wobbles but doesn't fall down.
   - (b) Text in a program that the compiler ignores.
   - (c) A place to store information in a program.

3. What is the process of fixing errors called?
   - (a) Defrosting
   - (b) Debugging
   - (c) Decomposing

2

Answers

1. b. Compiling converts a .java file into a .class file or set of .class files.

2. c. Variables are one place to store information; later you'll learn about others such as arrays and constants. Weebles wobble but they don't fall down, and comments are text in a program that the compiler ignores.

3. b. Because errors in a computer program are called bugs, fixing those errors is called debugging. Some programming tools come with a feature called a debugger that helps you fix errors.

Activities

If you'd like to explore the topics covered in this hour a little more fully, try the following activities:

☐ Write a program for megamillionaires: Calculate the amount the national debt increases in a week.

☐ Go back to the BigDebt program and add one or two errors. For example, take a semi-colon off the end of a line, or change the line that reads class BigDebt { into class bigDebt {. Save the program and try to compile it. Compare the error messages you get to the errors you caused.

PART

I

Hour 3

Vacationing in Java

"Java is a huge opportunity for all of us."
—*Marc Andreesen of Netscape at the JavaOne Conference, May 31, 1996*

Before you venture further into Java programming, it's worthwhile to learn more about the language and see what Java programmers are doing today. One of the reasons that Java has become popular quickly is that it can be used to offer programs on the World Wide Web. Because of this capability, the best examples of how to use Java are also on the Web. During this hour, we'll take a look at some sites that feature Java programs and talk about the history and development of the language.

To go on this vacation, you need a Web browser that can handle Java programs. Most current versions of Netscape Navigator and Microsoft Internet Explorer can run Java programs that are found on Web pages.

JUST A MINUTE

If you're using a current version of Netscape Navigator or Microsoft Internet Explorer and it isn't working with Java programs, check your setup configuration from one of the program's pull-down menus (select View | Options in Internet Explorer or Options | Network Preferences | Languages in Navigator). Make sure your browser software is configured to run Java programs.

Load your browser software of choice, put on your best Hawaiian shirt, and get ready to vacate. Because you won't be leaving your house, you won't get a chance to experience the simpler pleasures of tourism: odd driving rituals, exotic food, exotic members of the opposite sex, exotic members of the opposite sex with food, and so on. But look on the bright side: no antibacterial shots, traveler's checks, or passports are required either.

The following topics will be covered during this hour:

- A definition of the Java language
- The benefits of using Java
- Some examples of Java at work
- An explanation of object-oriented programming
- Sites of note for Java programmers

JUST A MINUTE

The Web site-seeing examples that you visit during this hour's vacation are just a small sampling of the Java programs in use on the Web. A search of the AltaVista Web search database finds more than 4,900 pages that have included a Java program as of this writing.

First Stop: JavaSoft

The Java vacation begins at a place you'll be visiting regularly now that you're a Java programmer: the Web site of JavaSoft, the group that developed the Java language. To get there, go to the following address:

http://java.sun.com

JavaSoft is the division of Sun Microsystems that is responsible for the advancement of the Java language and the development of related software. To see a simple example of Java in action, choose the hyperlink on the JavaSoft main page that offers a "Java version" of the site. If you can't find one, you can reach the Java front page by visiting the following Web address:

```
http://java.sun.com:81/index.html?
```

A Java program is used on this page to add pull-down menus on top of the page. Drag your mouse across the different section titles on the page to see the pull-down menus that appear. Figure 3.1 shows a pull-down menu that appears when the mouse is over the `Where Can I Read About…?` text.

Figure 3.1.

The JavaSoft Web site uses a Java program to add pull-down menus on top of a Web page.

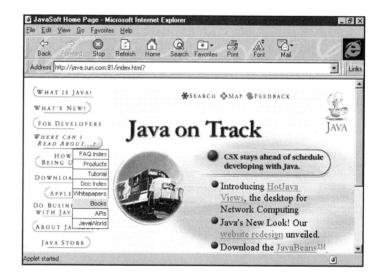

This Web site is the place to find the latest released versions of the Java Developer's Kit, as well as other programmer's resources. This site also has press releases about Java-related products, full documentation for Java, and sample Java programs that run on the Web. Sun Microsystems made Java available for free via this Web site in late 1995.

A Brief History of Java

Company cofounder Bill Joy called Java the end result of 15 years of work to produce a better, more reliable way to write computer programs. Java's creation was a little more complicated than that.

Java was invented five years ago by Sun engineer James Gosling as a language to use as the brains for smart appliances (interactive TVs, omniscient ovens, and the like). Gosling was unhappy with the results he was getting by writing programs with C++, another programming language, so he holed up in his office and wrote a new language to better suit his needs.

COFFEE BREAK

Most people who are holed up in their office aren't producing new programming languages or other achievements. They're playing Quake. How many lasting contributions to mankind have been lost because of Id Software?

At the time, Gosling named his language Oak after a tree he could see from his office window. The language was part of Sun's strategy to make millions when interactive TV became a multimillion-dollar industry. That still hasn't happened today (five years down the road), but something completely different took place. Just as Sun was ready to scrap Oak development and scatter its workers to other parts of the company, the World Wide Web became popular.

In a fortuitous circumstance, many of the qualities that made Gosling's language good on its appliance project made it suitable for adaptation to the World Wide Web. Sun developers devised a way for programs to be run safely from Web pages and chose a catchy new name to accompany the language's new focus: Java.

COFFEE BREAK

You might have heard that Java is an acronym that stands for Just Another Vague Acronym. You also might have heard that it was named for the developers' love of coffee, especially the percolating product of a shop near Sun's offices. Actually, the story behind Java's naming contains no secret messages or declarations of liquid love. Instead, Java was chosen for the same reason that comedian Jerry Seinfeld likes to say the word *salsa*. It sounds cool.

Although Java can be used for many other things, the Web provided the showcase that it needed to capture international attention. A programmer who puts a Java program on a Web page makes it instantly accessible to the entire Web-surfing planet. Because Java was the first tool that could offer this capability, it became the first computer language to receive as much press as Dennis Rodman, Madonna's baby, and the alien autopsy. In 1996, you had to be in solitary confinement or a long-term orbital mission to avoid hearing about Java.

Going to School with Java

As a medium that offers a potential audience of millions, the World Wide Web includes numerous resources for educators and schoolchildren. Because Java programs can offer a more interactive experience than standard Web pages, some programmers have used the language to write learning programs for the Internet.

3

For one of the strongest examples of this use of Java, visit the following address:

`http://www.npac.syr.edu/projects/vishuman/VisibleHuman.html`

This Web site uses data from the National Library of Medicine's Visible Human Project. The project is a database of thousands of cross-sectional images of human anatomy. A Java program is being used to enable users to search the collection and view images. Instead of making requests by text commands, users make the requests to see different parts of the body graphically, and the results are shown immediately in graphic detail. The Java program is shown in Figure 3.2.

Figure 3.2.

Images from the National Library of Medicine's Visible Human Project can be viewed interactively on the Web using a Java program.

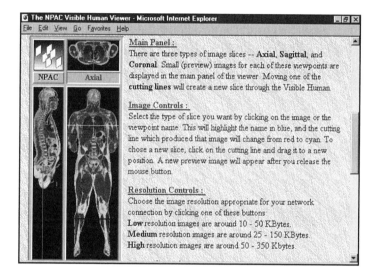

Numerous educational programs are available for many different computer systems, but what makes this program remarkable is its versatility. The Visible Human Project tool is similar in function and performance to CD-ROM software that users might run on their computer systems. However, it is run directly from a Web page. No special installation is needed, and unlike most CD-ROM software, it isn't limited to PC-compatible and Macintosh systems. Just like Web pages, Java programs can be run on any computer system that can handle them.

In order to handle Java programs, a Web browser must have a Java interpreter. The interpreter included with a browser serves a similar function as the interpreter that you used to run the `BigDebt` program during Hour 2, "Writing Your First Program." The difference is that a browser's interpreter can only run Java programs that are set up to run on Web pages and cannot handle programs set up to run from the command line. Currently, Java-enabled browsers are available for most common systems, including PCs running a version of Microsoft Windows, Apple Macintosh systems, SPARC workstations, and computers running the Linux operating system.

A Java program such as the Visible Human Project database does not have to be written for a specific computer system. This advantage is called *platform independence.* Java was created to work on multiple systems. Originally, Java's developers believed it needed to be multiplatform because it would be used on a variety of appliances and other electronic devices.

The programs that you write using Java can be run on a variety of computer systems without requiring any extra work from you. This advantage is one of the primary reasons that so many people are learning to write Java programs and are using them on software projects. Many professional software companies are using Java for the same reason. Under the right circumstances, Java can remove the need to create specific versions of a program for different computer systems. The potential audience for software grows with a multiplatform solution such as Java.

Lunch in *JavaWorld*

If you didn't lose your appetite after searching through the innards of a visible human, take a lunch break with *JavaWorld*, an online magazine for Java programmers and other Internet developers. The *JavaWorld* Web site is available at the following address:

```
http://www.javaworld.com
```

JavaWorld offers how-to articles, news stories related to Java development, and other features in each monthly edition. One of the advantages of the publication's Web format is that it can display functional Java programs in conjunction with articles. Figure 3.3 shows a working example from a tutorial on Java animation programming.

Figure 3.3.

A JavaWorld *how-to article on Java animation programming includes a working example of a program.*

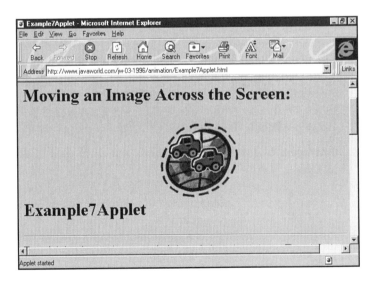

3

In addition to offering information of benefit to Java programmers, *JavaWorld* publishes articles and commentary about the language and its development. One issue that has been hotly debated since Java's release is whether the language is secure. Security is important because of the way Java programs work when they are placed on a Web page. The Java programs that you have tried during this hour were downloaded to your computer first. When the program was finished downloading, it ran on your computer. It was as though someone sat down at your computer, popped in a disk, and ran his own program.

Unless you know a whole lot of people, most of the Web pages you visit will be published by strangers. In terms of security, running their programs isn't a lot different than letting the general public use your computer on weekends. If the Java language did not have safeguards to prevent abuse, its programs could introduce viruses onto your system, delete files, and do other malicious things. Java includes several different types of security to make sure that its programs are safe when run from Web pages.

The main security is provided by the following restrictions on Java programs running over the Web:

☐ No program can open, read, write, or delete files on the user's system.

☐ No program can run other programs on the user's system.

☐ All windows created by the program will be identified clearly as Java windows. This identification prevents someone from creating a fake window asking for the user's name and password.

☐ Programs cannot make connections to Web sites other than the one they came from.

☐ All programs will be verified to make sure that nothing was modified after they were compiled.

At this time, the general consensus among Java developers is that the language has enough safeguards in place to be usable over the Web. Several security holes have been found, often by programming security experts, and these holes have been dealt with quickly by Sun or the Web browser programmers. Because *JavaWorld* covers the latest news of note in the Java development community, it is a good way to keep track of any security issues that arise.

CAUTION

> None of the safeguards in place are a complete block against malicious programs. Just as loopholes were found in the past year, more will undoubtedly be found in the future. If you are concerned about running Java programs through your Web browser, you might want to run programs only from a source such as Gamelan because it tests the programs before including them in the directory. You also should back up anything you can't afford to lose on your computer, which is good practice for anyone who runs programs received from the Internet.

Taking in a Ball Game at Instant Ballpark

The first afternoon stop on the Java tour will be a trip to the old ball game. Instant Sports, a Texas company that provides sports reporting information, is using Java to present baseball games as they happen in a visual, pitch-by-pitch fashion. To see how baseball is played in cyberspace, visit the following address:

http://www.instantsports.com/

The Java program called Instant Ballpark presents each pitch in a major league game. The ball travels from the pitcher's icon to the batter and goes out to the fielders when it's hit. Sound effects, such as the umpire's strike call and the ball hitting the bat, also are presented.

The program is a unique way to follow live games and past games that are available from the Instant Ballpark archive. Figure 3.4 shows the last play in a game between the Chicago White Sox and the Seattle Mariners from the 1996 season.

Figure 3.4.

Mariners shortstop Alex Rodriguez drives home the winning run in Instant Ballpark, a presentation of a live baseball game using a Java program.

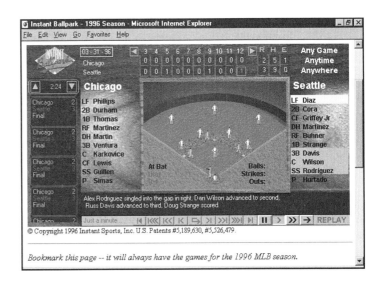

One of the things that you might notice about Instant Ballpark is that it updates the day's scores in other games as you are using the program to follow a game. This update is relatively easy to do because the Java language is multithreaded. *Multithreading* is a way for the computer to do more than one thing at the same time. One part of a program takes care of one task, another part takes care of a different task, and the two parts can pay no attention to each other. Each part of a program in this example is called a *thread*.

In a program such as Instant Ballpark, the league scoreboard along one side of the window could run in its own thread. The rest of the program could be another thread. If you use an operating system such as Microsoft Windows 95, you're using a type of this behavior when you run more than one program at the same time. If you're at work and you surf the Web for European aerobics videos in one window while running a company sales report in another window, congratulate yourself—you're multithreading!

Getting Down to Business

At this point in your travels, you might be getting the impression that Java is primarily of use to baseball fans and those who have body parts to show the world. Although those two subject areas are enough to keep most of us entertained for hours, the next stop on our trip shows an example of Java getting down to business.

Direct your Web browser to the following address:

```
http://www.engine.com/java/engbrowse/Employee.html
```

This example is an employee payroll database managed as a pair of Java programs. Employee information is viewed in one program, and the other program is used to edit items from the payroll record of a specific employee. Figure 3.5 shows Bart Simpson's record as it is being edited.

Unlike other payroll tracking systems that require the installation of software on the computers of each employee who needs access, the use of Java enables Software Engine to make the program available to any employee with a Web browser. With some kind of password security system in place, the program could even be used by employees who are away from the office on business trips. All the employees would have to do is access the company's Web site.

Figure 3.5.

A Java program from Software Engine that is used to maintain employee payroll records.

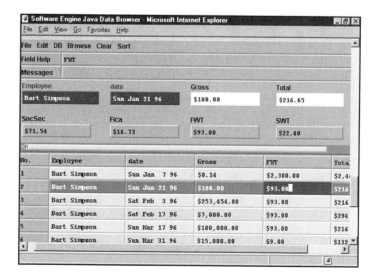

A database program such as Software Engine's can be thought of in several different ways. One way is to think of a program as an object—something that exists in the world, takes up space, and has certain things it can do. Java, like the C++ language, uses object-oriented programming, as you will see during Hour 10, "Creating Your First Object." Object-oriented programming (OOP) is a way of thinking about computer programs. A program is thought of as a group of objects. Each object handles a specific task and knows how to speak to other objects. For example, a word-processing program could be set up as the following group of objects:

- ☐ A document object, which is the area where you type in text
- ☐ A spell-checking object, which can look over the document object to find any possible spelling errors
- ☐ A printer object, which handles the printing of the document
- ☐ A menu object, a mouse object, and many others

Each of these objects is an independent computer program that doesn't need the others to do its job. The word-processing software is a collection of all the objects necessary to get work done.

OOP is a powerful way to create programs and it makes the programs you write more useful. Consider the word-processing software. If the programmer wants to use the spell-checking capabilities of that program with some other software, the spell-checking object is ready for use with the new program. No changes need to be made.

Stopping by Gamelan to Ask Directions

This world tour of Java programs is being led by a professional who is well-versed in the hazards and highlights of Web-based travel. You'll be venturing out on your own trips soon, so it's worthwhile to stop at the best tour guide currently available for the Java-hungry tourist, the Gamelan Web site:

```
http://www.gamelan.com
```

Gamelan is the most comprehensive directory of Java programs, programming resources, and other information related to the language. Most of the programs visited during this hour were originally found on a trek through the searchable database maintained by Gamelan. Updates are made on a daily basis, so this is another place that you'll be visiting often as you develop your Java programming skills.

One of the best uses of Gamelan for programmers is to see what programs are available that offer source code. In case you're unfamiliar with the term, *source code* is another name for the text files that are used to write computer programs. The BigDebt.java file that you created during Hour 2, "Writing Your First Program," is an example of source code.

3

Gamelan's directory listings indicate when a compiled Java program is accompanied by the source code used to create it. After you have finished your first 24 hours as a Java programmer, you ought to take a look at some of these programs. Figure 3.6 shows a Java program being used on Gamelan to provide instant access to the different areas that comprise the site.

Figure 3.6.

The Gamelan directory offers more than 4,000 Java resources and links to programs. It uses this Java program as a navigational aid.

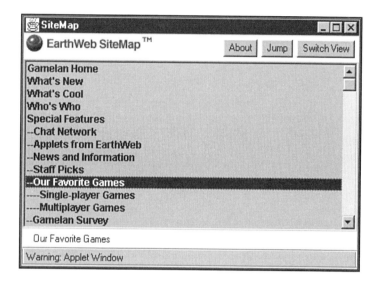

The large number of programs listed in Gamelan show that the language has been adopted quickly by thousands of programmers around the world. Part of the reason is that Java's popularity inspires people to learn it, which is the same principle that caused parachute pants and breakdancing to be briefly popular in the mid-'80s. Another reason for the swiftly growing population of Java programmers is the simplicity of the language.

One of the goals of Java's design was to make it easier to learn than C++, the language James Gosling was having fits with on Sun's smart-appliance project. Much of Java is based on C++, so programmers who have learned to use that language will find it easier to learn Java. However, some of the elements of C++ that are the hardest to learn—and the hardest to use correctly—have been removed from Java.

For people who are learning programming for the first time, Java is easier to learn than C++ would be. Also, Java will not work if its variables and other elements of a program are used incorrectly. This adherence to rules can be painful for experienced programmers, but it forces everyone to develop good habits as they create programs.

Some languages are created to make it easier for experienced programmers to harness the capabilities of the computer in their programs by including shortcuts and other features that programming veterans easily understand. Java does not use these features, preferring to make the language as simple as an object-oriented programming language can be. Java was created to be easy to learn, easy to debug, and easy to use.

A Big Finish with Castanets

The second-to-last stop on your Java vacation has a certain Caribbean flair to it—castanets, marimbas, and bongos are involved. If you packed a ruffly Cuban bandleader shirt just like the one Carmine Ragusa used to wear on episodes of *Laverne and Shirley*, now's the best chance you'll ever have to wear it. Visit the following Web address:

```
http://www.marimba.com
```

Unlike the other sightseeing locations you have visited, this site can't be viewed with a Web browser alone. Marimba, a startup company formed by several former Java developers at Sun, has used Java to create Castanet, a new way to receive and run software over the Internet.

Castanet is a way to send out computer programs that automatically update themselves on the computers of people who request them. It's a service not unlike television, where you turn to a channel and immediately start receiving the broadcast signal of that channel. In fact, the Java programs sent by this method are called *channels*. Figure 3.7 shows a Castanet channel offered by Excite that presents the lineup of other channels that are currently available. Like TV listings, Excite's guide offers previews of each channel and a way to immediately request them. If Excite updates its guide channel program, Castanet sends that update automatically over the Internet. No effort is required on the user's end to keep up with new versions of the software.

Figure 3.7.

The Excite guide to Castanet channels, which itself is a channel.

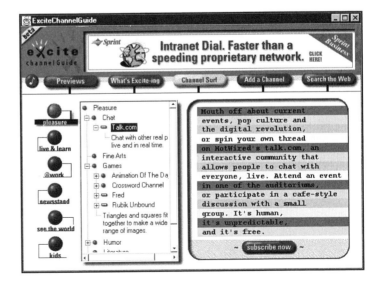

Java is not able to send out its programs in this manner, so Castanet requires the use of special software called the Tuner. The Castanet Tuner is a sophisticated Java program that runs from the command line. Although Netscape has announced plans to include the Tuner's functionality in a future version of its software, this feature has not become available at the time of this writing. To find out more about downloading the Tuner for your system, visit the following Web page:

```
http://www.marimba.com/products/castanet-tuner.html
```

The Tuner is several megabytes in size, so you might not want to install it on your system immediately. Visit the Marimba Web site to find out more about channels and what services they offer.

Castanet illustrates a point about Java that sometimes get lost: Although Java is most popular as a way to write Web page programs, it is not limited to use on the Internet. You can use it to write any kind of software.

Workshop: Putting Java on Your Desktop

The last stop on your whirlwind tour of Java is ESPNET SportsZone, the electronic edition of the cable sports channel. So far, your guides have asked nothing of you other than an occasional wardrobe change, but that's going to change. Redirect your Web browser to the following address:

```
http://espnet.sportszone.com
```

If you're using a browser such as Netscape Navigator or Microsoft Internet Explorer, your first assignment is to find the Java programs on this page. This assignment ought to be a lot easier than finding Waldo in those *Where's Waldo?* children's books, but if you need a hint, here it is: They're the parts with changing text and graphics.

ESPN uses Java programs to provide constant updates to scores and headlines in the same way it uses a sports ticker during some events. In the scoreboard program, scores are frequently updated in the program's window, along with graphical advertisements.

The scoreboard Java program is offered as part of a Web page, but it has a special feature that adds to its usefulness. It can be detached from the page and placed on your system's desktop as a stand-alone window. Click the Display on Desktop button and then minimize your Web browser. This might be more sports than you're able to handle in a short period of time, but it shows how Java can present information in a way much different from standard Web pages. Figure 3.8 shows the scoreboard program on a Windows 95 desktop.

Figure 3.8.

Scores are presented in a desktop window with the ESPNet SportsZone Scorepost program.

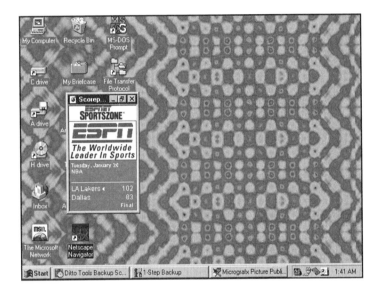

Once you're completely caught up on the sports events that have taken place during your world-in-an-hour jaunt, it's time to put away your luggage and get ready for a return to programming. More Web sites and other items of note for Java programmers are described in Appendix A, "Where to Go from Here: Java Resources."

Q&A

Q Can I use the sample Java programs from the JavaSoft Web site on my own home page?

A JavaSoft encourages the use of its sample programs on Web sites. Take a look at the directories that were created when you installed the Java Developer's Kit on your system. You will find more than a dozen sample programs along with the .java files that were used to compile them. These programs can be a valuable resource when you're working on your own Java programs later on.

Q What other ways have been devised to offer programs on Web pages?

A Several programming strategies are aimed at making Web pages smarter. The main competitor to Java is ActiveX, an extension of Microsoft technology called the Component Object Model. ActiveX programs are similar in function to Java programs—they are placed on Web pages and are run when browsers are equipped to handle them. The primary differences are that ActiveX uses a way to verify the identity of ActiveX programmers, and ActiveX programs are not downloaded each time they are encountered. Unlike Java programs, an ActiveX program stays on a

3

user's system. In addition to ActiveX, JavaScript and VBScript offer some programming capabilities on Web pages. These programs must be more simple than Java and ActiveX programs, however.

Q I ran a useful Java program on a Web page. Can I run it on my system without the browser?

A Under most circumstances, no. Java programs typically are developed either to run on a Web page or to run from the command line. A program can be written so that it works in both ways, but most of the programs you will find in a directory such as Gamelan do not include this functionality. You'll learn much more about the different types of Java programs during Hour 4, "Understanding How Java Programs Work."

Q If Java programs are platform-independent, why are some Java programs such as SunSoft Java WorkShop only available for specific systems?

A Java programs might be limited to specific systems such as PC compatibles because the programs include the use of non-Java programming for some features. For example, a Java program might use a program written in C++ to communicate with a modem because Java does not support this capability in its current version. Java is still relatively young in its development, and some of its goals concerning complete platform independence have not been achieved yet. Web programs are the area where Java's multiplatform promise is most fully realized. Anyone with a Java-capable Web browser can use one of Java's Web programs on a page.

Q Is there a print edition of *JavaWorld*?

A At present, *JavaWorld* is distributed strictly through the World Wide Web. However, several newsstand magazines are available that cover the language, including *Java Report, Dr. Dobb's Journal*, and others.

Q Can a Java program I run on a Web page give my computer a virus?

A Because of security restrictions that prevent Web programs from reading, writing, or modifying files, there's no way for a virus to be transmitted from a Java program on a Web page to your system. Java programs that you download and run from the command line have the same risk of viruses as any program you download. If you're using programs received over the Internet, you need to acquire a good antivirus program and use it regularly.

Quiz

If your mind hasn't taken a vacation by this point in the hour, test your knowledge of this chapter with the following questions.

Questions

1. How did object-oriented programming get its name?

    (a) Programs are considered to be a group of objects working together.

    (b) People often object because it's hard to master.

    (c) Its parents named it.

2. Which of the following isn't a part of Java's security?

    (a) Web programs cannot run programs on the user's computer.

    (b) The identity of a program's author is verified.

    (c) Java windows are labeled as Java windows.

3. What is a program's capability to handle more than one task called?

    (a) Schizophrenia

    (b) Multiculturalism

    (c) Multithreading

Answers

1. a. It's also abbreviated as OOP.

2. b. ActiveX programs verify the author of the program, but this security method is not implemented with Java.

3. c. This also is called multitasking, but the term *multithreading* is used in conjunction with Java because an independently running part of a program is called a thread.

Activities

Before unpacking your luggage, you can explore the topics of this hour more fully with the following activities:

☐ Use the Gamelan directory at `http://www.gamelan.com` to find out what card games have been developed using Java.

☐ Find the sample Java programs by searching the JavaSoft site, and download one of them to your computer.

3

Hour **4**

Understanding How Java Programs Work

An important distinction to make in Java programming is where your program is supposed to be running. Some programs are intended to work on your computer; you type in a command or click on an icon to start them up. Other programs are intended to run as part of a World Wide Web page. You encountered several examples of this type of program during the previous hour's whirlwind vacation.

Java programs that run locally on your own computer are called *applications*. Programs that run on Web pages are called *applets*. During this hour, you'll learn why that distinction is important, and the following topics will be covered:

☐ How applications work

☐ Organizing an application

☐ Sending arguments to an application

☐ How applets work

☐ The required parts of an applet

☐ Sending parameters to an applet

☐ Using HTML tags to put an applet on a page

Creating an Application

Although Java has become well-known because it can be used in conjunction with World Wide Web pages, you can also use it to write any type of computer program. The BigDebt program that you wrote during Hour 2, "Writing Your First Program," is an example of a Java application.

To try out another program, use your word processor to open up a new file and enter everything from Listing 4.1. Remember not to enter the line numbers and colons along the left-hand side of the listing; these items are used to make parts of programs easier to describe in the book. When you're done, save the file as Root.java.

Listing 4.1. The full text of Root.java.

```
1: class Root {
2:       public static void main(String[] arguments) {
3:               int number = 225;
4:               System.out.println("The square root of "
5:                       + number
6:                       + " is "
7:                       + Math.sqrt(number) );
8:       }
9: }
```

Before you can test out this application, you need to compile it with the javac compiler tool. While in the same directory as the Root.java file, compile it with the following command:

javac Root.java

If you have entered Listing 4.1 without any typos, including all punctuation and every word capitalized as shown, it should compile without any errors. The javac compiler responds to a successful compilation by not responding with any message at all.

You run Java applications in the same way you would run any program that's installed on your computer. Because they require the use of the java interpreter to run, the most common way that you'll run a Java program is probably by typing a command like the following at a command-line prompt:

java DrumMachine

This command would cause the java interpreter to look for a Java program called DrumMachine.class in the current directory. If it found one, it would start running it. To run the Root application, type the following:

java Root

4

The output should resemble the following:

```
The square root of 225 is 15.0
```

When you run a Java application, the interpreter looks for a main() block and starts handling Java statements at that point. If your program does not have a main() block, as most applets do not, the interpreter will respond with an error.

Sending Arguments to Applications

Because Java applications are usually run from a command line, you can send information to applications at the same time that you run them. The following example uses the java interpreter to run an application called DisplayTextFile.class, and it sends two extra items of information to the application: readme.txt and /p:

```
java DisplayTextFile readme.txt /p
```

The extra information you can send to a program is called *arguments*. The first argument, if there is one, is provided one space after the name of the application. Each additional argument is also separated by a space. You can send as many arguments as you want to a Java application. In order to do something with them, however, you have to write some statements in the application to handle them.

To see how arguments work in an application, create a new file in your word processor called NewRoot.java. Enter the text of Listing 4.2 into the file and save it when you're done. Compile the program with the javac compiler tool, while correcting any errors that are caused by typos.

Listing 4.2. The full text of NewRoot.java.

```
 1: class NewRoot {
 2:     public static void main(String[] arguments) {
 3:         int number = 0;
 4:         if (arguments.length > 0)
 5:             number = Integer.parseInt( arguments[0] );
 6:         System.out.println("The square root of "
 7:             + number
 8:             + " is "
 9:             + Math.sqrt(number) );
10:     }
11: }
```

This program is similar to the Root program except for Lines 3–5. Don't worry about the specific statements used in these lines; they use some advanced features. What's important to note is what these lines are accomplishing: If an argument is sent to the NewRoot program when it is run, the argument is stored in the number variable.

To try the program out, use the Java interpreter with a command such as the following:

```
java NewRoot 169
```

This command causes the output to report that the square root of 169 is 13.0. Try the program several times with different numbers.

Arguments are a useful way to customize the performance of a program. They are often used to configure a program so that it runs a specific way. Java applications use arguments, but applets use a different way to receive information as they are run.

Applet Basics

Applets—programs that can run on World Wide Web pages—were the thing that made Java a computer magazine cover subject upon its release. Applets put a spotlight on the ways that Java was different and remarkable. Before Java, World Wide Web pages were a combination of text, images, and forms that used gateway programs running on the computer that hosted the pages. These gateway programs required special access to the Web page server machine, so most Web users did not have the ability to use them. Writing them required even more expertise.

In contrast, programmers of all skill levels can write Java applets, and you'll write several during the span of these 24 hours. You can test applets with any Web browser that handles Java programs and put one on a Web page without any special access from a Web provider. The Java programs that you toured during the previous hour were all applets. Their structure differs from applications in several important ways, and they are designed specifically for presentation on the World Wide Web.

As stated previously, applets do not have a `main()` block like applications do. Applets have several different sections that are handled depending on what is happening in the applet. These sections are detailed fully during Hour 13, "Learning How Applets Work." Two of the sections are the `init()` block statement and the `paint()` block. `init()` is short for initialization, and it is used to set up anything that needs to be set up as an applet first runs. The `paint()` block is used to display anything that should be displayed.

To see an applet version of the `Root` application, create a new file in your word processor and call it `RootApplet.java`. Enter the code in Listing 4.3; save it when you're done. Compile the file with the `javac` compiler tool by typing the following:

```
javac RootApplet.java
```

4

Listing 4.3. The full text of `RootApplet.java`.

```
 1: public class RootApplet extends java.applet.Applet {
 2:         int number;
 3:
 4:         public void init() {
 5:             number = 225;
 6:     }
 7:
 8:         public void paint(java.awt.Graphics g) {
 9:             g.drawString("The square root of " +
10:                         number +
11:                         " is " +
12:                 Math.sqrt(number), 5, 50);
13:     }
14: }
```

This program contains a lot of the same statements as the Java application that did the same thing. The main difference is in how it is organized—the `main()` block has been replaced with an `init()` block and a `paint()` block.

JUST A MINUTE

> The sample programs in this hour are provided primarily to introduce you to the way Java programs are structured. Some aspects of these programs will be introduced fully later, so don't feel like you're falling behind. The main purpose of this hour is to get the programs to compile and see how they function when you run them.

Unlike applications, compiled Java applets cannot be tested using the `java` interpreter tool. You have to put them on a Web page and view that page in one of two ways:

- ☐ Use a Web browser that can handle Java applets, such as the current versions of Netscape Navigator or Microsoft Internet Explorer.
- ☐ Use the `appletviewer` tool that comes with the Java Developer's Kit.

To create a Web page that can display the `RootApplet` program, return to your word processor and create a new file. Enter Listing 4.4 in that file and save it as `RootApplet.html`.

Listing 4.4. The full text of `RootApplet.html`.

```
1: <applet code="RootApplet.class" height=100 width=300>
2: </applet>
```

This Web page contains the bare minimum needed to display a Java applet on a Web page. The <APPLET> tag is used to specify that a Java program is being put on the page, the code attribute provides the name of the applet, and the height and width attributes describe the size of the applet's display area. These items will be described in detail during Hour 13.

For now, use the appletviewer tool to take a look at this page. Type the following at the command line:

```
appletviewer RootApplet.html
```

Figure 4.1 shows what the applet looks like using appletviewer.

Figure 4.1.

The RootApplet *applet displayed with the* appletviewer *tool.*

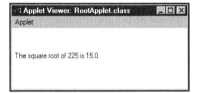

The square root of 225 is 15.0

Sending Parameters to Applets

Java applets are never run from the command line, so you can't specify arguments the way you can with applications. Applets use a different way to receive information at the time the program is run. This information is called *parameters*, and you can send parameters through the HTML page that runs the applet. You have to use a special HTML tag for parameters called <PARAM>.

Load the file RootApplet.java back into your word processor. The init() block of the program should resemble the following:

```
public void init() {
    number = 225;
}
```

Replace these three lines with the following statements:

```
public void init() {
            String parameter = getParameter("NUMBER");
            if (parameter != null)
                    number = Integer.parseInt(parameter);
}
```

Save the file and then compile it by typing the following at the command line:

```
javac RootApplet.java
```

4

Before you can try this change out, you need to modify the Web page RootApplet.html so that it sends a parameter. Load the page into your word processor and add a line between the <APPLET> line and the </APPLET> line, so that the code resembles the following:

```
<applet code="RootApplet.class" height=100 width=300>
<param name="NUMBER" value=196>
</applet>
```

Save the file when you're done, and load the page using appletviewer again. The output should resemble Figure 4.2. Change the value of the VALUE attribute in the RootApplet.html file and run the program again. Try this several times, and you'll see that your program is now flexible enough to handle any number.

Figure 4.2.

The modified RootApplet *program displayed with* appletviewer.

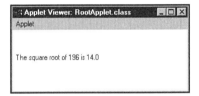

You can use as many parameters as needed to customize the operation of an applet, as long as each has a different NAME attribute specified along with the <PARAM> tag.

Workshop: Viewing the Code Used to Run Applets

As a brief workshop to better familiarize yourself with the <APPLET> tag and how it can be used to alter the performance of an applet, visit this book's World Wide Web site at the following address:

```
http://www.prefect.com/java24
```

Visit this site using either the current version of Netscape Navigator or Microsoft Internet Explorer. Go to the section of the site labeled Hour 4 Showcase, and you'll be given a guided tour through several working examples of applets. On each of these pages, you can use a pull-down menu command to view the HTML tags that were used to create the page. With Navigator, the command is View ¦ Document Source, and with Internet Explorer, the command is View ¦ Source. Compare the parameters that are used with each applet to the way the applet runs.

Appendix C, "This Book's Web Site," describes other things you can do on this book's site. The Web site is intended as a complement to the material covered in this book and a way to find out about corrections, revisions, or other information that makes these 24 hours more productive.

Summary

During this hour, you got a chance to create both a Java application and an applet. These two types of programs have several important differences in the way they function and the way they are created. The next several hours will continue to focus on applications as you become more experienced as a Java programmer. Applications are easier to test because they don't require you to create a Web page to view them; they can be easier to create as well. The last several hours of the book focus on applets, however, because that's the area where beginning programmers are most likely to want to put their skills to work.

Q&A

Q Can a single Java program be both an applet and an application?

A It is possible to make a program serve as both applet and application, but it's often an unwieldy solution unless the program is simple. An applet could be set up to run as an application also by including a main() block in the applet, but you would not be able to use the init() block or paint() block in the automatic fashion they are used in an applet. Most programs are written either as an application or as an applet, rather than attempting to do both.

Q Do all arguments sent to a Java application have to be strings?

A Java puts all arguments into strings for storage when an application runs. When you want to use one of these arguments as an integer or some other non-string type, you have to convert the value. You'll learn how to do this during the coming hours.

Q Why don't Java applets require the same kind of special access as gateway programs?

A Java applets don't have the same access requirements because they don't pose the same risk to a Web site provider. Gateway programs don't have any kind of security in place to prevent the program from attempting to do harmful things to the machine running the Web page. Java applets, on the other hand, have strict restrictions to prevent them from being used to write harmful programs. Also, Java programs do not run on the Web site's machine—they run on the system of the person viewing the page. This means that the Web site's machine will not slow down due to numerous people running a Java applet on a page.

4

Quiz

Test your knowledge of the material covered in this chapter by answering the following questions.

Questions

1. Which type of Java program can be run by the `java` interpreter tool?

   (a) Applets

   (b) Applications

   (c) none

2. What special HTML tag is used to put a Java program onto a Web page?

   (a) `<APPLET>`

   (b) `<PROGRAM>`

   (c) `<RUN>`

3. If you get into a fight with someone over the way to send information to a Java application, what are you doing?

   (a) Struggling over strings

   (b) Arguing about arguments

   (c) Feudin' on functionality

Answers

1. b. Applications are run with the interpreter tool, and Web pages containing applets can be run with the `appletviewer` tool as well as Java-capable World Wide Web browsers.

2. a. The `<APPLET>` tag is used along with the `<PARAM>` tag to send parameters to the applet.

3. b. Can't we all get along?

Activities

If you'd like to apply your acumen of applets and applications, do the following activities:

☐ Check out the Gamelan site at http://www.gamelan.com and use the search term *Marquee* to see links and descriptions to all of the applets that have been written to display text in a marquee sign format. Each of these applets use parameters to modify the text that is displayed.

☐ Write a Java applet that can handle a parameter named X and a parameter named Y. Display the two numbers in a drawString() statement like the one in the RootApplet program.

4

PART

II

Learning the Basics of Programming

Hour

Hour 5

Storing and Changing Information in a Program

In Hour 2, "Writing Your First Program," you used a *variable*, a special storage place that is used to hold information. The information stored in variables can be changed as your program runs, which is why they're called variables. Your first program stored an integer number in a variable called debt. Integers are only one of the types of information that can be stored in variables. Variables also can hold characters, lines of text, floating-point numbers, and other things.

Variables are the main way that a computer remembers something as it runs a program. The BigDebt program used the debt variable to tell the computer that the national debt increases by $59 million per day. The computer needed to remember that fact a little later so a minute's worth of debt increase could be calculated. During this hour, you'll learn more about using variables in your Java programs.

The following topics will be covered during this hour:

- ☐ Creating variables
- ☐ The different types of variables
- ☐ Storing values into variables
- ☐ Using variables in mathematical expressions
- ☐ Putting one variable's value into another variable
- ☐ Increasing and decreasing a variable's value

Statements and Expressions

Computer programs are a set of instructions that tell the computer what to do. Each of these instructions is called a *statement*. The following example from a Java program is a statement:

```
int HighScore = 400000;
```

In a Java program, you can use brackets to group statements. These groupings are called *block statements*. Consider the following portion of a program:

```
1: public static void main (String[] arguments) {
2:     int a = 3;
3:     int b = 4;
4:     int c = 8 * 5;
5: }
```

Lines 2–4 of this example are a block statement. The opening bracket on Line 1 denotes the beginning of the block, and the closing bracket on Line 5 denotes the end of the block.

Some statements are called *expressions* because they involve a mathematical expression. Line 4 in the preceding example is an expression because it sets the value of the c variable equal to 8 multiplied by 5. You'll be working with several different types of expressions throughout the coming sections.

Assigning Variable Types

In a Java program, variables are created with a statement that must include two things:

- ☐ The name of the variable
- ☐ The type of information the variable will store

To see the different types of variables and how they are created, load the word processor you're using to write programs and set it up to start a new file. You will be creating a program called `Variable`.

Give your new file the name Variable.java, and start writing the program by entering the following lines:

```
class Variable {
   public static void main (String[] arguments) {
           // Coming soon: variables
   }
}
```

Go ahead and save these lines before making any changes.

Integers and Floating-Point Numbers

So far, the Variable program has a main() block with only one statement in it—the comment line Coming soon: variables. Delete the comment line and enter the following statement in its place:

```
int tops;
```

This statement creates a variable named tops. This statement does not specify a value for tops, so the variable is an empty storage space for the moment. The int text at the beginning of the statement designates tops as a variable that will be used to store integer numbers. You can use the int type to store most of the nondecimal numbers that you will need in your computer programs. It can hold any integer from -2.14 billion to 2.14 billion.

Create a blank line after the int tops; statement and add the following statement:

```
float gradePointAverage;
```

This statement creates a variable with the name gradePointAverage. The float text stands for floating-point numbers. Floating-point variables are used to store numbers that might contain a decimal point.

JUST A MINUTE

A floating-point variable could be used to store a grade point average such as 2.25, to pick a number that's dear to my heart. It also could be used to store a number such as 0, which is the percentage chance of getting into a good graduate school with that grade point average, despite my really good cover letter and a compelling written recommendation from my parole officer.

Characters and Strings

Because all the variables you have dealt with so far are numeric, you might have the mistaken impression that all variables are used with numbers. You can also use variables to store text.

Two types of text can be stored as variables: characters and strings. A *character* is a single letter, number, punctuation mark, or other symbol. Most of the things you can use as characters are shown on your computer's keyboard. A *string* is a group of characters.

Your next step in creating the `Variable` program is to create a `char` variable and a `String` variable. Add these two statements after the line `float gradePointAverage;`:

```
char key = 'C';
String productName = "Orbitz";
```

When you are using character values in your program, such as in the preceding example, you must put single quote marks on both sides of the character value being assigned to a variable. You must surround string values with double quote marks. These quote marks are needed to prevent the character or string from being confused with a variable name or other part of a statement. Take a look at the following statement:

```
String productName = Orbitz;
```

This statement might look like a statement that tells the computer to create a `String` variable called `productName` and give it the text value of `Orbitz`. However, because there are no quote marks around the word `Orbitz`, the computer is being told to set the `productName` value to the same value as a variable named `Orbitz`.

After adding the `char` and `String` statements, your program should resemble Listing 5.1. Make any changes that are needed and be sure to save the file. This program does not produce anything to display, but you should compile it with the `javac` compiler tool to make sure it was created correctly.

Listing 5.1. The `Variable` program.

```
1: class Variable {
2:     public static void main (String[] arguments) {
3:         int tops;
4:         float gradePointAverage;
5:         char key = 'C';
6:         String productName = "Orbitz";
7:     }
8: }
```

The last two variables in the `Variable` program use the = sign to assign a starting value when the variables are created. You can use this option for any variables that you create in a Java program. For more information, see the section called "Storing Information in Variables."

5

JUST A MINUTE

Although the other variable types are all lowercase letters (`int`, `float`, `char`), the capital letter is required in the word `String` when creating `String` variables. A string in a Java program is somewhat different than the other types of information you will use in variables. You'll learn about this distinction in Hour 6, "Using Strings to Communicate."

Other Numeric Variable Types

The variables that you have been introduced to so far will be the main ones that you use during this book and probably for most of your Java programming. There are a few other types of variables you can use in special circumstances.

You can use three other variable types with integers. The first, `byte`, can be used for integer numbers that range from -128 to 127. The following statement creates a variable called `escapeKey` with an initial value of 27:

```
byte escapeKey = 27;
```

The second, `short`, can be used for integers that are smaller in size than the `int` type. A `short` integer can range from -32,768 to 32,767, as in the following example:

```
short roomNumber = 222;
```

The last of the special numeric variable types, `long`, is typically used for integers that are too big for the `int` type to hold. A `long` integer can be of almost any size; if the number has five commas or less when you write it down, it can fit into a `long`. Some six-comma numbers can fit as well.

Except for times when your integer number is bigger than 2.14 billion or smaller than -2.14 billion, you won't need to use any of these special variable types very often. If they're muddling your understanding of variable types, concentrate on `int` and `float`. Those types are the ones you'll be using most often.

The `boolean` Variable Type

Java has a special type of variable that can only be used to store the value `true` or the value `false`. This type of variable is called a `boolean`. At first glance, a `boolean` variable might not seem particularly useful unless you plan to write a lot of computerized true-or-false quizzes. However, `boolean` variables will be used in a variety of situations in your programs. The following are some examples of questions that `boolean` variables can be used to answer:

☐ Has the user pressed a key?

☐ Is the game over?

☐ Is this the first time the user has done something?

☐ Is the bank account overdrawn?

☐ Have all 10 images been displayed onscreen?

☐ Can the rabbit eat Trix?

The following statement is used to create a `boolean` variable called `gameOver`:

```
boolean gameOver = false;
```

This variable has the starting value of `false`, and a statement such as this one could be used in a game program to indicate that the game isn't over yet. Later on, when something happens to end the game (such as the destruction of all of the player's acrobatic Italian laborers), the `gameOver` variable can be set to `true`. Although the two possible `boolean` values—`true` and `false`—look like strings in a program, you should not surround them with quote marks. Hour 7, "Using Conditional Tests to Make Decisions," describes `boolean` variables more fully.

COFFEE BREAK   Boolean numbers are named for George Boole, who lived from 1815 to 1864. Boole, a British mathematician who was mostly self-taught until late adulthood, invented Boolean algebra, a fundamental part of computer programming, digital electronics, and logic.

Naming Your Variables

Variable names in Java can begin with a letter, underscore character (_), or a dollar sign ($). The rest of the name can be any letters or numbers, but you cannot use blank spaces. You can give your variables any names that you like under those rules, but you should be consistent in how you name variables. This section outlines the generally recommended naming method for variables.

CAUTION   Java is case-sensitive when it comes to variable names, so you must always capitalize variable names in the same way throughout a program. For example, if the `gameOver` variable is used as `GameOver` somewhere in the program, the `GameOver` statement will cause an error when you compile the program.

5

First, the name that you give a variable should describe its purpose in some way. The first letter should be lowercase, and if the variable name has more than one word, make the first letter of each word a capital letter. For instance, if you wanted to create an integer variable to store the all-time high score in a game program, you could use the following statement:

```
int allTimeHighScore;
```

You can't use punctuation marks or spaces in a variable name, so neither of the following would work:

```
int all-TimeHigh Score;
int all Time High Score;
```

If you tried to use these names in a program, the Java compiler would respond with an error.

Storing Information in Variables

As you have seen, in a Java program you can put a value into a variable at the same time that you create the variable. You also can put a value in the variable at any time later in the program.

To set up a starting value for a variable upon its creation, use the equals sign (=). The following is an example of creating a floating-point variable called pi with the starting value of 3.14:

```
float pi = 3.14;
```

All variables that store numbers can be set up in a similar fashion. If you're setting up a variable for a character or a string, you must place quote marks around the value as shown previously.

You also can set one variable equal to the value of another variable if they both are of the same type. Consider the following example:

```
int mileage = 300;
int totalMileage = mileage;
```

First, an integer variable called mileage is created with a starting value of 300. In the second line, an integer variable called totalMileage is created with the same value as mileage. Both variables will have the starting value of 300. In future hours, you will learn ways to convert one variable's value to the type of another variable.

5

CAUTION

If you do not give a variable a starting value, you must give it a value before you try to use it. If you don't, when you attempt to compile your program, the javac compiler will respond with an error message such as the following:

```
WarGame.java:7: Variable warships may not have been initialized.
                warships = warships + 10;
            ^
1 error
```

Workshop: Using Expressions

As you worked on a particularly unpleasant math problem in school, did you ever complain to a higher power, protesting that you would never use this knowledge again in your life? Sorry to break this to you, but all your teachers were right: Those math skills are going to be used in your computer programming.

That's the bad news. The good news is that the computer will do any of the math that you ask it to do. As mentioned earlier in this hour, any instructions you give a computer program involving math are called expressions. Expressions will be used frequently in your computer programs. You can use them for tasks such as the following:

☐ Changing the value of a variable

☐ Counting the number of times something has happened in a program

☐ Using a mathematical formula in a program

As you write computer programs, you will find yourself drawing upon your old math lessons as you use expressions. Expressions can use addition, subtraction, multiplication, division, and modulus division.

To see expressions in action, return to your word processor and close the Variable.java file if it is still open. Create a new file and save it as Elvis.java. The Elvis program creates a fictional person whose weight loss and weight gain can be tracked with mathematical expressions. Instead of adding statements to the program piece by piece, enter the full text of Listing 5.2 into the word processor. Each part of the program will be discussed in turn.

Listing 5.2. The Elvis program.

```
 1: class Elvis {
 2:     public static void main(String[] arguments) {
 3:         int weight = 250;
 4:         System.out.println("Elvis weighs " + weight);
 5:         System.out.println("Elvis visits a few all-you-can-eat rib joints.");
 6:         System.out.println("Elvis throws a Thanksgiving luau.");
 7:         weight = weight + 10;
 8:         System.out.println("Elvis now weighs " + weight);
 9:         System.out.println("Elvis discovers aerobics.");
10:         weight = weight - 15;
11:         System.out.println("Elvis now weighs " + weight);
```

5

```
12:        System.out.println("Elvis falls into a washing machine during the
13:        shrink cycle.");
14:        weight = weight / 3;
15:        System.out.println("Elvis now weighs " + weight);
16:        System.out.println("Elvis accidentally clones himself 12 times.");
17:        weight = weight + (weight * 12);
18:        System.out.println("The 13 Elvii now weigh " + weight);
19:    }
20: }
```

When you're done, save the file and use the javac tool to compile the program. In the same directory as the Elvis.java file, type the following command to compile the Elvis program:

```
javac Elvis.java
```

If it compiles without any errors, you will not see any output; javac responds only if something goes wrong. If you do see error messages, check the line number that is listed in the error message to look for typos. Correct any typos that you find and compile the program.

Next, run the program by typing the following command:

```
java Elvis
```

Listing 5.3 shows the output for this program.

Listing 5.3. The output of the Elvis program.

```
Elvis weighs 250
Elvis visits a few all-you-can-eat rib joints.
Elvis throws a Thanksgiving luau.
Elvis now weighs 260
Elvis discovers aerobics.
Elvis now weighs 245
Elvis falls into a washing machine during the shrink cycle.
Elvis now weighs 81
Elvis accidentally clones himself 12 times.
The 13 Elvii now weigh 1053
```

As in the other programs that you have created, the Elvis program uses a main() block statement for all of its work. This statement can be divided into the following five sections:

1. Lines 3–4: The initial weight of Elvis is set to 250.

2. Lines 5–8: Elvis gains weight.

3. Lines 9–11: Elvis loses weight.

4. Lines 12–14: Elvis reduces in size dramatically.

5. Lines 15–17: Elvis multiplies.

Line 3 creates the `weight` variable and designates it as an integer variable with `int`. The variable is given the initial value 250, and it is used throughout the program to monitor Elvis' weight.

The next line is similar to several other statements in the program:

```
System.out.println("Elvis weighs " + weight);
```

The `System.out.println()` command displays a string that is contained within the parentheses. In the preceding line, the text `Elvis weighs` is displayed, followed by the value of the `weight` variable. There are numerous `System.out.println()` statements in the program. If you're still unclear about how these statements work, look at each of them in Listing 5.2 and compare them to the corresponding lines in Listing 5.3.

All About Operators

Four different mathematical expressions are used in the `Elvis` program to add weight to Elvis, subtract weight from Elvis, divide it, and finish it off with some multiplication. Each of these expressions uses symbols (+, -, *, /, and %) called *operators*. You will be using these operators to crunch numbers throughout your Java programs.

An addition expression in Java uses the + sign, as in Line 7 of your program:

```
weight = weight + 10;
```

This line sets the `weight` variable equal to its current value plus 10. Because the `weight` was set to 250 when it was created, Line 7 changes `weight` to 260.

A subtraction expression uses the - sign, as in Line 10:

```
weight = weight - 15;
```

This expression sets the `weight` variable equal to its current value minus 15. The `weight` variable is now equal to 245.

A division expression uses the / sign, as in Line 13:

```
weight = weight / 3;
```

The `weight` variable is set to its current value divided by 3 and rounded down because `weight` is an integer. The `weight` variable is now equal to 81.

There's another expression that you can use to find the remainder of a division. When the value of the `weight` variable was divided by 3 in Line 13, a remainder of 2 was discarded in order for `weight` to remain as an integer value. To find a remainder from an expression, use

5

the % operator. You could use the following statement to find the remainder of 245 divided by 3:

```
remainder = 245 % 3;
```

A multiplication expression uses the * sign. Line 16 uses a multiplication expression as part of a more complicated statement:

```
weight = weight + (weight * 12);
```

The weight * 12 part of the expression multiplies weight by 12. The full statement takes the current value of weight and adds it to weight multiplied by 12. This example shows how more than one expression can be combined in a statement. The result is that weight becomes 1,053—in other words, 81 + (81 * 12).

Incrementing and Decrementing a Variable

One thing you will need to do often is to change the value of a variable by 1. Because this task is so common, there are special, simplified ways to accomplish it in your Java programs. You can increase the value by 1, which is called *incrementing* the variable, or decrease the value by 1, which is *decrementing* the variable. You use special operators for each of these tasks.

To increment the value of a variable by 1, use the ++ operator, as in the following statement:

```
x++;
```

This statement adds 1 to the value stored in the x variable.

To decrement the value of a variable by 1, use the -- operator:

```
y--;
```

This statement reduces y by 1.

COFFEE BREAK

During Hour 1, "Becoming a Programmer," the name of the C++ programming language was described as a joke you'd understand later on. Now that you've been introduced to the increment operator ++, you have all the information you need to figure out why C++ has two plus signs instead of just one. If you're still having trouble, C++ adds new features and functionality to the C programming language in the same way that the ++ operator adds 1 to a variable. Just think: After you work through all 24 hours of this book, you'll be able to tell jokes that are incomprehensible to more than 99 percent of the world's population.

5

Operator Precedence

When you are using an expression with more than one operator, you need to know what order the computer will use as it works out the expression. Consider the following statement:

```
x = y * 3 + 5;
```

Unless you know what order the computer will use when working out the math in this expression, you cannot be sure what the x variable will be set to. If y is equal to 10 and multiplication occurs before addition, x will equal 35. If y equals 10 and addition occurs before multiplication, x will equal 80.

The following order is used when working out an expression:

- ☐ Incrementing and decrementing take place first.
- ☐ Multiplication, division, and modulus division occur next.
- ☐ Addition and subtraction follow.
- ☐ Comparisons take place next.
- ☐ The equal sign = is used to set a variable's value.

Comparisons will be discussed during Hour 7. The rest has been described during this hour, so you should be able to figure out the result of the following statement:

```
int number = 5++ * 6 + 4 * 10 / 2;
```

This statement sets the number variable to 56. How does the computer come up with this number? First, the increment operator is handled, and 5++ is set to the value of 5 increased by 1—in other words, 6. The expression then becomes the following:

```
int number = 6 * 6 + 4 * 10 / 2;
```

Now, multiplication and division are handled from left to right. First, 6 is multiplied by 6. Then 4 is multiplied by 10 and that result is divided by 2 (4 * 10 / 2). The expression becomes the following:

```
int number = 36 + 20;
```

This expression results in the number variable being set to 56.

If you want an expression to be evaluated in a different order, you can use parentheses to group parts of an expression that should be handled first. For example, the expression x = 5 * 3 + 2; would normally cause x to equal 17 because multiplication is handled before addition. However, look at a modified form of that expression:

```
x = 5 * (3 + 2);
```

In this case, the expression within the parentheses is handled first, so the result equals 25. You can use parentheses as often as needed in a statement.

5

Summary

Now that you have been introduced to variables and expressions, you can give a wide range of instructions to your computer in a program. Programs that you write can accomplish many of the same tasks as a calculator by handling sophisticated mathematical equations with ease. Manipulating numbers is only one element of variable use. You also can handle characters, strings of characters, and special true-or-false values called `boolean` variables. The next hour will expand your knowledge of `String` variables and how they are used.

Q&A

Q Is a line in a Java program the same thing as a statement?

A No. Although the programs that you will create in this book put one statement on each line, this is done to make the programs easier to understand; it's not required. The Java compiler does not consider lines, spacing, or other formatting issues when compiling a program. The compiler just wants to see semicolons at the end of each statement. You can put more than one statement on a line, although this is not generally recommended.

Q Is there a reason to set up a variable without giving it a value right away?

A For many of the simple programs that you will be creating in the first several hours, no. However, there are many circumstances where it makes more sense to give a variable a value at some point later in the program. One example would be a calculator program. The variable that stores the result of a calculation will not be needed until a user tries out the program's calculator buttons. Therefore, you would not need to set up an initial value when creating a `result` variable.

Q What's the specific range for the `long` variable type?

A In Java, a `long` integer variable can be anything from -9,223,372,036,854,775,808 to 9,223,372,036,854,775,807. This range ought to give your mathematical expressions plenty of breathing room when you can't use `int`, which has a range of -2,147,483,648 to 2,147,483,647.

Q Why should the first letter of a variable name be lowercase, as in `gameOver`?

A It makes the variable easier to spot among all of the other elements of a Java program. Also, by following a consistent style in the naming of variables, you eliminate errors that can occur when you use a variable in several different places in a program. The style of naming used in this book has become popular since Java's release.

5

Q **Can two variables have the same letters but different capitalization, as in** `highScore` **and** `HighScore`**?**

A Each of the differently capitalized names would be treated as its own variable, so it's possible to use the same name twice in this way. However, it seems likely to cause a lot of confusion when you or someone else is attempting to figure out how the program works. It also increases the likelihood of using the wrong variable name somewhere in your program, which is an error that will not be caught during compilation. Errors like that make it into the finished product and are called *logic errors*. They must be caught by an attentive programmer during testing.

Quiz

Test your knowledge of variables, expressions, and the rest of the information in this hour by answering the following questions.

Questions

1. What do you call a group of statements contained with an opening bracket and a closing bracket?

   (a) A block statement

   (b) Groupware

   (c) Bracketed statements

2. A `boolean` variable is used to store true-or-false values.

   (a) True

   (b) False

   (c) No, thanks. I already ate.

3. What characters cannot be used to start a variable name?

   (a) A dollar sign

   (b) Two forward slash marks (//)

   (c) A letter

5

Answers

1. a. The grouped statements are called a *block statement* or a *block*.

2. a. True or false are the only answers a `boolean` variable can store.

3. b. Variables can start with a letter, dollar sign ($), or an underscore character (_). If you started a variable name with two slash marks, the rest of the line would be ignored because the slash marks are used to start a comment line.

Activities

You can review the topics of this hour more fully with the following activities:

☐ Expand the `Elvis` program to track the weight if it were incremented by one pound for three consecutive days.

☐ Create a short Java program that uses an x integer and a y integer and displays the result of x squared plus y squared.

5

Hour 6

Using Strings to Communicate

In the film *The Piano*, Holly Hunter portrays Ada, a young Scottish woman who marries badly. A mute since the age of 6, Ada can only express herself fully by playing her prized possession, a piano. Like Ada, your computer programs are capable of quietly doing their work and never stopping for a chat—or piano recital—with humans. However, if *The Piano* teaches us anything, it is that communication ranks up there with food, water, and shelter as essential needs. (It also teaches us that Harvey Keitel has a lot of body confidence, but that's a matter for another book.)

Java programs don't have access to a piano. They use strings as the primary means to communicate with users. *Strings* are collections of text—letters, numbers, punctuation, and other characters. During this hour, you will learn all about working with strings in your Java programs. The following topics will be covered:

☐ Using strings to store text
☐ Displaying strings in a program

☐ Including special characters in a string

☐ Pasting two strings together

☐ Including variables in a string

☐ Some uses for strings

☐ Comparing two strings

☐ Determining the length of a string

☐ Changing a string to uppercase or lowercase

Storing Text in Strings

Strings are a common feature in computer programming because they provide a way to store text and present it to users. The most basic element of a string is a character. A *character* is a single letter, number, punctuation mark, or other symbol.

In Java programs, a character is one of the types of information that can be stored in a variable. Character variables are created with the `char` type in a statement such as the following:

```
char keyPressed;
```

This statement creates a variable named `keyPressed` that can store a character. When you create character variables, you can set them up with an initial value, as in the following:

```
char quitKey = '@';
```

Note that the value of the character must be surrounded by single quotation marks. If it isn't, the `javac` compiler tool will respond with an error when the program is compiled.

A string is a collection of characters. You can set up a variable to hold a string value by using the `String` text and the name of the variable, as in the following statement:

```
String fullName = "Ada McGrath Stewart";
```

This statement creates a `String` variable called `fullName` and stores the text `Ada McGrath Stewart` in it, which is the full name of Hunter's pianist. In a Java statement, a string is denoted with double quotation marks around the text. These quote marks will not be included in the string itself.

Unlike the other types of variables that you have used—`int`, `float`, `char`, `boolean`, and so on—the `String` type is capitalized. The reason for this is that strings are somewhat different than the other variable types in Java. Strings are a special resource called objects, and the types of all objects are capitalized. You'll be learning about objects during Hour 10, "Creating Your First Object." The important thing to note during this hour is that strings are different than the other variable types, and because of this difference, `String` is capitalized when strings are used in a statement.

6

Displaying Strings in Programs

The most basic way to display a string in a Java program is with the `System.out.println()` statement. This statement takes any strings and other variables inside the parentheses and displays them. The following statement displays a line of text to the system output device, which is the computer's monitor:

```
System.out.println("Silence affects everyone in the end.");
```

The preceding statement would cause the following text to be displayed:

```
Silence affects everyone in the end.
```

Displaying a line of text on the screen is often called printing, which is what `println()` stands for—"print this line." You can use the `System.out.println()` statement to display text within double quotation marks and also to display variables, as you will see. Put all material that you want to be displayed within the parentheses.

Using Special Characters in Strings

When a string is being created or displayed, its text must be enclosed within double quotation marks to indicate the beginning and end of the string. These quote marks are not displayed, which brings up a good question: What if you want to display double quotation marks?

In order to display them, Java has created a special code that can be put into a string: `\"`. Whenever this code is encountered in a string, it is replaced with a double quotation mark. For example, examine the following:

```
System.out.println("Jane Campion directed \"The Piano\" in 1993.");
```

This code is displayed as the following:

```
Jane Campion directed "The Piano" in 1993.
```

You can insert several special characters into a string in this manner. The following list shows these special characters; note that each is preceded by a backslash (\).

Special characters	Display
\'	Single quotation mark
\"	Double quotation mark
\\	Backslash
\t	Tab
\b	Backspace
\r	Carriage return
\f	Formfeed
\n	Newline

The newline character causes the text following the newline character to be displayed at the beginning of the next line. Look at this example:

```
System.out.println("Music by\nMichael Nyman");
```

This statement would be displayed as the following:

```
Music by
Michael Nyman
```

Pasting Strings Together

When you use the System.out.println() statement and handle strings in other ways, you will sometimes want to paste two strings together. You do this by using the same operator that is used to add numbers: +.

The + operator has a different meaning in relation to strings. Instead of trying to do some math, it pastes two strings together. This action can cause strings to be displayed together, or it can make one big string out of two smaller ones. *Concatenation* is a word used to describe this action, because it means to link two things together. You'll probably see this term in other books as you build your programming skills, so it's worth knowing. However, pasting is the term used here to describe what happens when one string and another string decide to get together. Pasting sounds like fun. Concatenating sounds like something that should never be done in the presence of an open flame.

The following statement uses the + operator to display a long string:

```
System.out.println("\"\'The Piano\' is as peculiar and haunting as any film " +
         "I've seen.\"\n\t-- Roger Ebert, \'Chicago Sun-Times\'");
```

Instead of putting this entire string on a single line, which would make it harder to understand when you look at the program later, the + operator is used to break up the text over two lines of the program's Java text file. When this statement is displayed, it will appear as the following:

```
"'The Piano' is as peculiar and haunting as any film I've seen."
    -- Roger Ebert, 'Chicago Sun-Times'
```

Several special characters are used in the string: \", \', \n, and \t. To better familiarize yourself with these characters, compare the output with the System.out.println() statement that produced it.

6

Using Other Variables with Strings

Although you can use the + operator to paste two strings together, as demonstrated in the preceding section, you will use it more often to link strings and variables. Take a look at the following:

```
int length = 121;
char rating = 'R';
System.out.println("Running time: " + length + " minutes");
System.out.println("Rated " + rating);
```

This code will be displayed as the following:

```
Running time: 121 minutes
Rated R
```

This example displays a unique facet about how the + operator works with strings. It can allow variables that are not strings to be treated just like strings when they are displayed. The variable length is an integer set to the value 121. It is displayed between the strings Running time: and minutes. The System.out.println() statement is being asked to display a string plus an integer plus another string. This statement works because at least one part of the group is a string. The Java language offers this functionality to make displaying information easier.

One thing that you might want to do with a string is paste something to it several times, as in the following example:

```
String searchKeywords = "";
searchKeywords = searchKeywords + "drama ";
searchKeywords = searchKeywords + "romance ";
searchKeywords = searchKeywords + "New Zealand ";
```

This code would result in the searchKeywords variable being set to drama romance New Zealand. The first line creates the searchKeywords variable and sets it to be an empty string because there's nothing between the double quotation marks. The second line sets the searchKeywords variable equal to its current string plus the string drama added to the end. The next two lines add romance and New Zealand in the same way.

As you can see, when you are pasting more text at the end of a variable, the name of the variable has to be listed twice. Java offers a shortcut to simplify this process a bit: the += operator. The += operator combines the functions of the = and + operators. With strings, it is used to add something to the end of an existing string. The searchKeywords example can be shortened by using +=, as shown in the following code:

```
String searchKeywords = "";
searchKeywords += "drama ";
searchKeywords += "romance ";
searchKeywords += "New Zealand ";
```

This code produces the same result: searchKeywords is set to drama romance New Zealand.

6

Advanced String Handling

In addition to creating strings, pasting them together, and using them with other types of variables, there are several different ways you can examine a string variable and change its value. These advanced features are possible because strings are objects in the Java language. Working with strings develops skills that you'll be using to work with other objects later.

Comparing Two Strings

One thing you will be testing often in your programs is whether one string is equal to another. You do this by using `equals()` in a statement with both of the strings, as in this example:

```
String favorite = "piano";
String guess = "ukelele";
System.out.println("Is Ada's favorite instrument a " + guess + "?");
System.out.println("Answer: " + favorite.equals(guess));
```

This example uses two different string variables. One, `favorite`, is used to store the name of Ada's favorite instrument: a piano. The other, `guess`, is used to store a guess as to what her favorite might be. The guess is that Ada prefers the ukelele.

The third line displays the text `Is Ada's favorite instrument a` followed by the value of the `guess` variable and then a question mark. The fourth line displays the text `Answer:` and then contains something new:

```
favorite.equals(guess)
```

This part of the statement is known as a method. A *method* is a way to accomplish a task in a Java program. This method's task is to determine if one string, `favorite`, has the same value as another string, `guess`. If the two string variables have the same value, the text `true` will be displayed. If not, the text `false` will be displayed. The following is the output of this example:

```
Is Ada's favorite instrument a ukelele?
Answer: false
```

Determining the Length of a String

It can be useful at times to determine the length of a string in characters. You do this by using the `length()` method. This method works in the same fashion as the `equals()` method, except that only one string variable is involved. Look at the following example:

```
String cinematographer = "Stuart Dryburgh";
int nameLength = cinematographer.length();
```

This example sets `nameLength`, an integer variable, equal to 15. The `cinematographer.length()` method counts the number of characters in the string variable called `cinematographer`, and this count is assigned to the `nameLength` integer variable.

6

Changing a String's Case

Because computers take everything literally, it's easy to confuse them. Although a human would recognize that the text *Harvey Keitel* and the text *HARVEY KEITEL* are referring to the same thing, most computers would disagree. For instance, the equals() method discussed previously in this hour would state authoritatively that *Harvey Keitel* is not equal to *HARVEY KEITEL*.

To get around some of these obstacles, Java has methods that display a string variable as all uppercase letters (toUpperCase()) or all lowercase letters (toLowerCase()). The following example shows the toUpperCase() method in action:

```
String baines = "Harvey Keitel";
String change = baines.toUpperCase();
```

This code sets the string variable change equal to the baines string variable converted to all uppercase letters—HARVEY KEITEL, in other words. The toLowerCase() method works in the same fashion but returns an all-lowercase string value.

Workshop: Presenting Credits

Ada McGrath Stewart was thrown into unfamiliar territory when she moved from Scotland to New Zealand to marry a stranger who didn't appreciate her ivory tickling. You might have felt similarly lost with some of the topics introduced during this hour.

As a workshop to reinforce the string handling features that have been covered, you will write a Java program to display credits for a feature film. You have three guesses as to the movie chosen, and if you need a hint, it starts with a *The* and ends with a musical instrument that can be used to express the repressed passion of attractive mutes.

Load the word processor you're using to write Java programs and create a new file called Credits.java. Enter the text of Listing 6.1 into the word processor and save the file when you're done.

Listing 6.1. The Credits program.

```
1: class Credits {
2:     public static void main(String[] arguments) {
3:         // set up film information
4:         String title = "The Piano";
5:         int year = 1993;
6:         String director = "Jane Campion";
7:         String role1 = "Ada";
8:         String actor1 = "Holly Hunter";
```

continues

6

Listing 6.1. continued

```
 9:          String role2 = "Baines";
10:          String actor2 = "Harvey Keitel";
11:          String role3 = "Stewart";
12:          String actor3 = "Sam Neill";
13:          String role4 = "Flora";
14:          String actor4 = "Anna Paquin";
15:          // display information
16:          System.out.println(title + " (" + year + ")\n" +
17:                    "A " + director + " film.\n\n" +
18:                    role1 + "\t" + actor1 + "\n" +
19:                    role2 + "\t" + actor2 + "\n" +
20:                    role3 + "\t" + actor3 + "\n" +
21:                    role4 + "\t" + actor4);
22:      }
23: }
```

Before you attempt to compile the program with the javac tool, look over the program and see whether you can figure out what it's doing at each stage. Here's a breakdown of what's taking place:

☐ Line 1 gives the Java program the name Credits.

☐ Line 2 begins the main() block statement in which all of the program's work gets done.

☐ Line 3 is a comment statement explaining that you're going to set up the film's information in subsequent lines.

☐ Lines 4–14 set up variables to hold information about the film, its director, and its stars. One of the variables, year, is an integer. The rest are string variables.

☐ Line 15 is another comment line for the benefit of humans like us examining the program.

☐ Lines 16–21 are one long System.out.println() statement. Everything between the first parenthesis on Line 16 and the last parenthesis on Line 21 is displayed on-screen. The newline text (\n) causes the text after it to be displayed at the beginning of a new line. The Tab text (\t) inserts Tab spacing in the output. The rest is either text or string variables that should be shown.

☐ Line 22 ends the main() block statement.

☐ Line 23 ends the program.

Attempt to compile the program by going to the directory that contains Credits.java and typing this command:

```
javac Credits.java
```

6

If you do not see any error messages, the program has compiled successfully, and you can run it with the following command:

```
java Credits
```

If you do encounter error messages, correct any typos that you find in your version of the Credits program and try again to compile it.

Listing 6.2 shows the output of the Credits program: a rundown of the film, year of release, director, and the four lead performers from *The Piano*. Be glad that you didn't have to present the credits for an ensemble film. A program detailing Robert Altman's *Short Cuts*, the 1993 film with more than 25 lead characters, could hog an hour on typing alone.

Listing 6.2. The output of the Credits program.

```
The Piano 1993
A Jane Campion film.
Ada      Holly Hunter
Baines   Harvey Keitel
Stewart  Sam Neill
Flora    Anna Paquin
```

COFFEE BREAK

If this hour's trivia related to *The Piano* and the films of director Jane Campion has sparked your curiosity, or if you just dig quiet women in braids, visit the following World Wide Web sites:

☐ Magnus Hjelstuen's unofficial The Piano Web site, with cast descriptions, storyline discussion, and comprehensive details about his favorite movie:

http://www.ifi.uio.no/~magnush/Piano/

☐ The Internet Movie Database, a voluminous yet searchable database of movies, TV shows, actors, directors, yet other related topics:

http://www.imdb.com

Summary

Once your version of Credits works like the one shown in Listing 6.2, give yourself some credits, too. You're writing longer Java programs and dealing with more sophisticated issues each hour. Like variables, strings are something you'll use every time you sit down to write a program.

At the beginning of *The Piano*, Holly Hunter's Ada lost her piano when her new husband refused to make his Maori laborers carry it home. Luckily for you, the ability to use strings in your Java programs cannot be taken away by an insensitive newlywed or anyone else. You'll be using strings in many ways to communicate with users.

Q&A

Q In addition to `System.out.println()`, what are some other ways to display strings in Java programs?

A Strings can be displayed using different means in Java programs that run on World Wide Web pages and in programs that have a graphical user interface. Web page Java programs, which are called applets, rely on a method called `drawString()` to display text. Hour 13, "Learning How Applets Work," covers several programming features that are specific to applet programming. Programs that have a graphical user interface display strings by putting them into a text-entry field or displaying them as a label next to some other part of the program's window.

Q How can I set the value of a string variable to be blank?

A A pair of double quotation marks without any text between them is considered to be an empty string. You can set a string variable equal to this upon its creation or in other parts of your programs. The following code creates a new string variable called `adaSays` and sets it to nothing:

```
String adaSays = "";
```

Q Is there a way to make the text in one `println()` statement start right at the end of the text in the preceding `println()` statement? I don't want the second `println()` statement to start at the beginning of a new line, but it always does.

A Java automatically starts each `System.out.println()` statement on its own new line, so the only way to prevent this is to use a statement that includes all of the text you want to display. The `Credits` program from the workshop has an example of a `println()` statement that includes several different lines of output. Take a look at it and see whether it fits what you want to do.

Q If the + operator is used with strings to link up two different strings, can you add the numeric value of one string to the value of another?

A You can use the value of a `String` variable as an integer only by using a method that converts the string's value into a numeric form. This procedure is called casting because it recasts existing information, in this case a string, as a different type of information.

6

Q **Is it necessary to use += instead of + when adding some text to a string variable?**

A Not at all. The += operator is strictly for the benefit of programmers who want to use it as a shortcut. If you're more comfortable using the + operator when pasting some added text to a string variable, you ought to stick with it. The time and convenience you can gain by using += will be lost pretty quickly if it causes you to make errors in your program.

Q **Isn't there some kind of == operator that can be used to determine whether two strings have the same value, as in `daughter == "Flora"`?**

A As you will discover during the next hour, "Using Conditional Tests to Make Decisions," the == operator can be used with all of the variable types except for strings. The reason for the difference is that strings are objects. Java treats objects differently than other types of information, so special methods are necessary to determine whether one string is equal to another.

Q **Do all methods in Java display `true` or `false` in the same way that the `equals()` method does in relation to strings?**

A Methods have different ways of making a response after they are used. When a method sends back a value, as the `equals()` method does, this is called *returning* a value. The `equals()` method is set to return a Boolean value. Other methods might return a string, an integer, another type of variable, or nothing at all.

Quiz

The following questions will test your knowledge of the care and feeding of a string.

Questions

1. My friend concatenates. Should I report him to the authorities?
   (a) No. It's illegal only during the winter months.
   (b) Yes, but not until I sell my story to *Hard Copy* first.
   (c) No. All he's doing is pasting two strings together in a program.
2. Why is the word `String` capitalized while `int` and others are not?
   (a) `String` is a full word, but `int` ain't.
   (b) Like all objects in Java, `String` has a capitalized name.
   (c) Poor quality control at JavaSoft.

3. Which of the following characters will put a single quote in a string?

    (a) `<QUOTE>`

    (b) `\'`

    (c) `'`

Answers

1. c. Concatenation is just another word for pasting, joining, melding, or otherwise connecting two strings together. It uses the + and += operators.

2. b. The types of objects available in Java are all capitalized, which is the main reason variable names have a lowercase first letter. It makes it harder to mistake them for objects.

3. b. The single backslash is what begins one of the special characters that can be inserted into strings.

Activities

You can review the topics of this hour more fully with the following activities:

☐ Write a short Java program called `Favorite` that puts the code from this hour's "Comparing Two Strings" section into the `main()` block statement. Test it out to make sure it works as described and says that Ada's favorite instrument is not the ukelele. Then, change the initial value of the `guess` variable from `ukelele` to `piano`. See what happens.

☐ Modify the `Credits` program so that the names of the director and all performers are displayed entirely in uppercase letters.

6

Hour 7

Using Conditional Tests to Make Decisions

Writing a computer program has been compared to telling a household robot what to do. You provide the computer a list of instructions, called *statements*, and these instructions are followed to the letter. You can tell the computer to work out some unpleasant mathematical formulas, and it will work them out for you. Tell it to display some information, and it will dutifully respond.

However, there are times when you need the computer to be more selective about what it does. For example, if you have written a program to balance your checkbook, you might want the computer to display a warning message if your account is overdrawn. The warning could be something along the lines of `Hear that bouncing noise? It's your checks`. The computer should display this message only if your account is overdrawn. If it isn't, the message would be both inaccurate and emotionally upsetting.

The way to accomplish this task in a Java program is to use a statement called a conditional. *Conditionals* cause something to happen in a program only if a specific condition is met. Country star Kenny Rogers sang with the hippie-rock group The First Edition in the late '60s, and one of the group's singles hit the top 5 in 1968: "Just Dropped In (To See What Condition My Condition Was In)". During this hour, you'll be dropping in to check the condition of several things in your Java programs using the conditional statements `if`, `else`, `switch`, `case`, and `break`. You also will be using several conditional operators: `==`, `!=`, `<`, `>`, and `?`. The following topics will be covered:

☐ Testing to see whether conditions are met

☐ Using the `if` statement for basic conditional tests

☐ Using other statements in conjunction with `if`

☐ Testing whether one value is greater than or less than another

☐ Testing whether two values are equal or unequal

☐ Using `else` statements as the opposite of `if` statements

☐ Chaining several conditional tests together

☐ Using the `switch` statement for complicated conditional tests

☐ Creating complicated tests with the ternary operator

`if` Statements

If you want to test a condition in a Java program, the most basic way is with an `if` statement. As you learned previously, the `boolean` variable type is used to store only two possible values: `true` or `false`. The `if` statement works along the same lines, testing to see whether a condition is true or false and taking action only if the condition is true.

You use `if` along with a condition to test, as in the following statement:

```
if (account < 0.01)
    System.out.println("Hear that bouncing noise? It's your checks");
```

Although this code is listed on two lines, it's one statement. The first part uses `if` to determine whether the `account` variable is less than 0.01 by using the `<` operator. The second part displays the text `Hear that bouncing noise? It's your checks`. The second part of the `if` statement will be run only if the first part is true. If the `account` variable has a value of 0.01 (1 cent) or higher, the `println` statement will be ignored. Note that the condition that you test with an `if` statement must be surrounded by parentheses, as in (`account < 0.01`).

7

JUST A MINUTE

> If you're not sure why if (account < 0.01) is not a statement on its own, note that there is no semicolon at the end of the line. In Java programs, semicolons are used to show where one statement ends and the next one begins. In the preceding example, the semicolon does not appear until after the println portion of the statement. If you put a semicolon after the if portion, as in if (account < 0.01);, you'll cause an error in your program that can be hard to spot. Take care regarding semicolons when you start using the if statement.

The less than operator, <, is one of several different operators that you can use with conditional statements. You'll become more familiar with the if statement as you use it with some of the other operators.

Less Than and Greater Than Comparisons

In the preceding section, the < operator is used the same way it was used in math class, as a less-than sign. There also is a greater-than conditional operator, >. This operator is used in the following statements:

```
if (elephantWeight > 780)
    System.out.println("This elephant is too fat for your tightrope act.");
if (elephantTotal > 12)
    cleaningExpense = cleaningExpense + 150;
```

The first if statement tests whether the value of the elephantWeight variable is greater than 780. The second if statement tests whether the elephantTotal variable is greater than 12.

One thing to learn about if statements is that they often cause nothing to happen in your programs. If the preceding two statements are used in a program where elephantWeight is equal to 600 and elephantTotal is equal to 10, the rest of the statements will be ignored. It's as though you are giving an order to a younger sibling who is subject to your whims: "Jerry, go to the store. If they have Everlasting Gobstopper candy, buy some for me. If not, do nothing and await further orders."

There will be times when you will want to determine whether something is less than or equal to something else. You can do this with the <= operator, as you might expect; use the >= operator for greater-than-or-equal-to tests. Here's an example:

```
if (account <= 0)
    System.out.println("Hear that bouncing noise? It's your checks");
```

This revision of the checkbook example mentioned previously should be a bit easier to understand. It tests whether account is less than or equal to the value 0 and taunts the user if it is.

7

Equal and Not Equal Comparisons

Another condition to check on in a program is equality. Is a variable equal to a specific value? Is one variable equal to the value of another? These questions can be answered with the == value, as in the following statements:

```
if (answer == rightAnswer)
    studentGrade = studentGrade + 10;
if (studentGrade == 100)
    System.out.println("Congratulations — a perfect score!");
```

CAUTION

> The operator used to conduct equality tests has two equal signs: ==. It's very easy to confuse this operator with the = operator, which is used to give a value to a variable. Always use two equal signs in a conditional statement.

You also can test inequality—whether something is not equal to something else. You do this with the != operator, as shown in the following example:

```
if (team != "New York Jets")
    chanceToWin = 50;
if (answer != rightAnswer)
    score = score - 5;
```

You can use the == and != operators with every type of variable except for one, strings. To see whether one string has the value of another, use the equals() method described during Hour 6, "Using Strings to Communicate."

Organizing a Program with Block Statements

Up to this point, all of the if statements have been followed with a single instruction, such as the println() method. In many cases, you will want to do more than one action in response to an if statement. To do this, you'll use the squiggly bracket marks { and } to create a block statement.

Block statements are statements that are organized as a group. Previously, you have seen how block statements are used to mark the beginning and end of the main() block of a Java program. Each statement within the main() block is handled when the program is run. Listing 7.1 is an example of a Java program with a block statement used to denote the main() block. The block statement begins with the opening bracket { on Line 2 and ends with the closing bracket } on Line 11. Load your word processor and enter the text of Listing 7.1 as a new file.

7

Listing 7.1. A Java program using a `main()` block statement.

```
1: class Game {
2:     public static void main(String[] arguments) {
3:         int total = 0;
4:         int score = 7;
5:         if (score == 7)
6:             System.out.println("You score a touchdown!");
7:         if (score == 3)
8:             System.out.println("You kick a field goal!");
9:         total = total + score;
10:        System.out.println("Total score: " + total);
11:    }
12: }
```

Save this file as `Game.java` and compile it with the `javac` compiler tool. The output should resemble Listing 7.2.

Listing 7.2. The output of the `Game` program.

```
You score a touchdown!
Total score: 7
```

You can also use block statements in conjunction with `if` statements to make the computer do more than one thing if a conditional statement is true. The following is an example of an `if` statement that includes a block statement:

```
if (playerScore > 9999) {
    playerLives++;
    System.out.println("Extra life!");
    difficultyLevel = difficultyLevel + 5;
}
```

The brackets are used to group all statements that are part of the `if` statement. If the variable `playerScore` is greater than 9,999, three things will happen:

☐ The value of the `playerLives` variable increases by one (because the increment operator `++` is used).

☐ The text `Extra life!` is displayed.

☐ The value of the `difficultyLevel` variable is increased by 5.

If the variable `playerScore` is not greater than 9,999, nothing will happen. All three statements inside the `if` statement block will be ignored.

7

if-else **Statements**

There are times when you want to do something if a condition is true and do something else if the condition is false. You can do this by using the `else` statement in addition to the `if` statement, as in the following example:

```
if (answer == correctAnswer) {
    score += 10;
    System.out.println("That's right. You get 10 points.");
}
else {
    score -= 5;
    System.out.println("Sorry, that's wrong. You lose 5 points.");
}
```

The `else` statement does not have a condition listed alongside it, unlike the `if` statement. Generally, the `else` statement is matched with the `if` statement that immediately comes before it in a Java program. You also can use `else` to chain several `if` statements together, as in the following example:

```
if (grade == "A")
    System.out.println("You got an A. Great job!");
else if (grade == "B")
    System.out.println("You got a B. Good work!");
else if (grade == "C")
    System.out.println("You got a C. You'll never get into a good college!");
else
    System.out.println("You got an F. You'll do well in Congress!");
```

By putting together several different `if` and `else` statements in this way, you can handle a variety of conditions. In the preceding example, a specific message is sent to A students, B students, C students, and future legislators.

switch **Statements**

The `if` and `else` statements are good for situations with only two possible conditions, but there are times when you have more than two options that need to be considered. With the preceding grade example, you saw that `if` and `else` statements can be chained to handle several different conditions.

Another way to do this is to use the `switch` statement. You can use it in a Java program to test for a variety of different conditions and respond accordingly. In the following example, the grade example has been rewritten with the `switch` statement to handle a complicated range of choices:

```
switch (grade) {
    case 'A':
        System.out.println("You got an A. Great job!");
        break;
```

7

```
        case 'B':
            System.out.println("You got a B. Good work!");
            break;
        case 'C':
            System.out.println("You got a C. You'll never get into a good col-
lege!");
            break;
        default:
            System.out.println("You got an F. You'll do well in Congress!");
    }
```

The first line of the switch statement specifies the variable that will be tested—in this example, grade. Then the switch statement uses the { and } brackets to form a block statement.

Each of the case statements checks the test variable from switch against a specific value. In this example, there are case statements for values of A, B, and C. Each of these has one or two statements that follow it. When one of these case statements matches the variable listed with switch, the computer handles the statements after the case statement until it encounters a break statement. For example, if the grade variable has the value of B, the text You got a B. Good work! will be displayed. The next statement is break, so no other part of the switch statement will be considered. The break statement tells the computer to break out of the switch statement.

The default statement is used as a catch-all if none of the preceding case statements is true. In this example, it will occur if the grade variable does not equal A, B, or C. You do not have to use a default statement with every switch block statement that you use in your programs. If it is omitted, nothing will happen if none of the case statements has the correct value.

The Conditional Operator

The most complicated conditional statement is one that you might not find reasons to use in your programs, the ternary operator. If you find it too confusing to implement in your own programs, take heart: You can use other conditionals to accomplish the same thing.

You can use the ternary operator when you want to assign a value or display a value based on a conditional test. For example, in a video game, you might need to set the numberOfEnemies variable based on whether the skillLevel variable is greater than 5. One way to do this is with an if-else statement:

```
if (skillLevel > 5)
    numberOfEnemies = 10;
else
    numberOfEnemies = 5;
```

7

A shorter way to do this is to use the ternary operator, which is ?. A ternary operator has the following parts:

- [ ] The condition to test, surrounded by parentheses, as in (skillLevel > 5)
- [ ] A question mark (?)
- [ ] The value to use if the condition is true
- [ ] A colon (:)
- [ ] The value to use if the condition is false

To use the ternary operator to set the value of numberOfEnemies based on skillLevel, you could use the following statement:

```
numberOfEnemies = ( skillLevel > 5) ? 10 : 5;
```

You can also use the ternary operator to determine what information to display. Consider the example of a program that displays the text Mr. or Ms. depending on the value of the gender variable. You could do this action with another if-else statement:

```
if (gender == "male")
    System.out.print("Mr.");
else
    System.out.print("Ms.");
```

A shorter method is to use the ternary operator to accomplish the same thing, as in the following:

```
System.out.print( (gender == "male") ? "Mr." : "Ms." );
```

The ternary operator can be useful, but it's also the hardest element of conditional tests in Java to understand. Feel free to use the longer if and else statements if you want.

Workshop: Watching the Clock

This hour's workshop gives you another look at each of the conditional tests you can use in your programs. For this project, you will use Java's built-in timekeeping feature, which keeps track of the current date and time, and will present this information in sentence form.

Run the word processor that you're using to create Java programs and give a new document the name ClockTalk.java. This program is long, but most of it consists of long conditional statements. Type the full text of Listing 7.3 into the word processor and save the file when you're done.

7

Listing 7.3. The full text of `ClockTalk.java.`

```
 1: import java.util.*;
 2:
 3: class ClockTalk {
 4:         public static void main(String[] arguments) {
 5:                 // get current time and date
 6:                 GregorianCalendar now = new GregorianCalendar();
 7:                 int hour = now.get(Calendar.HOUROFDAY);
 8:                 int minute = now.get(Calendar.MINUTE);
 9:                 int month = now.get(Calendar.MONTH) + 1;
10:                 int day = now.get(Calendar.DAYOFMONTH);
11:                 int year = now.get(Calendar.YEAR);
12:
13:                 // display greeting
14:                 if (hour < 12)
15:                         System.out.println("Good morning.\n");
16:                 else if (hour < 17)
17:                         System.out.println("Good afternoon.\n");
18:                 else
19:                         System.out.println("Good evening.\n");
20:
21:                 // begin time message by showing the minutes
22:                 System.out.print("It's");
23:                 if (minute != 0) {
24:                         System.out.print(" " + minute + " ");
25:                         System.out.print( (minute != 1) ? "minutes" :
26:                         "minute");
27:                         System.out.print(" past");
28:                 }
29:
30:                 // display the hour
31:                 System.out.print(" ");
32:                 System.out.print( (hour > 12) ? (hour - 12) : hour );
33:                 System.out.print(" o'clock on ");
34:
35:                 // display the name of the month
36:                 switch (month) {
37:                         case (1):
38:                                 System.out.print("January");
39:                                 break;
40:                         case (2):
41:                                 System.out.print("February");
42:                                 break;
43:                         case (3):
44:                                 System.out.print("March");
45:                                 break;
46:                         case (4):
47:                                 System.out.print("April");
48:                                 break;
49:                         case (5):
50:                                 System.out.print("May");
51:                                 break;
```

continues

Listing 7.3. continued

```
52:                             case (6):
53:                                     System.out.print("June");
54:                                     break;
55:                             case (7):
56:                                     System.out.print("July");
57:                                     break;
58:                             case (8):
59:                                     System.out.print("August");
60:                                     break;
61:                             case (9):
62:                                     System.out.print("September");
63:                                     break;
64:                             case (10):
65:                                     System.out.print("October");
66:                                     break;
67:                             case (11):
68:                                     System.out.print("November");
69:                                     break;
70:                             case (12):
71:                                     System.out.print("December");
72:                     }
73:
74:                     // display the date and year
75:                     System.out.println(" " + day + ", " + year + ".");
76:             }
77: }
```

Once you have saved the file, try to compile it by entering `javac ClockTalk.java` at the command line. Correct any typos that cause error messages to occur during the attempted compilation. After the program compiles correctly, look over Lines 14–75 before going over the description of the program. See whether you can get a good idea about what is taking place in each of these sections and how the conditional tests are being used.

The `ClockTalk` program is made up of the following sections:

☐ Line 1 enables your program to use two classes that are needed to track the current date and time: `java.util.Calendar` and `java.util.GregorianCalendar`.

☐ Lines 3–4 begin the `ClockTalk` program and its `main()` statement block.

☐ Line 6 creates a variable called `now` with a special type of variable called a `GregorianCalendar`. The `now` variable stores the current date and current time and will change each time you run this program (unless, of course, the physical laws of the universe are altered and time stands still).

☐ Lines 7–11 create variables to hold the `hour`, `minute`, `month`, `day`, and `year`. These variables are used in the subsequent sections as the program displays information.

- Lines 14–19 display one of three possible greetings: Good morning., Good afternoon., or Good evening. The greeting to display is selected based on the value of the hour variable.

- Lines 22–28 display the current minute along with some accompanying text. First, the text It's is displayed in Line 22. If the value of minute is equal to 0, Lines 24–27 are ignored because of the if statement in Line 23. This statement is necessary because it would not make sense for the program to tell someone that it's 0 minutes past an hour. Line 24 displays the current value of the minute variable. A ternary operator is used in Line 25 to display either the text minutes or minute, depending on whether minute is equal to 1. Finally, in Line 27 the text past is displayed.

- Lines 30–33 display the current hour by using another ternary operator. This ternary conditional statement in Line 32 causes the hour to be displayed differently if it is larger than 12, which prevents the computer from stating things like 15 o'clock.

- Lines 36–72, almost half of the program, are a long switch statement that displays a different name of the month based on the integer value stored in the month variable.

- Lines 74–75 finish off the display by showing the current date and the year.

- Lines 76–77 close out the main() statement block and then the entire ClockTalk program.

When you run this program, the output should resemble the following code, with changes based on the current date and time. For example, if today's date is 4-13-1997 and the time is 8:30 a.m., your program would display the following text:

```
Good morning.
It's 30 minutes past 8 o'clock on April 13, 1997.
```

Run the program several times to see how it keeps up with the clock.

COFFEE BREAK

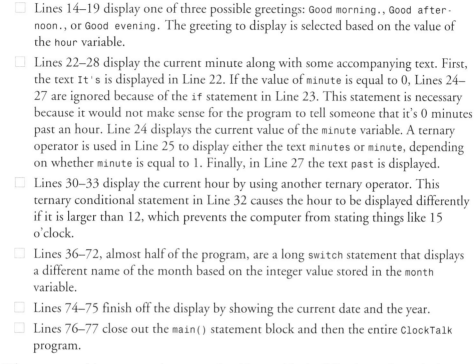

The ClockTalk program uses the Gregorian calendar system that has been used throughout the Western world for many years to determine the date and time. It was introduced in 1582 when Pope Gregory XIII moved the Julian calendar system forward 10 days—turning Oct. 5, 1582, into Oct. 15, 1582. This was needed because the calendar was moving out of alignment with the seasons due to discrepancies in the Julian system. Changes introduced with version 1.1 of the Java language make it possible to create other calendar systems for use with Java programs. Check Gamelan at http://www.gamelan.com or other Java programming resources for these calendar systems as they become available.

7

Summary

Now that you can use conditional statements, the overall intelligence of your Java programs has improved greatly. Your programs can now evaluate information and use it to react differently in different situations, even if information changes as the program is running. They can decide between two or more alternatives based on specific conditions.

Using the if statement and other conditionals in programming also promotes a type of logical thinking that can reap benefits in other aspects of your life. ("*If* she's attractive, I'll take her to an expensive restaurant, *else* we're using my two-for-one Taco Barn burrito coupon.") Programming a computer forces you to break down a task into a logical set of steps to undertake and decisions that must be made, and it provides interesting insight.

One thing that conditional statements do not offer insight about is the thinking of the lyricist who penned "Just Dropped In (To See What Condition My Condition Was In)". There may be no rational explanation for lyrics such as, "I tred on a cloud, I fell eight miles high. Told my mind I'm gonna sky. I just dropped in to see what condition my condition was in."

Q&A

Q **The if statement seems like the one that's most useful. Is it possible to use only if statements in programs and never use the others?**

A It's possible to do without else or switch, and many programmers never use the ternary operator ?. However, else and switch often are beneficial to use in your programs because they make them easier to understand. A set of if statements chained together can become unwieldy.

Q **An if statement is described as a single statement or as a conditional statement followed by another statement to handle if the condition is true. Which is it?**

A The point that might be confusing is that if statements and other conditionals are used in conjunction with other statements. The if statement makes a decision, and the other statements do work based on the decision that is made. The if statement combines a conditional statement with one or more other types of Java statements, such as statements that use the println() method or create a variable.

Q **During this hour, opening and closing brackets { and } are not used with an if statement if it is used in conjunction with only one statement. Is this mandatory?**

A No. Brackets can be used as part of any if statement to surround the part of the program that's dependent on the conditional test. Using brackets is a good practice to get into because it prevents a common error that might take place when you revise the program. If you add a second statement after an if conditional and don't add brackets, unexpected errors will occur when the program is run.

7

Q Will the Java compiler `javac` catch the error when an = operator is used with a conditional instead of an ==?

A Often no, and it results in a real doozy of a logic error. These errors only show up when a program is being run and can be discovered only through observation and testing. Because the = operator is used to assign a value to a variable, if you use `name = "Fernando"` in a spot in a program where you mean to use `name == "Fernando"`, you could wipe out the value of the `name` variable and replace it with `Fernando`. When the value stored in variables changes unexpectedly, the result is subtle and unexpected errors that you must debug.

Q Does `break` have to be used in each section of statements that follow a case?

A You don't have to use `break`. If you do not use it at the end of a group of statements, all of the remaining statements inside the `switch` block statement will be handled, regardless of the `case` value they are being tested with.

Q What's the difference between `System.out.println()` and `System.out.print()`?

A The `println()` statement displays a line of text and ends the line with a newline character. The newline character has the same behavior as the carriage return key on a manual typewriter. It causes the next text to begin displaying at the leftmost edge of the next line. The `print()` statement does not use a newline character, making it possible to use several `print()` statements to display information on the same line.

Quiz

The following questions will see what condition your knowledge of conditions is in.

Questions

1. Conditional tests result in either a true or false value. Which variable type does this remind you of?
    (a) None. They're unique.
    (b) The `long` variable type.
    (c) The `boolean` type.

2. Which statement is used as a catch-all category in a `switch` block statement?
    (a) `default`
    (b) `otherwise`
    (c) `onTheOtherHand`

3. What's a conditional?

    (a) The thing that repairs messy split ends and tangles after you shampoo.

    (b) Something in a program that tests whether a condition is true or false.

    (c) The place where you confess your sins to a neighborhood religious figure.

Answers

1. c. The `boolean` variable type can only equal `true` or `false`, making it similar to conditional tests.

2. a. `default` statements will be handled if none of the other `case` statements matches the `switch` variable.

3. b. The other descriptions are conditioner and confessional.

Activities

To improve your conditioning in terms of Java conditionals, review the topics of this hour with the following activities:

☐ Remove the `break` statement from one of the lines in the `ClockTalk` program, and then compile it and see what happens when you run it. Try it again with a few more `break` statements removed.

☐ Create a short program that stores a value of your choosing from 1 to 100 in an integer variable called `grade`. Use this `grade` variable with a conditional statement to display a different message for all A, B, C, D, and F students. Try it first with an `if` statement, and then try it with a `switch` statement.

7

Hour 8

Repeating an Action with Loops

One of the more annoying punishments for schoolchildren is to make them write something over and over again on paper or, for a capital offense, on the chalkboard. In one of his frequent trips to the board, cartoon problem child Bart Simpson had to write "I will not trade pants with others" dozens of times. This kind of punishment might work on children, but it definitely would fail on a computer. They can repeat a task with ease.

COFFEE BREAK

As you might expect, every one of Bart Simpson's chalkboard punishments has been documented on the World Wide Web. Visit the following address to see the list:

```
http://www.ncf.carleton.ca/~co378/HomePage.Chalk.html
```

Computer programs are ideally suited to do the same thing over and over again because of loops. A *loop* is a statement or set of statements that will be repeated in a program. Some loops are set to occur a fixed number of times. Others can loop indefinitely. In the Java programs that you write, you will find many circumstances in which a loop is useful. You can use them to wait until a specific thing has taken place, such as a user clicking on a button. You can also use them to cause the computer to wait and do nothing for a brief period, such as in an animation program.

To create and control loops, you use a *loop statement*. A loop statement causes a computer program to return to the same place more than once. If the term seems unusual to you, think of what a stunt plane does when it loops: It completes a circle and returns to the place it started the loop. There are three loop statements in Java: `for`, `do`, and `do-while`. These loop statements are often interchangeable in a program because each can be made to work like the others. The choice of which loop statement to use in a program often depends on personal preference, but it's beneficial to learn how all three work. You frequently can simplify a loop section of a program by choosing the right statement.

The following topics will be covered during this hour:

- ☐ Using the `for` loop
- ☐ Using the `do` loop
- ☐ Using the `do-while` loop
- ☐ Exiting a loop prematurely
- ☐ Naming a loop

for **Loops**

The most complex of the loop statements is `for`. The `for` loop is often used in cases where you want to repeat a section of a program for a fixed amount of times. It also can be used if the number of times the loop should be repeated is variable. The following is an example of a `for` loop:

```
for (int number = 0; number < 1000; number++) {
    if (number % 12 == 0)
        System.out.println("#: " + number);
}
```

This loop displays every number from 0 to 999 that is evenly divisible by 12. Every `for` loop has a variable that is used to determine when the loop should begin and end. This variable often is called the counter. The counter in the preceding loop is `number`.

The example illustrates the three parts of a `for` statement:

- ☐ The initialization section: In the first part, the `number` variable is initialized with a value of 0.

8

☐ The conditional section: In the second part, there is a conditional test like one you might use in an if statement. The test is number < 10000.

☐ The change section: The third part is a statement that changes the value of the number variable by using the increment operator.

In the initialization section, you can set up the counter variable that you want to use in the for statement. You can create the variable inside the for statement, as the number variable was created in the example, or you can create the variable elsewhere in the program. In either case, the variable should be given a starting value in this section of the for statement. The variable will have this value when the loop starts.

The conditional section contains a test that must remain true for the loop to continue looping. Once the test is false, the loop will end. In this example, the loop will end when the number variable is no longer smaller than 1,000.

The last section of the for statement contains a Java statement that changes the value of the counter variable in some way. This statement is handled each time the loop goes around. The counter variable has to change in some way, or the loop will never end. For instance, in this example, number is incremented by one using the increment operator ++ in the change section. If number were not changed, it would stay at its original value, 0, and the conditional number < 1000 would always be true.

The statements inside the bracket marks({ }) are also executed during each trip through the loop. The bracketed area is usually where the main work of the loop takes place, although some loops do all of their work in the change section.

The preceding example had two statements within the { and } marks:

```
if (number % 12 == 0)
        System.out.println("#: " + number);
```

These statements will be executed 1,000 times. The loop starts by setting the number variable equal to 0. It then adds 1 each pass through the loop and stops when number is no longer less than 1000. Every time number is evenly divisible by 12, the number is displayed next to the text #:.

JUST A MINUTE

> An unusual term that you might hear in connection with loops is iteration. An *iteration* is a single trip through a loop. The counter variable that is used to control the loop is often called an *iterator*.

Each section of a for loop is set off from the other sections with a semicolon (;). A for loop can have more than one variable set up during the initialization section and more than one statement in the change section, as in the following:

```
for (i = 0, j = 0; i * j < 1000; i++, j += 2) {
    System.out.println(i + " * " + j + " = " i * j);
}
```

These multiple statement sections of the for loop are set off by commas, as in i = 0, j = 0. This loop will display a list of equations where the i variable is multiplied by the j variable. The i variable increases by 1, and the j variable increases by 2 during each trip through the loop. Once i multiplied by j is no longer less than 1,000, the loop will end.

Sections of a for loop can be empty. An example of this would be if the counter variable has already been created with an initial value in another part of the program, as in the following:

```
for ( ; displayCount < endValue; displayCount++) {
    // loop statements would be here
}
```

CAUTION

Because many Java statements end with a semicolon, an easy mistake to make is putting a semicolon at the end of a for statement, as in the following:

```
for (int i = 0; i < 100; i++); {
    value = value + i;
}
```

In this example, the semicolon puts the statements in the brackets, value = value + i;, outside of the loop. As a result, nothing will happen as the for loop is handled. The program will compile without any errors, but you won't get the results you expect when it runs.

while **Loops**

The while loop does not have as many different sections to set up as the for loop. The only thing it needs is a conditional test, which accompanies the while statement. The following is an example of a while loop:

```
while ( gameLives > 0) {
    // the statements inside the loop go here
}
```

This loop will continue repeating until the gameLives variable is no longer greater than 0. The while statement tests the condition at the beginning of the loop, before any statements of the loop have been handled.

When a program reaches the while statement for the first time, if the tested condition is false, the statements inside the loop will be ignored. If the while condition is true, the loop goes around once and tests the `while` condition again. If the tested condition never changes inside the loop, the loop will keep looping indefinitely.

do-while **Loops**

The `do-while` loop is similar in function to the `while` loop, but the conditional test goes in a different place. The following is an example of a `do-while` loop:

```
do {
    // the statements inside the loop go here
} while ( gameLives > 0 );
```

Like the previous `while` loop, this loop will continue looping until the `gameLives` variable is no longer greater than 0. The `do-while` loop is different because the conditional test is conducted after the statements inside the loop instead of before them.

When the `do` loop is reached for the first time as a program runs, the statements between the `do` and the `while` are handled automatically. Then the `while` condition is tested to determine whether the loop should be repeated. If the `while` condition is true, the loop goes around one more time. If the condition is false, the loop ends. Something must happen inside the `do` and `while` statements that changes the condition tested with `while`, or the loop will continue indefinitely. The statements inside a `do-while` loop will always be handled at least once.

If you're still confused about the difference between a `while` loop and a `do-while` loop, engage in a little role-playing and pretend you're a teenager who wants to borrow your father's car. If you are a teenager with a case of car envy, all the better. There are two strategies that you can take:

1. Borrow the car first and tell Dad later that you did it.
2. Ask Dad before you borrow the car.

Strategy 1 has an advantage over Strategy 2 because you get to use the car once even if Dad doesn't want to let you use it. The `do-while` loop is like Strategy 1 because something happens once even if the loop condition is false the first time `while` is encountered. The `while` loop is like Strategy 2 because nothing will happen unless the `while` condition at the beginning is true. It all depends on the situation in your program. Sams.net makes no warranties express nor implied that your father will be happy if you borrow his car without telling him first.

Exiting a Loop

The normal way to exit a loop is for the condition that is tested to become false. This is true of all three types of loops in Java: `for`, `while`, and `do-while`. However, there might be times when you want a loop to end immediately even if the condition being tested is still true. You can do this with a break statement, as shown in the following code:

```
while (index <= 1000) {
    index = index + 5;
    if (index == 400)
        break;
    System.out.println("The index is " + index);
}
```

This loop will continue looping until the value of the index variable is greater than 1,000. However, a special case causes the loop to end even if the index variable is less than or equal to 1,000: If index equals 400, the loop ends immediately.

Another special-circumstance statement that you can use inside a loop is continue. The continue statement causes the loop to exit its current trip through the loop and start over at the first statement of the loop. Consider the following loop:

```
while (index <= 1000) {
    index = index + 5;
    if (index == 400)
        continue;
    System.out.println("The index is " + index);
}
```

In this loop, the statements will be handled normally unless the value of index equals 400. In that case, the continue statement causes the loop to go back to the while statement instead of the System.out.println() statement. Because of the continue statement, the loop will never display the following text:

```
The index is 400
```

You can use the break and continue statements with all three kinds of Java loop statements.

Naming a Loop

Like other statements in Java programs, loops can be put inside of each other. The following shows a for loop inside of a while loop:

```
while ( totalCoconuts < 100) {
    for ( int count = 0; count < 10; count++) {
        totalCoconuts = totalCoconuts + count;
        if (totalCoconuts > 400)
            break;
    }
}
```

The break statement will cause the for loop to end if the totalCoconuts variable equals 400 or greater. However, there might be a case where you want to break out of both loops for some

8

reason. To make this possible, you have to give the outer loop—the while statement—a name. To name a loop, put the name on the line before the beginning of the loop and follow it with a colon (:).

Once the loop has a name, you can use the name after the break or continue statement to indicate which loop the break or continue statement applies to. Note that although the name of the loop is followed by a colon at the spot where the loop begins, the colon is not used with the name in a break or continue statement. The following example repeats the previous one with the exception of one thing: If the totalCoconuts variable equals 400 or more, both loops are ended.

```
coconutLoop:
while ( totalCoconuts < 100) {
    for ( int count = 0; count < 10; count++) {
        totalCoconuts = totalCoconuts + count;
        if (totalCoconuts > 400)
            break coconutLoop;
    }
}
```

Workshop: Teaching Your Computer a Lesson

This hour's workshop provides evidence that you cannot punish your computer in the same way that Bart Simpson is punished at the beginning of each episode of *The Simpsons*. Pretend you're a teacher, and the computer is the kid who contaminated your morning cup of coffee with Thorium 230. Even if you're the most strident liberal, you realize that the computer must be taught a lesson—it's not acceptable behavior to give the teacher radiation poisoning. Your computer must be punished, and the punishment is to display the same sentence over and over again.

The Repeat program will use a loop statement to handle a System.out.println() statement again and again. Once the computer has been dealt this punishment for 25,000 sentences or one minute, whichever comes first, it can stop running and think about the error of its ways.

COFFEE BREAK

A topic of heated debate here at Sams.net concerns whether the punishment is severe enough. Thorium is a silver-white metal that has a half-life of 80,000 years. Some scientists believe that it is as toxic as plutonium, and if it finds a home in someone's liver, bone marrow, or lymphatic tissue, Thorium 230 can cause cancer, leukemia, or lung cancer. A student who irradiates a teacher probably should receive three hours of in-school detention, at least.

Use your word processor to create a new file called Repeat.java. Enter the text of Listing 8.1 and save the file when you're done.

Listing 8.1. The full source code of Repeat.java.

```
 1: import java.util.*;
 2:
 3: class Repeat {
 4:     public static void main(String arguments[]) {
 5:         String sentence = "Thorium 230 is not a toy.";
 6:         int count = 0;
 7:         GregorianCalendar start = new GregorianCalendar();
 8:         int startMinute = start.get(Calendar.MINUTE);
 9:         int startSecond = start.get(Calendar.SECOND);
10:         start.roll(Calendar.MINUTE, true);
11:         int nextMinute = start.get(Calendar.MINUTE);
12:         int nextSecond = start.get(Calendar.SECOND);
13:         while (count++ <= 25000) {
14:             System.out.println(sentence);
15:             GregorianCalendar now = new GregorianCalendar();
16:             if (now.get(Calendar.MINUTE) >= nextMinute)
17:                 if (now.get(Calendar.SECOND) >= nextSecond)
18:                     break;
19:         }
20:         System.out.println("\nI wrote the sentence " + count + " times.");
21:         System.out.println("I have learned my lesson.");
22:     }
23: }
```

The following things are taking place in this program:

☐ Line 1: The import statement makes the java.util group of classes available to this program. You're going to use two of them, Calendar and GregorianCalendar, in order to keep track of time while the program is running.

☐ Lines 2 and 3: The Repeat class is declared, and the main() block of the program begins.

☐ Lines 5 and 6: The sentence variable is set up with the text of the punishment sentence, and the count variable is created with a value of 0.

☐ Line 7: Using the GregorianCalendar class, which is used to retrieve the time information, the start variable is created with the current time.

☐ Lines 8 and 9: The get() method of the GregorianCalendar class is used to retrieve the current minute and second and store them in the variables startMinute and startSecond.

8

☐ Line 10: The GregorianCalendar roll() method is used to roll the value of the start variable one minute forward in time.

☐ Lines 11 and 12: The get() method is used again to retrieve the minute and second for start and store them in the variables nextMinute and nextSecond.

☐ Line 13: The while statement begins a loop using the count variable as the counter. When count hits 25,000, the loop will end.

☐ Line 14: The punishment text, stored in the string variable sentence, is displayed.

☐ Line 15: Using the GregorianCalendar class, the now variable is created with the current time.

☐ Lines 16–18: Using one if statement inside of another, the program tests to see whether one minute has passed by comparing the current minute and second to the values of nextMinute and nextSecond. If it has passed, break ends the while loop.

☐ Line 19: The } marks the end of the while loop.

☐ Lines 20 and 21: The computer displays the number of times it repeated the punishment sentence and claims to be rehabilitated.

☐ Lines 22 and 23: The main() block of the program and the program are closed out with } marks.

Compile the program with the javac compiler tool and then give it a try by typing the following at the command line:

```
java Repeat
```

Run this program several times to see how many sentences are displayed in a minute's time. The Repeat program is an excellent way to see whether your computer is faster than mine. During the testing of this workshop program, Repeat usually displayed from 8,700 to 9,100 sentences in a minute's time. If your computer displays the sentence more times than mine does, don't just send me your condolences. Buy more of my books so I can upgrade.

CAUTION

Although most of the programs that you will write in this book will work under version 1.0.2 of the Java Developer's Kit, the Repeat program will not compile successfully unless you use version 1.1 of the Kit. This program uses the GregorianCalendar class, which, like many other new features, was introduced with 1.1 and does not exist in 1.0.2. JavaSoft encourages the use of new features like this because they make improvements on the language. For example, GregorianCalendar is part of JavaSoft's effort to enable programmers to use different calendar systems in Java programs.

Summary

The information presented in this chapter is information that you will be coming back to again and again and again when you write programs. Loops are a fundamental part of most programming languages. In several of the hours to come, you'll get a chance to manipulate graphics so that you can produce animated effects. You couldn't do this without loops.

Q&A

Q Should the counter variable used in a `for` loop be created inside the `for` statement or before the loop begins?

A The only time the counter should be created outside of the `for` loop, or any other loop for that matter, is when it needs to be used in another part of the program. A variable that is created in a loop or other kind of block statement only exists inside that block. You can't use the value in any other part of the program. This is good programming practice because it makes it harder to misuse variables—you can't set their value in one part of the program and use them somewhere else incorrectly. The concept of a variable existing in one part of a program and not existing anywhere else is called *scope*, and it's covered fully during Hour 11, "Describing What Your Object Is Like."

Q The term *initialization* has been used in several places. What does it mean?

A It means to give something an initial value and set it up. When you create a variable and assign a starting value to it, you are initializing the variable.

Q If a loop never ends, how does the program stop running?

A Usually in a program where a loop does not end, something else in the program is set up to stop execution in some way. For example, a loop could continue indefinitely while the program waits for the user to click a button labeled `Quit`. However, if a program isn't working correctly, one bug you'll run into during testing is a loop that cannot be stopped. This bug is called an *infinite loop* because the program will loop happily forever. If one of the Java programs you run from the command line is stuck in an infinite loop, press Ctrl + C.

Quiz

The following questions will test your knowledge of loops. In the spirit of the subject matter, repeat each of these until you get them right.

8

Questions

1. What must be used to separate each section of a for statement?

    (a) Commas

    (b) Semicolons

    (c) Off-duty police officers

2. Which statement causes a program to go back to the statement that began a loop and then keep going from there?

    (a) continue

    (b) next

    (c) skip

3. When it comes to borrowing a car from your father, what lesson did you learn during this hour?

    (a) Don't even think about it.

    (b) Speak softly and carry a big stick.

    (c) It's better to beg forgiveness than to ask permission.

Answers

1. b. Commas are used to separate things within a section, but semicolons separate sections.

2. a. The break statement ends a loop entirely, and continue skips to the next go-around of the loop.

3. c.

Activities

If your head isn't going in circles from all this looping, review the topics of this hour with the following activities:

☐ Modify the Repeat program so that it uses a for loop instead of a while loop and compare the efficiency of each approach.

☐ Write a short program using loops that finds the first 400 prime numbers.

PART

III

Moving Into
Advanced Topics

Hour

Hour 9

Storing Information with Arrays

No one benefits more from the development of the computer than Santa Claus. For centuries, humankind has put an immense burden on him to gather and process information. Old St. Nick has to keep track of the following things:

☐ Naughty children

☐ Nice children

☐ Gift requests

☐ Homes with impassable chimneys

☐ Women who want more from Santa than Mrs. Claus is willing to let him give

☐ Countries that shoot unidentified aircraft first and ask questions later

Computers must have been a great boon at the North Pole because they are ideal for the storage, categorization, and study of information.

The most basic way that information is stored in a computer program is by putting it into a variable. However, this method is limited to relatively simple usage. If Santa had to give each naughty child his or her own variable name, he'd be working on the program for the next 12 holiday seasons at least, to say nothing of the effect on his jolly disposition or his carpal tunnel nerves. The list of naughty children is an example of a collection of similar information. Each child's name is a string of text or some kind of Santa Information System ID number. In order to keep track of a list of this kind, you can use arrays.

Arrays are groups of related variables that share the same type. You can have arrays of any type of information that can be stored as a variable. Arrays can be used to keep track of more sophisticated types of information than a single variable, but they are almost as easy to create and manipulate as variables are.

The following topics will be covered during this hour:

- Creating an array
- What a dimension of an array is
- Giving a value to an array element
- Changing the information in an array
- Making multidimensional arrays

Creating Arrays

Arrays are variables that are grouped together under a common name. The term should be familiar to you though the meaning might not be so clear—think of a salesman showing off his array of fabulous cleaning products or a game show with a dazzling array of prizes. Like variables, arrays are created by stating the type of the variable being organized into an array and the name of the array. The difference lies in the addition of the square bracket marks [and].

You can create arrays for any type of information that can be stored as a variable. For example, the following statement creates an array of string variables:

```
String[] naughtyChild;
```

Here are a few more examples:

```
int[] reindeerWeight;
boolean[] hostileAirTravelNations;
```

9

JUST A MINUTE

Java is flexible about where the square brackets are placed when an array is being created. You can put them after the variable name instead of after the variable type, as in the following:

```
String niceChild[];
```

To make arrays easier for humans to spot in your programs, you probably should stick to one style rather than switching back and forth, though Java allows both styles of usage.

The previous examples create arrays, but they do not store any values in them initially. To do this, you must use the new statement along with the variable type or store values in the array within { and } marks. You also must specify how many different items will be stored in the array. Each item in an array is called an *element*. The following statement creates an array and sets aside space for the values that it will hold:

```
int[] elfSeniority = new int[250];
```

This example creates an array of integers called `elfSeniority`. The array has 250 elements in it that can be used to store the number of months that each of Santa's elves has been employed at the Pole. If the rumors are true and Santa runs a union shop, this information is extremely important to keep track of.

When you create an array with the new statement, you must specify the number of elements. Each element of the array is given an initial value when it is set up with new; the value depends on the type of the array. All numeric arrays have the value 0, char arrays have the value '\0', and boolean arrays have the value false. A String array and all other objects are created with the initial value of null.

For arrays that are not extremely large, you can set up their initial values at the same time that you create them. The following example creates an array of strings and gives them initial values:

```
String[] reindeerNames = { "Dasher", "Dancer", "Prancer", "Vixen", "Comet", "Cupid",
"Donner", "Blitzen" };
```

The information that should be put into elements of the array is put between { and } brackets, and commas separate each element. The number of elements in the array is not specified in the statement because it is set to the number of elements in the comma-separated list. Each element of the array in the list must be of the same type. The preceding example uses a string for each of the reindeer names.

Once the array is created, you cannot make more space and add another variable to the array. Even if you recall the most famous reindeer of all, you couldn't add "Rudolph" as the ninth element of the `reindeerNames` array. The `javac` compiler won't let poor Rudolph join in any `reindeerNames`.

Using Arrays

You use arrays in a program as you would use any variable, except for the element number in between the square brackets next to the array's name. Once you refer to the element number, you can use an array element anywhere that a variable could be used. The following statements all use arrays that have been defined already in this hour's examples:

```
elfSeniority[193] += 1;
niceChild[94287612] = "Jonathan Bourne";
if ( hostileAirTravelNations[currentNation] == true)
    sendGiftByMail();
```

An important thing to note about arrays is that the first element of an array is numbered 0 instead of 1. This means that the highest number is one less than you might expect. For example, consider the following statement:

```
String[] topGifts = new String[10];
```

This statement creates an array of `String` variables that are numbered from 0 to 9. If you referred to a `topGifts[10]` somewhere else in the program, you would get an error message like the following when you run the program:

```
java.lang.ArrayIndexOutOfBoundsException:
        at SantaGifts.main(SantaGifts.java:4);
```

Like all of the error messages Java generates, this one's a bit hard to decipher. The key thing to note is the part that mentions an exception because exceptions are another word for errors in Java programs. This exception is an "array out of bounds" error, which means that the array has gone beyond its defined boundaries.

If you want to see what the upper limit of an array is during a program so that you can avoid going beyond the limit, you can use a variable called `length` that is associated with each array that is created. The `length` variable is an integer that returns the number of elements that an array can hold. The following example creates an array and then reports its length:

```
String[] reindeerNames = { "Dasher", "Dancer", "Prancer", "Vixen",
    "Comet", "Cupid", "Donner", "Blitzen", "Rudolph" };
System.out.println("There are " + reindeerNames.length + " reindeer.");
```

In this example, the value of `reindeerNames.length` is 9, which means that the highest element number you can specify is 8.

9

Multidimensional Arrays

The arrays you have been introduced to thus far in the hour all have one dimension; one line of numbers ranging from 0 to the largest element number is used to refer to an array. But some types of information require more dimensions to store adequately as arrays. An example would be the (x,y) coordinate system that's a staple of any math class. If you needed to store a list of x and y coordinates that have a point marked on them, you could use a two-dimensional array. One dimension of the array could store the x coordinate, and the other dimension could store the y coordinate.

To create an array that has two dimensions, you must use an additional set of square brackets when creating and using the array. Consider the following:

```
boolean[][] selectedPoint = new int[50][50];
selectedPoint[4][13] = true;
selectedPoint[7][6] = true;
selectedPoint[11][22] = true;
```

This example creates an array of Boolean values called `selectedPoint`. The array has 50 elements in its first dimension and 50 elements in its second dimension, so there are 2,500 individual array elements that can hold values (50 multiplied by 50). When the array is created, each element is given the default value of `false`. Three elements are then given the value of `true`: A point at the (x,y) position of (4,13), one at (7,6), and one at (11,22).

Arrays can have as many dimensions as you need, but keep in mind that they take up a lot of memory if they're extremely large. Creating the 50 by 50 `selectedPoint` array was equivalent to creating 2,500 individual variables.

Workshop: Array of Prizes Indeed

Watch the syndicated game show *Wheel of Fortune* for any length of time and you'll be surprised at how predictable the contestants are. In the years that this show has been one of the world's most successful television programs, fortune seekers have worked the puzzle-solving process into an exact science. *Wheel* contestants typically guess the same letters when they are starting out on a puzzle: R, S, T, L, and N. In the final round, when these letters and the vowel E are given to the players right away, they usually choose four other letters: C, D, M, and the vowel O. The reason for this predictablity is that these are the letters that appear most often in English words. The contestants are stifling their desire for spontaneity in order to better their chances to win a trip to Bermuda, cash, and a Yamaha Waverunner.

COFFEE BREAK

In case you're unfamiliar with the show, *Wheel of Fortune* is a game in which three contestants try to guess the letters of a phrase, name, quote, or other memorable item. If they get a letter right and it's a consonant, they win the amount of money they spun on a big wheel. To re-create the experience, play hangman with some of your friends in front of a studio audience, hand out random amounts of money when someone guesses a letter in the secret word or phrase, and give the winner a new Ford Explorer.

Your Java workshop during this hour will test the most-common-letter theory by looking at as many different phrases and expressions as you care to type. An array will be used to count the number of times that each letter appears. When you're done, the program will present each letter and the number of times it appears in the phrases you entered. It also will present some clues about which letters to avoid entirely unless you suspect that a puzzle's answer is the Aztec priest-ruler Quetzalcoatl or the fire god Xiuhtecuhtle.

Open up a new file in your word processor and call it `Wheel.java`. Enter Listing 9.1 and save the file when you're done.

Listing 9.1. The full source code of `Wheel.java`.

```
 1: class Wheel {
 2:     public static void main(String arguments[]) {
 3:         String phrase[] = {
 4:             "A STITCH IN TIME SAVES NINE",
 5:             "DON'T EAT YELLOW SNOW",
 6:             "JUST DO IT",
 7:             "EVERY GOOD BOY DOES FINE",
 8:             "I WANT MY MTV",
 9:             "HOW 'BOUT THEM COWBOYS",
10:             "PLAY IT AGAIN, SAM",
11:             "FROSTY THE SNOWMAN",
12:             "ONE MORE FOR THE ROAD",
13:             "HOME FIELD ADVANTAGE",
14:             "VALENTINE'S DAY MASSACRE",
15:             "GROVER CLEVELAND OHIO",
16:             "WONDERFUL WORLD OF DISNEY",
17:             "COAL MINER'S DAUGHTER",
18:             "WILL IT PLAY IN PEORIA"
19:         };
20:         int[] letterCount = new int[26];
21:         for (int count = 0; count < phrase.length; count++) {
22:             String current = phrase[count];
23:             char[] letters = current.toCharArray();
24:             for (int count2 = 0;  count2 < letters.length; count2++) {
25:                 char lett = letters[count2];
```

```
26:                    if ( (lett >= 'A') & (lett < 'Z') ) {
27:                        letterCount[lett - 'A']++;
28:                    }
29:                }
30:            }
31:            for (char count = 'A'; count <= 'Z'; count++) {
32:                System.out.print(count + ": " +
33:                    letterCount[count - 'A'] +
34:                    "\t");
35:            }
36:            System.out.println();
37:        }
38: }
```

After you compile the file and run it, the output should resemble Listing 9.2.

Listing 9.2. The output of the Wheel program.

```
A: 22  B: 3   C: 5   D: 13  E: 28  F: 6   G: 5   H: 8   I: 18  J: 1
K: 0   L: 13  M: 10  N: 19  O: 27  P: 3   Q: 0   R: 13  S: 15  T: 19
U: 4   V: 7   W: 9   X: 0   Y: 10  Z: 0
```

The following things are taking place in the Wheel program:

- [ ] Lines 1 and 2: The Wheel program and the main() block of the program begin.
- [ ] Lines 3–19: Phrases are stored in a String array called phrase. Every phrase between the { on Line 3 and the } on Line 19 will be stored in its own element of the array, beginning with A STITCH IN TIME SAVES NINE in phrase[0].
- [ ] Line 20: An integer array called letterCount is created with 26 elements. This array will be used to store the number of times each letter appears. The order of the elements is from A to Z. letterCount[0] will store the count for letter A, letterCount[1] will store the count for B, and so on up to letterCount[25] for Z.
- [ ] Line 21: A for loop is begun that cycles through the phrases stored in the phrase array. The phrase.length variable is used in the for statement to end the loop after the last phrase is reached.
- [ ] Line 22: A String variable named current is created and set with the value of the current element of the phrase array.
- [ ] Line 23: A character array is created that stores all of the characters in the current phrase.
- [ ] Line 24: A for loop is begun that cycles through the letters of the current phrase. The letters.length variable is used to end the loop after the last letter is reached.

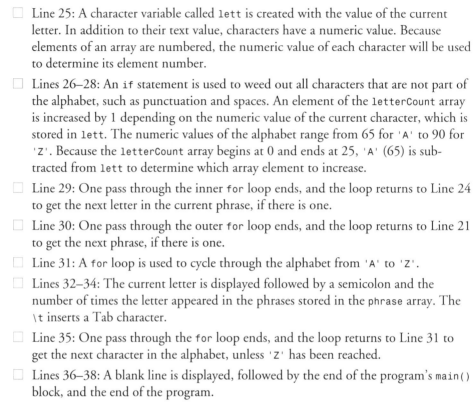

□ Line 25: A character variable called `lett` is created with the value of the current letter. In addition to their text value, characters have a numeric value. Because elements of an array are numbered, the numeric value of each character will be used to determine its element number.

□ Lines 26–28: An `if` statement is used to weed out all characters that are not part of the alphabet, such as punctuation and spaces. An element of the `letterCount` array is increased by 1 depending on the numeric value of the current character, which is stored in `lett`. The numeric values of the alphabet range from 65 for `'A'` to 90 for `'Z'`. Because the `letterCount` array begins at 0 and ends at 25, `'A'` (65) is subtracted from `lett` to determine which array element to increase.

□ Line 29: One pass through the inner `for` loop ends, and the loop returns to Line 24 to get the next letter in the current phrase, if there is one.

□ Line 30: One pass through the outer `for` loop ends, and the loop returns to Line 21 to get the next phrase, if there is one.

□ Line 31: A `for` loop is used to cycle through the alphabet from `'A'` to `'Z'`.

□ Lines 32–34: The current letter is displayed followed by a semicolon and the number of times the letter appeared in the phrases stored in the `phrase` array. The `\t` inserts a Tab character.

□ Line 35: One pass through the `for` loop ends, and the loop returns to Line 31 to get the next character in the alphabet, unless `'Z'` has been reached.

□ Lines 36–38: A blank line is displayed, followed by the end of the program's `main()` block, and the end of the program.

This workshop project shows how two nested `for` loops can be used to cycle through a group of phrases one letter at a time. Java attaches a numeric value to each character; this value is easier to use than the character inside arrays. Using the `length` variable makes it possible for you to add as many phrases as desired within the { and } marks. The letters in each of the new phrases that you add will be analyzed, and you can build up a better idea of what it takes to make a small fortune in 30 minutes on television.

Summary

Arrays make it possible to store complicated types of information in a program and manipulate that information. They're ideal for anything that can be arranged in a list and can be accessed easily using the loop statements that you learned about during Hour 8, "Repeating an Action with Loops."

The information processing needs of Santa Claus possibly have outgrown arrays. There are more children being manufactured each year, and the gifts they want are increasing in complexity and expense. Tickle Me Elmo alone created a logistical nightmare for him in Christmas 1996. Your programs are likely to use arrays to store information that is unwieldy to work with through variables, even if you're not making any lists or checking them twice.

Q&A

Q **Do arrays have to begin with an element 0, or could they range from a higher minimum number to a higher maximum number, such as 65 to 90?**

A No, but it is more efficient to do so because it takes up less memory in the computer to store arrays that begin with 0. You can use arrays of a higher index number simply by referring to the numbers you want to use. For example, if you created a for loop that cycled from array element 65 to element 90, you could disregard any other element numbers. However, there still will be array elements numbered from 0 to 64 taking up space in memory, even if you don't use them for anything.

Q **Why are some errors called exceptions?**

A The significance of the term is that a program normally runs without any problems, and the exception signals an exceptional circumstance that must be dealt with. Exceptions are warning messages that are sent from within a Java program.

Q **Can the length variable be set to increase or decrease the size of an array after it has been created?**

A There's no way to modify the size of an array after it has been created; length is strictly used to find out an array's upper boundary.

Quiz

If the brain were an array, you could test its length by answering each of the following questions about arrays.

Questions

1. What types of information are arrays best suited for?

   (a) Lists

   (b) Pairs of related information

   (c) Trivia

2. What variable can be used to check the upper boundary of an array?

    (a) `top`

    (b) `length`

    (c) `limit`

3. Who is the famous Aztec priest-ruler?

    (a) Quisp

    (b) Quetzalcoatl

    (c) Quichelorraine

Answers

1. a. Lists that contain nothing but the same type of information—strings, numbers, and so on—are well-suited for storage in arrays.

2. b.

3. b. It's also the name of a god of learning and civilization who is depicted as an approaching storm whose winds kick up dust before the rain comes.

Activities

To give yourself an array of experiences to draw from later on, you can expand your knowledge of this hour's topics with the following activities:

☐ Create a program that uses a multidimensional array to store student grades. The first dimension should be a number for each student, and the second dimension should be for each student's grades. Display the average of all the grades earned by each student and an overall average for every student.

☐ Write a program that stores the first 400 prime numbers in an array.

Hour 10

Creating Your First Object

One of the more fearsome items of jargon that you'll encounter during these 24 hours is *object-oriented programming*. This is a complicated term for an elegant way of describing what a computer program is and how it works. Before object-oriented programming, computer programs were usually described under the simplest definition you've learned in this book: sets of instructions that are listed in a file and handled in some kind of reliable order. Whether the program is big or small, the programmer's job is largely the same—write instructions for each thing the computer must do. By thinking of a program as a collection of objects instead, you can figure out the tasks a program must accomplish and assign the tasks to the objects where they belong best.

During this hour, the following topics will be covered:

☐ Understanding objects

☐ How attributes describe an object

☐ What determines how objects behave

☐ Combining objects
☐ Inheriting from other objects
☐ Creating an object

How Object-Oriented Programming Works

The programs that you create with Java can be thought of as objects just like any other objects in the world, such as nails, skateboards, Liquid Paper, glue, or *60 Minutes* cohost Morley Safer. An object is made up of smaller objects—in the case of Mr. Safer, two legs, two arms, a torso, a head, and a reporter's notebook. Each object has things that make it different from other objects. Morley's legs are long and angular; they bend in the middle and end in feet. His arms end in hands and are shorter than the legs. Each object also has specific jobs it has to do. Morley's legs are used for movement and support, and his arms are used to grab things, take notes, and hail taxicabs. If you break down computer programs in the same way that you have broken down Morley Safer, you are engaging in object-oriented programming. It's a much less complicated concept than it originally sounds.

In object-oriented programming, an object contains two things: attributes and behavior. *Attributes* are things that describe the object and show how it is different from other objects. *Behavior* is what an object does.

You create objects in Java by using a class as a template. The *class* is a master copy of the object that is consulted to determine which attributes and behavior an object should have. The term *class* should be familiar to you because every Java program that you have written thus far has been called a class. Every program that you create with Java will be a class because each one could be used as a template for the creation of new objects. As an example, any Java program that uses strings is using the String class. This class contains attributes that determine what a String object is and behavior that controls what String objects can do.

With object-oriented programming, any computer program is a group of objects that work together to get something done. Some simple programs may seem as though they consist of only one object—the class file. However, even those programs are using other objects to get their work done.

Objects in Action

Consider the case of a dice-rolling program. Rolling a six-sided die is a simple thing to do in the real world—you toss a cube and check the uppermost side of the cube when it stops rolling. When you make a computer do the same thing, you can think of the die as an object. In fact, during Hour 21, "Playing Games with Java," you will be using a Die object as you teach the computer to play the dice-rolling game called craps.

A Die object could consist of the following:

- [ ] A behavior to roll the die and figure out the result
- [ ] An attribute to store the result of a die roll

When you compare a six-sided die in the real world to a Die object in a computer program, it might seem odd to ask the Die object to roll itself. Dice don't roll themselves in the real world. However, objects in object-oriented programming work for themselves whenever possible. This quality makes them more useful because you can incorporate them in other programs without having as many things to teach them. If a Die object did not know how to roll itself, for instance, every time you used that Die object somewhere you would have to create behavior to roll it.

For another example of object-oriented programming, consider the autodialer program that Matthew Broderick's character used in *WarGames* to find computers he could hack into. If you're unfamiliar with the term, an *autodialer* is software that uses a modem to dial a series of phone numbers in sequence. The purpose of such a program is to find other computers that answer their own phone, so you can call them up later to see what they are.

Using an autodialer today practically guarantees you'll be on a first-name basis with your local phone company. In the early '80s, it was a good way to be rebellious without actually leaving the house. David Lightman (Broderick) used his autodialer to look for a videogame company's private computer system. He wanted to play the new game they were working on. Instead, Lightman found a secret government computer that could play everything from chess to Global Thermonuclear War.

An autodialer, like any computer program, can be thought of as a group of objects that work together. It could be broken down into the following:

- [ ] A Modem object, which knows how to make the modem dial a number and how to report when another computer system has answered a call
- [ ] A Monitor object, which keeps track of what numbers were called and which ones were successful and can save this information for inspection later

Each object exists independently of the other. The Modem object does its job without requiring any help from the Monitor object.

One of the advantages of having a completely independent Modem object is that it could be used in other programs that need modem functionality. If Broderick's character returns to hacking in *WarGames 1997* after a bitter divorce from Ally Sheedy's character, he could use the Modem object as part of an elaborate ATM fraud scheme.

Another reason to use self-contained programs such as objects is that they are easier to debug. Computer programs quickly become unwieldy in size. If your program is just one big list of instructions, you can't change one part without making sure it won't damage the performance of other parts that are dependent on it. If you're debugging something like a Modem object, though, you know it's not dependent on anything else. You can focus on making sure the Modem object does the job it's supposed to do and holds the information that it needs to do its job.

For these reasons, object-oriented programming is becoming the norm in many areas of software development. Learning an object-oriented language like Java as your first programming language can be an advantage in some ways because you're not unlearning the habits of other styles of programming. The main disadvantage is that an object-oriented language can be more challenging to learn than a non-object-oriented language such as Visual Basic.

What Objects Are

As stated, objects are created by using a class of objects as a guideline. The following is an example of a class:

```
public class Dog {
}
```

Any object created from this class can't do anything because it doesn't have any attributes or behavior yet. You need to add those or this class that won't be terribly useful. You could expand the class into the following:

```
public class Dog {
    String name;

    public void speak() {
        System.out.println("Arf! Arf!");
    }
}
```

The Dog class now should be recognizable to you because it looks a lot like the programs you have written during Hours 1 through 9. The Dog class begins with a class statement, as your programs have, except that it has a public statement alongside it. The public statement means that the class is available for use by the public—in other words, by any program that wants to use Dog objects.

The first part of the Dog class creates a string variable called name. This variable is an attribute of the object; the name is one of the things that distinguishes a dog from other dogs. The second part of the Dog class is a method called speak(). This method has one statement, a System.out.println() statement that displays the text, Arf! Arf!

10

If you wanted to use a Dog object in a program, you would create the object much like you would create a variable. You could use the following statement:

```
Dog firstDog = new Dog();
```

This statement creates a Dog object called firstDog. You can now use the object in the program; you can set its variables and call its methods. To set the value of the name variable of the firstDog object, you could use the following statement:

```
firstDog.name = "Checkers";
```

To make this dog speak by calling the speak() method, you could use the following code:

```
firstDog.speak();
```

Like a well-trained pet, the Dog object would respond to this statement by displaying the text, Arf! Arf!

Understanding Inheritance

The final selling point to object-oriented programming is called inheritance. *Inheritance* is the way one object can inherit behavior and attributes from other objects that are similar to it.

When you start creating objects for use in other programs, you will find that some new objects you want are a lot like other objects that have already been developed. For example, if David Lightman does not run afoul of the law because of his ATM scheme, he might want to create an object that can handle error correction and other advanced modem features that weren't around back in 1983 when *WarGames* was released.

Lightman could create a new ErrorCorrectionModem object by copying the statements of the Modem object and revising them. However, if most of the behavior and attributes of ErrorCorrectionModem are the same as those of Modem, this is a lot of unnecessary work. It also means that Lightman will have to maintain two separate programs if something needs to be changed or debugged later on. Through inheritance, a programmer can create a new class of objects by defining only how it is different from an existing class. Lightman could make ErrorCorrectionModem inherit from Modem, and all he would have to write are the things that make error-correction modems different than previous modems.

The way that a class of objects inherits from another class is through the extends statement. The following is a skeleton of an ErrorCorrectionModem class that inherits from the Modem class:

```
class ErrorCorrectionModem extends Modem {
        // program goes here
}
```

Building an Inheritance Hierarchy

Inheritance enables a variety of related classes to be developed without a lot of redundant work. Inheritance can be passed down from one class to another class to another class. This system of classes is called a class hierarchy, and all of the standard classes that you can use in your Java programs are part of a hierarchy.

Understanding a hierarchy is easier if you understand what subclasses and superclasses are. A class that inherits from another class is called a *subclass*, and the class that it is inherited from is called a *superclass*. In the preceding *WarGames* example, the Modem class is the superclass of the ErrorCorrectionModem class, and ErrorCorrectionModem is the subclass of Modem. A class can have more than one class that inherits from it in the hierarchy—another subclass of Modem might be ISDNModem, for example, if ISDN modems have behavior or attributes that make them different from error-correcting modems. If there were a subclass of ErrorCorrectionModem, such as InternalErrorCorrectionModem, it would inherit from all the classes above it—both ErrorCorrectionModem and Modem.

The programs that you write as you are learning about Java won't use complicated class hierarchies. However, the classes that are part of the standard Java language make full use of inheritance. Understanding it is essential to making the most of the classes that come with Java. You'll learn more about inheritance during Hour 12, "Inheriting Methods from Other Classes."

Workshop: Creating an Object

To see a working example of classes and inheritance, you will create classes that represent two types of objects: dogs and Morley Safer. For the sake of simplicity, the workshop will focus on a few simple attributes and behavior for these objects:

1. Each object should have a name and be able to remember it.
2. Each object should snore when it sleeps.
3. Each object should speak in an accurate way. Although dogs and Morley Safer can remember their own names and snore in the same manner, they do not speak in the same manner.

The first two things are shared in common between dogs and Morley Safer. Because of this, you can create a superclass that both the Dog class and the MorleySafer class can inherit from. Call this class Mammal. Using your word processor, create a new file and save it as Mammal.java. Enter Listing 10.1 and save the file.

10

Listing 10.1. The full text of `Mammal.java`.

```
1: public class Mammal {
2:     String name;
3:
4:     public void sleep() {
5:         System.out.println("ZZZZ ZZZZZZ ZZZZ");
6:     }
7: }
```

Compile this file with the `javac` compiler tool to produce a file called `Mammal.class`. Although you cannot run this program with the interpreter, you will be able to use it in other classes. You now have a `Mammal` class that can handle both of the things that the `Dog` and `MorleySafer` class have in common. By using the `extends` statement when you are creating the `Dog` and `MorleySafer` classes, you can make each of them a subclass of `Mammal`.

Start a new file in your word processor and save it as `Dog.java`. Enter Listing 10.2, and then save and compile the file.

Listing 10.2. The full text of `Dog.java`.

```
1: public class Dog extends Mammal {
2:     public void speak() {
3:         System.out.println("Arf! Arf!");
4:     }
5: }
```

Create a third file with your word processor, and save it as `MorleySafer.java`. Enter Listing 10.3, and then save and compile the file when you're done.

Listing 10.3. The full text of `MorleySafer.java`.

```
1: public class MorleySafer extends Mammal {
2:     public void speak() {
3:         System.out.println("Can I ask you a few questions about your 1987 tax
statement?");
4:     }
5: }
```

Once you have compiled all three of these files with the `javac` compiler tool, you will have three class files: `Mammal.class`, `Dog.class`, and `MorleySafer.class`. However, you cannot run any of these class files at the command line with the `java` interpreter tool because they do not have `main()` blocks. You need to create a short Java program to test out the class hierarchy you have just built. Return to your word processor and create a new file called `Speak.java`. Enter Listing 10.4.

Listing 10.4. The full text of `Speak.java`.

```
1: class Speak {
2:     public static void main(String arguments[]) {
3:         Dog doggie = new Dog();
4:         MorleySafer morley = new MorleySafer();
5:         doggie.name = "Cujo";
6:         morley.name = "Morley Safer";
7:         System.out.println("First we'll get the dog to speak:");
8:         doggie.speak();
9:         System.out.println("Now it's Morley's turn to speak:");
10:        morley.speak();
11:        System.out.println("Time for both to sleep:");
12:        doggie.sleep();
13:        morley.sleep();
14:     }
15: }
```

Save and compile the file when you're done. When you run it, the output should resemble the following:

```
First we'll get the dog to speak:
Arf! Arf!
Now it's Morley's turn to speak:
Can I ask you a few questions about your 1987 tax statement?
Time for both to sleep:
ZZZZ ZZZZZZ ZZZZ
ZZZZ ZZZZZZ ZZZZ
```

Note the following statements in this program:

- ☐ Lines 3 and 4: Two new objects are created, a `Dog` object called `doggie` and a `MorleySafer` object called `morley`.

- ☐ Line 5: The `name` variable of the `Dog` object `doggie` is set to `Cujo`.

- ☐ Line 6: The `name` variable of the `MorleySafer` object `morley` is set to `Morley Safer`.

- ☐ Line 8: The `speak()` method of the `doggie` object is called. Looking at the `speak()` method of the `Dog` class of objects, you can see that it displays the text, `Arf! Arf!`.

☐ Line 10: The speak() method of the morley object is called, resulting in the display of the following text: Can I ask you a few questions about your 1987 tax statement?

☐ Lines 12 and 13: The sleep() methods of doggie and then morley are called. If you look at the Dog class or the MorleySafer class, you won't find a sleep() method. However, because Dog and MorleySafer both inherit from the Mammal class, you should look there to see if it has a sleep() method that could have been inherited by its subclasses. The Mammal class does have a sleep() method, so the snoring text, zzzz zzzzzz zzzz, is displayed twice.

Summary

After creating your first class of objects and arranging several classes into a hierarchy, you ought to be more comfortable with the term *object-oriented programming*. You will be learning more about object behavior and attributes in the next two hours as you start creating more sophisticated objects.

Terms such as *program*, *class*, and *object* will make more sense as you have more experience with object-oriented development. It's a concept that takes some time to get used to. Once you have mastered it, you'll find that it's an effective way to design, develop, and debug computer programs.

Q&A

Q Can classes inherit from more than one class?

A It's possible with some programming languages but not Java. Multiple inheritance is a powerful feature, but it also makes object-oriented programming a bit harder to use and to learn. Java's developers decided to limit inheritance to one superclass for any class, although a class can have numerous subclasses.

Q Why are object-oriented programs easier to debug?

A Object-oriented programs enable you to focus on a smaller part of a computer program when figuring out where an error is happening. Because a related group of tasks are handled by the same object, you can focus on that object if the tasks aren't being performed correctly. You don't have to worry about any other parts of the program.

10

Q When would you want to create a class that isn't `public`?

A The main time you would not want to make a class of objects available to other programs is when the class is strictly for the use of one program you're writing. If you're creating a game program and your `ReloadGun` class of objects is highly specific to the game you're writing, it could be a private class. To make a class private, leave off the `public` statement in front of `class`.

Quiz

The following questions will test your knowledge of objects and the programs that use them.

Questions

1. What statement is used to enable one class to inherit from another class?

    (a) `inherits`

    (b) `extends`

    (c) `handitover`

2. Why are compiled Java programs saved with the `.class` file extension?

    (a) Java's developers think it's a classy language.

    (b) It's a subtle tribute to the world's teachers.

    (c) Every Java program is a class.

3. What are the two things that make up an object?

    (a) attributes and behavior

    (b) commands and data files

    (c) spit and vinegar

Answers

1. b. The `extends` statement is used because the subclass is an extension of the attributes and behavior of the superclass and of any superclasses above that in the class hierarchy.

2. c. Your programs will always be made up of at least one main class and any other classes that are needed.

3. a. In a way, b is also true because commands are comparable to behavior, and data files are analogous to attributes.

 10

Activities

If you don't object, you can extends your knowledge of this hour's topics with the following activity:

☐ Create a few more classes of objects to go under the Mammal class alongside Dog and MorleySafer. Add classes for ducks, horses, *60 Minutes* correspondent Mike Wallace, and owls that do not snore. By creating an Owl class that inherits from Mammal and putting a new sleep() method in Owl, you can create your own special snoring statement for that creature.

10

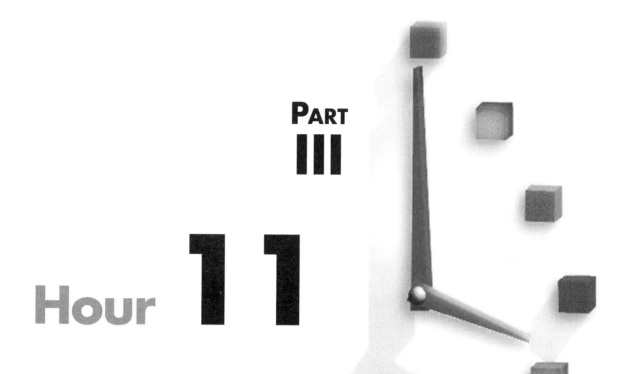

Hour 11

Describing What Your Object Is Like

As you learned during last hour's introduction to object-oriented programming, an object is a way of organizing a program so that it has everything it needs to accomplish a task. Objects need two things to do their jobs: attributes and behavior.

Attributes are the information stored within an object. They can be variables such as integers, characters, Boolean values, or even other objects. Behavior is the groups of statements used to handle specific jobs within the object. Each of these groups is called a *method*.

Up to this point, you have been working with the methods and variables of objects without knowing it. Any time your statement had a period in it that wasn't a decimal point or part of a string, chances are an object was involved. You'll see this during this hour as the following topics are covered:

- ☐ Creating variables for an object
- ☐ Creating variables for a class
- ☐ Using methods with objects and classes

☐ Calling a method in a statement

☐ Returning a value with a method

☐ Creating constructor methods

☐ Sending arguments to a method

☐ Using this to refer to an object

☐ Creating new objects

For the purposes of this hour's examples, you'll be looking at a class of objects called Virus whose sole purpose in life is to reproduce in as many places as possible—much like some of the people I went to college with. A Virus has several different things it needs in order to do its work, and these will be implemented as the behavior of the class. The information that's needed for the methods will be stored as attributes.

CAUTION

The example in this hour will not teach actual virus writing, though it might provide some insight into how virus programs work as they wreak havoc on the file systems of the computer-loving world. Sams.net had scheduled *Teach Yourself Virus Programming in a Three-Day Weekend* for spring of this year, but the book has been postponed because the author's hard drive was unexpectedly erased on Michaelangelo's birthday.

Creating Variables

The attributes of an object represent any variables that are needed in order for the object to function. These variables could be simple data types such as integers, characters, and floating-point numbers, or they could be arrays or objects of the String or Graphics classes. An object's variables can be used throughout its program in any of the methods the object includes. You create variables immediately after the class statement that creates the class and before any methods.

One of the things that a Virus object needs is a way to indicate that a file has already been infected. Some computer viruses change the field that stores the time a file was last modified; for example, a virus might move the time from 13:41:20 to 13:41:61. Because no normal file would be saved on the 61st second of a minute, the time is a sign that the file was infected. The Virus object will use 86 as the seconds field of a file's modification time because "86 it" is slang that means to throw something away—exactly the kind of unpleasant antisocial connotation we're going for. The value will be stored in an integer variable called newSeconds.

11

The following statements begin a class called `Virus` with an attribute called `newSeconds` and two other attributes:

```
public class Virus {
    public integer newSeconds = 86;
    public String author = "Sam Snett";
    integer maxFileSize = 30000;
```

All three variables are attributes for the class: `newSeconds`, `maxFileSize`, and `author`.

The `newSeconds` variable has a starting value of 86, and the statement that creates it has `public` in front of it. Making a variable `public` makes it possible to modify the variable from another program that is using the `Virus` object. If the other program attaches special significance to the number 92, for instance, it can change `newSeconds` to that value. If the other program creates a `Virus` object called `influenza`, it could set that object's `newSeconds` variable with the following statement:

```
influenza.newSeconds = 92;
```

The `author` variable also is `public`, so it can be changed freely from other programs. The other variable, `maxFileSize`, can only be used within the `Virus` class itself.

When you make a variable in a class `public`, the class loses control over how that variable is used by other programs. In many cases, this might not be a problem. For example, the `author` variable can be changed to any name or pseudonym that identifies the author of the virus, and the only restriction is aesthetic. The name might eventually be used on court documents if you're prosecuted, so you don't want to pick a dumb one. *The State of Ohio v. LoveHandles* doesn't have the same ring to it as *Ohio v. April Mayhem.*

Restricting access to a variable keeps errors from occurring if the variable is set incorrectly by another program. With the `Virus` class, if `newSeconds` is set to a value of 60 or less, it won't be reliable as a way to tell that a file is infected. Some files may be saved with that number of seconds regardless of the virus, and they'll look infected to `Virus`. If the `Virus` class of objects needs to guard against this problem, you need to do these two things:

☐ Switch the variable from `public` to `private protected` or `private`.

☐ Add behavior to change the value of the variable and report the value of the variable to other programs.

A `private protected` variable can only be used in the same class as the variable or any subclasses of that class. A `private` variable is restricted even further—it can only be used in the same class. Unless you know that a variable can be changed to anything without affecting how its class functions, you probably should make the variable `private` or `private protected`.

The following statement makes newSeconds a private protected variable:

```
private protected int newSeconds = 86;
```

If you want other programs to use the newSeconds variable in some way, you'll have to create behavior that makes it possible. This task will be covered later in the hour.

Creating Class Variables

When you create an object, it has its own version of all the variables that are part of the object's class. Each object created from the Virus class of objects has its own version of the newSeconds, maxFileSize, and author variables. If you modified one of these variables in an object, it would not affect the same variable in another Virus object.

There are times when an attribute has more to do with an entire class of objects than a specific object itself. For example, if you wanted to keep track of how many Virus objects were being used in a program, it would not make sense to store this value repeatedly in each Virus object. Instead, you can use a class variable to store this kind of information. You can use this variable with any object of a class, but only one copy of the variable exists for the whole class. The variables you have been creating for objects thus far can be called *object variables*, because they are tied to a specific object. *Class variables* refer to a class of objects as a whole.

Both types of variables are created and used in the same way, except that static is used in the statement that creates class variables. The following statement creates a class variable for the Virus example:

```
static int virusCount = 0;
```

Changing the value of a class variable is no different than changing an object's variables. If you have a Virus object called tuberculosis, you could change the class variable virusCount with the following statement:

```
tuberculosis.virusCount++;
```

Because class variables apply to an entire class instead of a specific object, you can use the name of the class instead:

```
Virus.virusCount++;
```

Both statements accomplish the same thing, but there's an advantage to using the second one. It shows immediately that virusCount is a class variable instead of an object's variable because you can't refer to object variables with the name of a class. That's only possible with class variables.

11

Creating Behavior with Methods

Attributes are the way to keep track of information about a class of objects, but they don't take any action. For a class to do the things it was created to do, you must create behavior. Behavior describes all of the different sections of a class that accomplish specific tasks. Each of these sections is called a *method*.

You have been using methods throughout your programs up to this point without knowing it, including two in particular: `println()` in Java applications and `drawString()` in applets. These methods display text on-screen. Like variables, methods are used in connection with an object or a class. The name of the object or class is followed by a period and the name of the method, as in `screen.drawString()` or `Integer.parseInt()`.

JUST A MINUTE

The `System.out.println()` method might seem confusing because it has two periods instead of one. This is because two classes are involved in the statement—the `System` class and the `PrintStream` class. The `System` class has a variable called out that is a `PrintStream` object. `println()` is a method of the `PrintStream` class. The `System.out.println()` statement means, in effect, "Use the `println()` method of the out variable of the `System` class." You can chain together references to variables and methods in this way.

Declaring a Method

You create methods with a statement that looks similar to the statement that begins a class. Both can take arguments between parentheses after their names, and both use { and } marks at the beginning and end. The difference is that methods can send back a value after they are handled. The value can be one of the simple types such as integers or Booleans, or it can be a class of objects. If a method should not return any value, use the statement `void`.

The following is an example of a method the `Virus` class can use to infect files:

```
boolean public infectFile(String filename) {
    boolean success = false;
    // file-infecting statements would be here
    return success;
}
```

The `infectFile()` method is used to add a virus to a file. This method takes a single argument, a string variable called `filename`, and this variable represents the file that should be attacked.

The actual code to infect a file is omitted here due to the author's desire to stay on the good side of the U.S. Secret Service. The only thing you need to know is that if the infection is a success, the success variable is set to a value of true.

By looking at the statement that begins the method, you can see boolean preceding the name of the method, infectFile. This statement signifies that a boolean value will be sent back after the method is handled. The return statement is what actually sends a value back. In this example, the value of success is returned.

When a method returns a value, you can use the method as part of an assignment statement. For example, if you created a Virus object called malaria, you could use statements such as these:

```
if (malaria.infectFile(currentFile))
    System.out.println(currentFile + " has been infected!");
else
    System.out.println("Curses! Foiled again!");
```

Any method that returns a value can be used at any place a value or variable could be used in a program.

Earlier in the hour, you switched the newSeconds variable to private to prevent it from being set by other programs. However, because you're a virus writer who cares about people, you still want to make it possible for newSeconds to be used if it is used correctly. The way to do this is to create public methods in the Virus class that use newSeconds. Because these methods are public, they can be used by other programs. Because they're in the same class as newSeconds, they can modify it.

Consider the following two methods:

```
int public getSeconds() {
    return newSeconds;
}

void public setSeconds(int newValue) {
    if (newValue > 60)
        newSeconds = newValue;
}
```

The getSeconds() method is used to send back the current value of newSeconds. The getSeconds() method is necessary because other programs can't even look at newSeconds because it is private. The getSeconds() method does not have any arguments, but it still must have parentheses after the method name. Otherwise, when you were using getSeconds in a program, the method would look no different than a variable.

The setSeconds() method takes one argument, an integer called newValue. This integer contains the value that a program wants to change newSeconds to. If newValue is 61 or greater, the change will be made. The setSeconds() method has void preceding the method name, so it does not return any kind of value.

Similar Methods with Different Arguments

As you have seen with the setSeconds() method, you can send arguments to a method to affect what it does. Different methods in a class can have different names, but methods can also have the same name if they have different arguments.

Two methods can have the same name if they have a different number of arguments, or the specific arguments are of different variable types. For example, it might be useful for the Virus class of objects to have two tauntUser() methods. One could have no arguments at all and would deliver a generic taunt. The other could specify the taunt as a string argument. The following statements could implement these methods:

```
void tauntUser() {
    System.out.println("The problem is not with your set, but with
    yourselves.");
}

void tauntUser(String taunt) {
    System.out.println(taunt);
}
```

Constructor Methods

When you want to create an object in a program, use the new statement, as in the following:

```
Virus typhoid = new Virus();
```

This statement creates a new Virus object called typhoid, and it uses a special method in the Virus class called a constructor. Constructors are methods that are used when an object is first being created. The purpose of a constructor is to set up any variables and other things that need to be established.

The following are two constructor methods for the Virus class of objects:

```
public Virus() {
    maxFileSize = 30000;
}

public Virus(String name, int size) {
    author = name;
    maxFileSize = size;
}
```

Like other methods, constructors can use the arguments they are sent as a way to have more than one constructor in a class. In this example, the first constructor would be used with a statement such as the following:

```
Virus mumps = new Virus();
```

The other constructor could be used only if a string and an integer were sent as arguments, as in this statement:

```
Virus rubella = new Virus("April Mayhem", 60000);
```

If you only had the preceding two constructor methods, you could not use the new statement with any other type or number of arguments within the parentheses.

Class Methods

Like class variables, class methods are a way to provide functionality associated with an entire class instead of a specific object. Use a class method when the method does nothing that affects an individual object of the class. One example that you have used in a previous hour was the parseInt() method of the Integer class. This method is used to convert a string to a variable of the type int, as in the following:

```
int time = Integer.parseInt(timeText);
```

To make a method into a class method, use static in front of the method name, as in the following:

```
static void showVirusCount() {
    System.out.println("There are " + virusCount + " viruses.");
}
```

The virusCount class variable was used earlier to keep track of how many Virus objects have been created by a program. The showVirusCount() method is a class method that displays this total, and it should be called with a statement such as the following:

```
Virus.showVirusCount();
```

Variable Scope Within Methods

When you create a variable or an object inside a method in one of your classes, it is usable only inside that method. The reason for this is the concept of *variable scope*. Scope is the section in which a variable exists in a program. If you go outside of the part of the program defined by the scope, you can no longer use the variable.

The { and } statements in a program define the boundaries for a variable. Any variable created within these marks cannot be used outside of them. For example, consider the following statements:

```
if (numFiles < 1) {
    String warning = "No files remaining.";
}
System.out.println(warning);
```

This example does not work correctly because the `warning` variable was created inside the brackets of the `if` block statement. The variable does not exist outside of the brackets, so the `System.out.println()` method cannot use `warning` as an argument.

One of the areas that can lead to errors in a program is when a variable has a different value than you expected it to have. In a large program written with many programming languages, this area can be difficult to fix because any part of the program might use the variable. Rules that enforce scope make programs easier to debug because scope limits the area in which a variable can be used.

This concept applies to methods because a variable created inside a method cannot be used in other methods. You can only use a variable in more than one method if it was created as an object variable or class variable after the `class` statement at the beginning of the program.

Using the `this` Keyword

Because you can refer to variables and methods in other classes along with variables and methods in your own class, it can easily become confusing. One way to make things a little clearer is with the `this` statement. The `this` statement is a way to refer in a program to the program's own object.

When you are using an object's methods or variables, you put the name of the object in front of the method or variable name, separated by a period. Consider these examples:

```
Virus chickenpox = new Virus();
chickenpox.name = "LoveHandles";
chickenpox.setSeconds(75);
```

These statements create a new `Virus` object called `chickenpox`, set the `name` variable of `chickenpox`, and then use the `setSeconds()` method of `chickenpox`.

There are times in a program where you need to refer to the current object—in other words, the object represented by the program itself. For example, inside the `Virus` class, you might have a method that has its own variable called `author`:

```
void public checkAuthor() {
    String author = null;
}
```

A variable called `author` exists within the scope of the `checkAuthor()` method, but it isn't the same variable as an object variable called `author`. If you wanted to refer to the current object's `author` variable, you have to use the `this` statement, as in the following:

```
System.out.println(this.author);
```

11

By using this, you make it clear which variable or method you are referring to. You can use this anywhere in a class that you would refer to an object by name. If you wanted to send the current object as an argument in a method, for example, you could use a statement such as the following:

```
verifyData(this);
```

In many cases, the this statement will not be needed to make it clear that you're referring to an object's variables and methods. However, there's no detriment to using this any time you want to be sure you're referring to the right thing.

Workshop: Using Class Methods and Variables

At the insistence of every attorney and management executive in the Macmillan family of computer publishers, the workshop for this hour will not be the creation of a working virus program. Instead, you'll create a simple Virus object that can do only one thing: Count the number of Virus objects that a program has created and report the total.

Load your word processor and create a new file called Virus.java. Enter Listing 11.1 into the word processor and save the file when you're done.

Listing 11.1. The full text of Virus.java.

```
 1: public class Virus {
 2:     static int virusCount = 0;
 3:
 4:     public Virus() {
 5:         virusCount++;
 6:     }
 7:
 8:     static int getVirusCount() {
 9:         return virusCount;
10:     }
11: }
```

Compile the file, and then return to your word processor. You need to create a short program that will create Virus objects and ask the Virus class to count them. Open up a new file and enter Listing 11.2. Save the file as VirusLook.java when you're done.

11

Listing 11.2. The full text of VirusLook.java.

```
1: class VirusLook {
2:     public static void main(String arguments[]) {
3:         Virus smash = new Virus();
4:         Virus crash = new Virus();
5:         Virus crumble = new Virus();
6:         System.out.println("There are " + Virus.getVirusCount() + "
7:         viruses.");
8:     }
9: }
```

Compile the VirusLook.java file, and then run it with the java interpreter by typing the following command:

```
java VirusLook
```

The output should be the following:

```
There are 3 viruses.
```

Summary

You now have completed two of the three hours devoted to object-oriented concepts in this book. You've learned how to create an object and give behavior and attributes to the object and to its own class of objects. Thinking in terms of objects is one of the tougher challenges of the Java programming language. Once you start to understand it, however, you realize that the entire language makes use of objects and classes.

During the next hour, you'll learn how to give your objects parents and children.

Q&A

Q Can constructor methods send back a value like other methods?

A No, because there's no way to receive that value. Unlike other methods that can be used as part of an equation, the argument of a method, or other statements, constructors are only handled in response to a new statement. There's no way for that statement to receive a value that would be sent by the method.

Q Do you have to create an object to use class variables or methods?

A Because class variables and methods aren't associated with a specific object, you don't need to create an object solely for the purpose of using them. The use of the Integer.parseInt() method is an example of this because you don't have to create a new Integer object just to convert a string to an int value.

Q **What's the difference between the Integer object and the int variable type?**

A The first is an object, and the second is a simple variable type. Each of the variable types such as char, int, and float has a corresponding object. The object is used when you want to use an object's methods or treat the variable like an object. Because an Integer object can do things in a program that the int variable type cannot, it is convenient to have both.

Quiz

The following questions will test whether you have the attributes and behavior to understand object-oriented programming techniques.

Questions

1. What is a method an example of in a Java class?

   (a) attributes

   (b) statements

   (c) behavior

2. If you want to make a variable a class variable, what statement must you use when it is created?

   (a) new

   (b) public

   (c) static

3. What is the name for the part of a program in which a variable lives?

   (a) its nest

   (b) the scope

   (c) variable valley

Answers

1. c. A method is made up of statements, but it's an example of behavior.

2. c.

3. b.

11

Activities

If all this talk of viruses didn't make you sick, you can increase your knowledge of this hour's topics with the following activity:

☐ Add a `private` variable to the `Virus` class that stores an integer called `newSeconds`. Create methods to return the value of `newSeconds` and change the value of `newSeconds` only if the new value is between 60 and 100.

Hour 12

Inheriting Methods from Other Classes

This might be a surprise to you, but your Java objects are ideally suited for childbearing. When you create a program as an object—a set of attributes and behavior—you have designed something that's ready to pass these qualities on to offspring. Like most offspring, these child objects will take on a lot of the attributes and behavior of their parent. They also can do some things differently than their parent does and can add some extra attributes and behavior that pop is incapable of.

This system is called *inheritance*, and it's something every superclass parent gives to its subclass children. Inheritance is one of the most useful aspects of object-oriented programming, and you'll be learning more about it during this hour.

The following topics will be covered:

- ☐ Superclasses and subclasses
- ☐ An inheritance hierarchy
- ☐ Overriding methods
- ☐ Creating a subclass
- ☐ Positioning behavior

The Power of Inheritance

Without knowing it, you have used inheritance every time you used one of the standard Java classes such as String or Math. Java classes are organized into a pyramid-shaped hierarchy of classes in which all classes descend from the Object class.

A class of objects inherits from all superclasses that are above it. To get a working idea of how this works, look at the Applet class. This class is the superclass of all applets, which are Java programs that you will write for the World Wide Web. The family tree of Applet is shown in Figure 12.1. Each of the boxes is a class, and the lines connect a superclass above to any subclasses that it has below.

Figure 12.1.

The family tree of the Applet *class.*

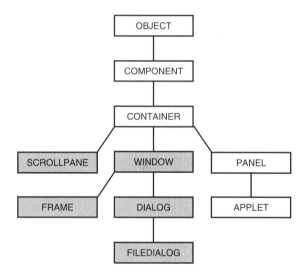

At the top is the Object class. Applet has four superclasses above it in the hierarchy: Panel, Container, Component, and Object. The Applet class inherits attributes and behavior from each of these classes because each is directly above it in the hierarchy of superclasses. Applet does not inherit anything from the five shaded classes in Figure 12.1, which include Dialog and Frame, because they are not above it in the hierarchy.

If this seems confusing, think of the hierarchy as a family tree. Applet will inherit from its parents, their parents, and on upward. It even might inherit some things from its great-great-grandparent Object. The Applet class won't inherit from its siblings or its cousins, however.

Setting up a complicated hierarchy of classes is a difficult thing, but it makes it easier to create new programs later on. The amount of work you need to do to write a new class of objects is reduced. Creating a new class boils down to the following task: You only have to define the ways in which it is different from an existing class. The rest of the work is done for you.

12

As an example, consider the popular video game Tetris. It has been adapted for dozens of different operating systems, processors, and programming languages since being written by Soviet mathematician Alexey Pajitnov and has been created as a Java class by several programmers. In case you somehow avoided Tetris during the past decade by lapsing into a coma or falling into a deep meditative trance, the game works as follows: Blocks of different shapes fall from the top of the screen, and you must organize them into unbroken horizontal lines before they stack up too high.

The Java source file for several adaptations of Tetris is available for your use. If you wanted to create a new version of Tetris based on one of these existing classes, you could make your game a subclass of an existing Tetris game. All you would have to do is create the things that are new or different about your version, and you'd end up with a new game.

Inheriting Behavior and Attributes

The behaviors and attributes of a class are a combination of two things: its own behavior and attributes and all behavior and attributes it inherited from its superclasses.

The following are some of the behavior and attributes of `Applet`:

- ☐ The `equals()` method determines whether an `Applet` object has the same value as another object.
- ☐ The `setBackground()` method sets the background color displayed on the applet window.
- ☐ The `add()` method adds user interface components such as buttons and text fields to the applet.
- ☐ The `showStatus()` method displays a line of text in a Web browser's status bar.

The `Applet` class can use all of these methods, even though `showStatus()` is the only one it didn't inherit from another class. The `equals()` method is defined in `Object`, `setBackground()` comes from `Component`, and `add()` comes from `Container`.

Overriding Methods

Some of the methods defined in the `Applet` class of objects also were defined in one of its superclasses. As an example, the `resize()` method is set up in the `Applet` class and the `Component` class. This method calls on the Web browser displaying the applet to resize the applet's display area. When a method is defined in a subclass and its superclass, the subclass method is used. This enables a subclass to change, replace, or completely wipe out some of the behavior or attributes of its superclasses.

Creating a new method in a subclass to change behavior inherited from a superclass is called overriding the method. You need to override a method any time the inherited behavior will produce an undesired result.

Establishing Inheritance

You establish a class as the subclass of another class with the extends statement, as in the following:

```
class AnimatedLogo extends java.applet.Applet {
    // program goes here
}
```

This statement establishes the AnimatedLogo class of objects as a subclass of Applet, using the full class name of java.applet.Applet. As you will see during the next hour, all applets in Java must be subclasses of Applet because they need the functionality this class provides in order to run on a World Wide Web page.

One method that AnimatedLogo will have to override is the paint() method, which is used to redraw all things that are shown on the program's display area. The paint() method is implemented by the Component class and is passed all the way down to AnimatedLogo. However, the paint() method does not do anything. It exists so that subclasses of Component have a method they can use when the display must be redrawn.

To override a method, you must start the method in the same way it started in the superclass it was inherited from. A public method must remain public, the value sent back by the method must be the same, and the number and type of arguments to the method must not change.

The paint() method of the Component class begins as follows:

```
public void paint(Graphics g) {
```

When AnimatedLogo overrides this method, it must begin with a statement like this:

```
public void paint(Graphics screen) {
```

The only difference is in the name of the Graphics object, which does not matter when determining if the methods are created in the same way. Because both paint() methods are public, return no value because of the void statement, and have a Graphics object as their only parameter, they match.

12

Workshop: Creating a Subclass

To see an example of inheritance at work, you will create a class called Point3D that represents a point in three-dimensional space. A two-dimensional point can be expressed with an (x,y) coordinate. Applets use an (x,y) coordinate system to determine where text and graphics should be displayed. Three-dimensional space adds a third coordinate, which can be called z.

The Point3D class of objects should do three things:

- ☐ Keep track of an object's (x,y,z) coordinate.
- ☐ Move an object to a new (x,y,z) coordinate when needed.
- ☐ Move an object by a certain amount of x, y, and z values as needed.

Java already has a standard class that represents two-dimensional points; it's called Point. It has two integer variables called x and y that store a Point object's (x,y) location. It also has a move() method to place a point at the specified location and a translate() method to move an object by an amount of x and y values.

Run your word processor and create a new file called Point3D.java. Enter the text of Listing 12.1 into the file, and save it when you're done.

Listing 12.1. The full text of Point3D.java.

```
 1: import java.awt.*;
 2:
 3: public class Point3D extends Point {
 4:     public int z;
 5:
 6:     public Point3D(int x, int y, int z) {
 7:         super.x = x;
 8:         super.y = y;
 9:         this.z = z;
10:     }
11:
12:     public void move(int x, int y, int z) {
13:         this.z = z;
14:         super.move(x, y);
15:     }
16:
17:     public void translate(int x, int y, int z) {
18:         this.z += z;
19:         super.translate(x, y);
20:     }
21: }
```

12

Compile this file with the javac compiler tool, and you will have a class you can use in programs. The Point3D class does not have a main() block statement, so you cannot run it with the java interpreter.

The Point3D class only has to do work that isn't being done by its superclass, Point. This work primarily involves keeping track of the integer variable z and receiving it as an argument to the move() method, translate() method, and Point3D() constructor method.

All of the methods use the statements super and this. The this statement is used to refer to the current Point3D object, so this.z = z; in Line 9 sets the object variable z equal to the z value that was sent as an argument to the method in Line 6.

The super statement refers to the superclass of the current object, Point. It is used to set variables and call methods that were inherited by Point3D. A subclass that overrides a method still can call the original method with the super statement. An example of this is Line 14, which calls the move() method of Point to set the (x,y) coordinates of the Point3D object. Because Point already is equipped to handle the x and y axes, it would be redundant for the Point3D class of objects to do the same thing.

To test out the Point3D class that you have compiled, create a program that uses Point and Point3D objects and moves them around. Create a new file in your word processor and enter Listing 12.2 into it. Save the file as TryPoints.java.

Listing 12.2. The full text of TryPoints.java.

```
 1: import java.awt.*;
 2:
 3: class TryPoints {
 4:     public static void main(String[] arguments) {
 5:         Point object1 = new Point(11,22);
 6:         Point3D object2 = new Point3D(7,6,64);
 7:
 8:         System.out.println("The 2D point is located at (" + object1.x + ", "
 9:             + object1.y + ")");
10:         System.out.println("\tIt's being moved to (4, 13)");
11:         object1.move(4,13);
12:         System.out.println("The 2D point is now at (" + object1.x + ", "
13:             + object1.y + ")");
14:         System.out.println("\tIt's being moved -10 units on both the x and y
15:         axes");
16:         object1.translate(-10,-10);
17:         System.out.println("The 2D point ends up at (" + object1.x + ", "
18:             + object1.y + ")\n");
19:
20:         System.out.println("The 3D point is located at (" + object2.x + ", "
21:             + object2.y + ", " + object2.z +")");
22:         System.out.println("\tIt's being moved to (10, 22, 71)");
23:         object2.move(10,22,71);
24:         System.out.println("The 3D point is now at (" + object2.x + ", "
25:             + object2.y + ", " + object2.z +")");
```

12

```
26:         System.out.println("\tIt's being moved -20 units on the x, y and z
27:         axes");
28:         object2.translate(-20,-20,-20);
29:         System.out.println("The 3D point ends up at (" + object2.x + ", "
30:             + object2.y + ", " + object2.z +")");
31:     }
32: }
```

After you compile this file and run it with the java interpreter, the following should be shown:

```
The 2D point is located at (11, 22)
    It's being moved to (4, 13)
The 2D point is now at (4, 13)
    It's being moved -10 units on both the x and y axes
The 2D point ends up at (-6, 3)

The 3D point is located at (7, 6, 64)
    It's being moved to (10, 22, 71)
The 3D point is now at (10, 22, 71)
    It's being moved -20 units on the x, y and z axes
The 3D point ends up at (-10, 2, 51)
```

Summary

When people talk about the miracle of birth, they're probably not speaking of the way a superclass can give birth to subclasses or the way behavior and attributes are inherited in a hierarchy of classes. However, if the real world worked the same way that object-oriented programming does, every grandchild of Mozart would get to choose whether to be a brilliant composer. All descendants of Mark Twain could wax poetic about Mississippi riverboat life. Every skill your direct ancestors worked to achieve would be handed to you without an ounce of toil.

On the scale of miracles, inheritance isn't quite up to par compared with continuing the existence of a species and getting a good tax break. However, it's an effective way to design software with a minimum of redundant work.

Q&A

Q Can a class have more than one superclass so that it inherits additional methods and behavior?

A It is possible with some object-oriented programming languages but not Java. One of the goals when Java was developed was to provide a simpler language than an object-oriented language such as C++, and limiting inheritance to a single super-class was one way to acheive this. You can use a special type of class called an interface to inherit behavior that isn't received from superclasses.

Q Most Java programs created up to this point have not used `extends` to inherit from a superclass. Does this mean they exist outside of the class hierarchy?

A All classes that you create in Java are part of the hierarchy because the default superclass for the programs you write is `Object`. The `equals()` and `toString()` methods are part of the behavior that automatically is inherited from `Object`.

Q When is the full name of a class, such as `java.applet.Applet`, needed in an `extends` clause instead of a shorter name such as `Applet`?

A You must use the full name whenever you don't use an `import` `java.applet.Applet;` or `import.java.applet.*;` statement at the beginning of your program. The `import` statement is used solely to make it easier to refer to class names in programs. Each class of objects in Java has a full name that identifies the group of classes it belongs to. For instance, the `Math` class is part of the `java.lang` group of classes. A group of classes is also called a *package*.

Quiz

To determine what kind of knowledge you inherited from the past hour's work, answer the following questions.

Questions

1. If a superclass handles a method in a way you don't want to use in the subclass, what can you do?

    (a) Delete the method in the superclass.

    (b) Override the method in the subclass.

    (c) Write a nasty letter to the editor of the *San Jose Mercury News* hoping that Java's developers will read it.

2. Which of the following is not a superclass of `Applet`?

    (a) `Dialog`

    (b) `Container`

    (c) `Component`

3. What statement can you use to refer to the methods and variables of a superclass?

    (a) `this`

    (b) `call`

    (c) `super`

12

Answers

1. b. Because you can override the method, you don't have to change any aspect of the superclass or the way it works.

2. a. `Dialog` has some common superclasses with `Applet`, but it isn't a superclass, so `Applet` does not inherit any behavior or attributes from it.

3. c. A `this` statement refers to the current object, and `super` refers to the superclass.

Activities

If a fertile imagination has birthed in you a desire to learn more, you can spawn more knowledge of inheritance with the following activities:

☐ Create a `Point4D` class that adds a `t` coordinate to the (x,y,z) coordinate system created by the `Point3D` class. The `t` coordinate stands for time, so you need to ensure that it does not get set to a negative value.

☐ Take the members of a football team's offense—lineman, wide receiver, tight end, running back, and quarterback. Design a hierarchy of classes that represent the skills of these players, putting common skills higher up in the hierarchy. For example, blocking is behavior that should probably be inherited by the linemen and tight end classes, and speed is something that should be inherited by wide receivers and running backs.

12

PART

IV

Creating Applets for the World Wide Web

Hour

Hour **13**

Learning How Applets Work

Now that Java is making the transition from a child prodigy to an established language, it is being used for all kinds of large-scale business software and other applications. However, the core of interest in the language remains in a new type of program that Java made possible: the applet. *Applets* are programs designed to run as part of a World Wide Web page. When a Java applet is encountered on a page, it is downloaded to the user's computer and begins running.

During this hour you'll be introduced to applet programming. Programming applets with Java is much different from creating applications with Java. Because applets must be downloaded off a page each time they are run, applets are smaller than most applications to reduce download time. Also, because applets run on the computer of the person using the applet, they have numerous security restrictions in place to prevent malicious or damaging code from being run.

The following topics will be covered:

- ☐ Setting up an applet
- ☐ Displaying information in an applet
- ☐ Stopping and starting an applet
- ☐ Putting an applet on a Web page
- ☐ Using applet HTML tags and attributes

Standard Applet Methods

All applets are subclasses of the Applet subclass, which is part of the java.applet package of classes. Being part of this hierarchy enables the applets that you write to use all the behavior and attributes they need to be run off of a World Wide Web page. Before you begin writing any other statements in your applets, they will be able to interact with a Web browser, load and unload themselves, redraw their window in response to changes in the browser window, and other functions.

In applications, programs begin running with the first statement of the main() block statement and end with the last } that closes out the block. There is no main() method in a Java applet, so there is no set starting place for the program. Instead, an applet has a group of standard methods that are handled in response to specific events as the applet runs.

The following are the events that could prompt one of the applet methods to be handled:

- ☐ The program is loaded for the first time
- ☐ Something happens that requires the applet window to be redisplayed
- ☐ The program stops at a specific point
- ☐ The program restarts after a stop
- ☐ The program is unloaded as it finishes running

The following is an example of a bare-bones applet:

```
public class Skeleton extends java.applet.Applet {
    // program will go here
}
```

Note that unlike applications, applet class files must be public in order to work. (However, if your applet uses other class files of your own creation, they do not have to be declared public.) This class inherits all of the methods that are handled automatically when needed: init(), paint(), start(), stop(), and destroy(). However, none of these methods do anything. If you want something to happen in an applet, you have to override these methods with new versions in your applet program. The two methods you will override most often are paint() and init().

13

The `paint()` Method

The `paint()` method should be a part of almost every applet that you write because you can't display anything without it. Whenever something needs to be displayed or redisplayed on the applet window, the `paint()` method handles the task. You also can force `paint()` to be handled with the following statement:

```
repaint();
```

Otherwise, the main reason `paint()` occurs is when something is changed in the browser or the operating system running the browser. For example, if a Windows 95 user minimizes a Web page containing an applet, the `paint()` method will be called to redisplay everything that was on-screen in the applet when the applet is later restored to full-size.

Unlike the other methods that you will be learning about during this hour, `paint()` takes an argument. The following is an example of a simple `paint()` method:

```
public class paint(Graphics screen) {
    // display statements go here
}
```

The argument is a `Graphics` object. The `Graphics` class of objects is used to handle all attributes and behavior that are needed to display text, graphics, and other information on-screen. (You'll learn about `drawString()`, one of the methods of the `Graphics` class, later this hour.) If you are using a `Graphics` object in your applet, you have to add the following `import` statement before the `class` statement at the beginning of the source file:

```
import java.awt.Graphics;
```

JUST A MINUTE

If you are using several classes that are a part of the `java.awt` package of classes, use the statement `import java.awt.*;` instead. It makes all of these classes available for use in your program.

The `init()` Method

The `init()` method is handled once—and only once—when the applet is run. As a result, it's an ideal place to set up values for any objects and variables that are needed for the applet to run successfully. This method is also a good place to set up fonts, colors, and the screen's background color.

CAUTION

Variables and objects should not be created inside an `init()` method
because they will only exist within the scope of that method. For example,
if you create an integer variable called `displayRate` inside the `init()`
method and try to use it in the `paint()` method, you'll get an error when
you attempt to compile the program. Create any variables that you need
to use throughout a class as object variables right after the `class` statement and before any methods.

The `start()` and `stop()` Methods

At any point when the applet program starts running, the `start()` method will be handled.
When a program first begins, the `init()` method is followed by the `start()` method. After
that, in many instances there will never be a cause for the `start()` method to be handled again.
In order for `start()` to be handled a second time or more, the applet has to stop execution
at some point.

The `stop()` method is called when an applet stops execution. This event can occur when a user
leaves the Web page containing the applet and continues to another page. It also can occur
when the `stop()` method is called directly in a program.

In the programs that you'll write as you're starting out with the Java language, `start()` and
`stop()` will have the most use in animation. You'll learn more about this use during Hour
18, "Creating Animation."

The `destroy()` Method

The `destroy()` method is an opposite of sorts to the `init()` method. It is handled just before
an applet completely closes down and completes running. This method is used in rare
instances when something has been changed during a program and should be restored to its
original state. It's another method that you'll use more often with animation than with other
types of programs.

Putting an Applet on a Web Page

Applets are placed on a Web page in the same way that anything unusual is put on a page:
HTML commands are used to describe the applet, and the Web browser loads it along with
the other parts of the page. If you have used HTML to create a Web page, you know that it's
a way to combine formatted text, images, sound, and other elements together. HTML uses

special commands called tags that are surrounded by < and > marks, including <IMG> for the display of images, <P> for the insertion of a paragraph mark, and <CENTER> to center the text that follows until a </CENTER> tag is reached.

The performance of some of these HTML tags can be affected by attributes that determine how they function. For example, SRC is an attribute of the <IMG> tag, and it provides the name of the image file that should be displayed. The following is an example of an <IMG> tag:

```
<IMG SRC="Graduation.jpg">
```

You can place applets on a Web page by using an <APPLET> tag and several attributes. The following is an example of the HTML required to put an applet on a page:

```
<APPLET CODE="StripYahtzee.class" CODEBASE="javadir" HEIGHT=300 WIDTH=400>
Sorry, no dice ... this requires a Java-enabled browser.
</APPLET>
```

The CODE attribute identifies the name of the applet's class file. If more than one class file is being used with an applet, CODE should refer to the main class file that is a subclass of the Applet class.

If there is no CODEBASE attribute, all files associated with the applet should be in the same directory as the Web page that loads the program. CODEBASE should contain a reference to the directory or subdirectory where the applet and any related files can be found. In the preceding example, CODEBASE indicates that the StripYahtzee applet can be found in the javadir subdirectory.

The HEIGHT and WIDTH attributes designate the exact size of the applet window on the Web page and must be big enough to handle the things you are displaying in your applet.

In between the opening <APPLET> tag and the closing </APPLET> tag, you can provide an alternate of some kind for Web users whose browser software cannot run Java programs. In the preceding example, a line of text is displayed indicating that Java is required to play the game.

Another attribute that you can use with applets is ALIGN. It designates how the applet will be displayed in relation to the surrounding material on the page, including text and graphics. Values include ALIGN="Left", ALIGN="Right", and others.

A Sample Applet

The first program that you wrote was a Java application that revealed a depressing fact about the U.S. financial condition—one minute's worth of the national debt. If it isn't too painful a prospect, you'll take a look at how applets are structured by writing the same program as an applet.

13

Load your word processor and create a new file called BigDebtApplet.java. Enter the text of Listing 13.1 into the file and save it when you're done.

Listing 13.1. The full text of BigDebtApplet.java.

```
 1: import java.awt.*;
 2:
 3: public class BigDebtApplet extends java.applet.Applet {
 4:     int debt;
 5:
 6:     public void init() {
 7:         debt = 59000000;
 8:         debt = debt / 1440;
 9:     }
10:
11:     public void paint(Graphics screen) {
12:         screen.drawString("A minute's worth of debt is $" + debt, 5, 50);
13:     }
14: }
```

This applet does not need to use the start(), stop(), or destroy() methods, so they are not included in the program. Compile the program with the javac compiler tool.

Using the drawString() Method

The drawString() method is one of the things you can use in a paint() method to display information. It is similar in function to System.out.println() statement, which cannot be used in an applet. The drawString() method is part of the Graphics class, so you must use it in the paint() method or another method that has the Graphics object that was sent to the paint() method.

The following three arguments are sent to drawString():

☐ The text to display, which can be several different strings and variables strung together with the + operator

☐ The x position (in an (x,y) coordinate system) where the string should be displayed

☐ The y position where the string should be displayed

The (x,y) coordinate system in an applet is used with several methods. It begins with the (0,0) point in the upper-left corner of the applet window. Figure 13.1 shows how the (x,y) coordinate system works in conjunction with the statement on Line 12 of BigDebtApplet.java.

13

Figure 13.1.

Drawing a string to an (x,y) position.

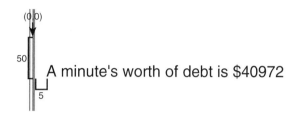

Testing the `BigDebtApplet` **Program**

Although you have compiled the `BigDebtApplet` program into a class file, you cannot run it using the `java` interpreter. If you do, you'll get an error message such as the following:

```
In class BigDebtApplet: void main(String argv[]) is not defined
```

The error occurs because the `java` interpreter runs Java applications beginning with the first statement of the `main()` block. To run an applet, you need to create a Web page that loads the applet. To create a Web page, open up a new file on your word processor and call it `BigDebtApplet.html`. Enter Listing 13.2 and then save the file.

Listing 13.2. The full text of `BigDebtApplet.html`.

```
 1: <html>
 2: <head>
 3: <title>The Big Debt Applet</title>
 4: </head>
 5: <body bgcolor="#000000" text="#FF00FF">
 6: <center>
 7: This a Java applet:<br>
 8: <applet code="BigDebtApplet.class" height=150 width=300>
 9: You need a Java-enabled browser to see this.
10: </applet>
11: </body>
12: </html>
```

Normally, you can test the Java applets that you write using the `appletviewer` tool that comes with the Java Developer's Kit. You can see the output of the `BigDebtApplet` applet by typing the following:

```
appletviewer BigDebtApplet.html
```

However, `appletviewer` only runs the applets that are included in a Web page and does not handle any of the other elements such as text and images. To see the `BigDebtApplet.html` file, load it into a browser that can handle Java programs, such as the current versions of Microsoft

13

Internet Explorer and Netscape Navigator. Figure 13.2 shows a screen capture of `BigDebtApplet.html` loaded into Internet Explorer.

Figure 13.2.

The `BigDebtApplet`
program on a Web page
displayed by Microsoft
Internet Explorer.

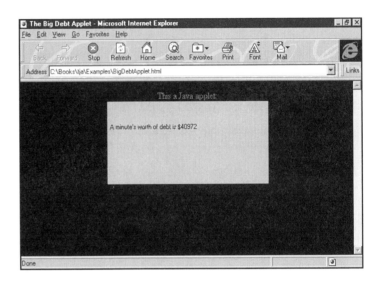

CAUTION

At the time of this writing, the current versions of Netscape Navigator and Microsoft Internet Explorer do not support any new feature introduced with version 1.1 of the Java language. This hour's applet works, but many others in later hours do not. Use the `appletviewer` tool to run applets unless you know your browser software fully supports Java 1.1.

Workshop: Enhancing the `BigDebtApplet` Project

As a short exercise to close out the hour, you'll enhance the `BigDebtApplet` program by making it accumulate the debt over time, displaying how much the national debt grows each second.

Open up a new file with your word processor and call it `Ouch.java`. Enter Listing 13.3 and save the file when you're done.

Listing 13.3. The full text of `Ouch.java`.

```
 1: import java.awt.*;
 2: import java.util.*;
 3:
 4: public class Ouch extends java.applet.Applet {
 5:     int debt = 683;
 6:     int totalTime = 1;
 7:
 8:     public void paint(Graphics screen) {
 9:         screen.drawString(totalTime + " second's worth of debt is $"
10:             + (debt * totalTime), 5, 30);
11:         for (int i = 0; i < 5000000; i++);
12:         totalTime++;
13:         repaint();
14:     }
15: }
```

This file uses an empty `for` loop in Line 11 to approximate the passage of a second's time. Whether it actually pauses for a second depends on your processor speed and anything else that's currently running on your computer. The call to `repaint()` in Line 13 at the end of the `paint()` method causes the `paint()` method to be called again, starting over at the beginning of the method on Line 9.

To try out the program, you need to compile it with the `javac` compiler tool and create a Web page that runs the applet. Create a new file on your word processor and enter Listing 13.4 into the file. Save it when you're done.

Listing 13.4. The full text of `Ouch.html`.

```
1: <applet code="Ouch.class" height=300 width=300>
2: </applet>
```

This Web page only contains the HTML tags that are required to add an applet to a page. Load this Web page into the `appletviewer` tool by typing the following at a command line:

```
appletviewer Ouch.html
```

You will see an applet that begins with the calculation of a second's worth of debt. At a regular interval, another second's debt will be added. The following is an example of the text that is displayed as the applet runs:

```
13 second's worth of debt is $8879
```

13

Summary

This hour was the first of several that will focus on the development of applets. You got a chance to become acquainted with the init() and paint() methods, which you will be using frequently when you're developing applets.

Writing applets is a good way for beginners to develop their skills as Java programmers for the following reasons:

- Applets are usually smaller in scope, making their creation a less daunting task.
- You can find thousands of sample applets on the World Wide Web, including many with the source file available to learn from.
- You can make applets available to a global audience at low to no cost through the Web, exposing your work to more people who can offer comments and suggestions.

There's a "code war" of sorts afoot among the hundreds of Java programmers who are putting their work on the Web, and many new applets announced on sites like http://www.jars.com demonstrate new things that can be done with the language.

Q&A

Q Can arguments be sent to applets, as they can to applications?

A You can't use arguments, but parameters serve a similar function to arguments in applet programming. You can use the <PARAM> tag with its NAME and VALUE attributes to send parameters to Java programs. It's described fully in Hour 15, "Sending Parameters to Applets."

Q Is there a reason why the CODEBASE attribute should be used in an <APPLET> tag?

A If all Java programs are grouped into their own subdirectory, as indicated by CODEBASE, this structure might improve the way a Web site is organized, but there's no other reason why using CODEBASE is better than omitting it. The choice is a matter of personal preference.

Q What happens if the height and width specified for an applet don't leave enough room for the information that is displayed in the paint() method?

A The information will be drawn off-screen beyond the edges of the applet window and won't be visible at any point while the applet runs. Choosing the right dimensions for an applet is largely a matter of trial-and-error until you find the right size for both the HEIGHT and WIDTH attributes of the <APPLET> tag. Fortunately, you can change the Web page's HTML without having to recompile the Java program.

13

Quiz

The following questions test your knowledge of applets.

Questions

1. What type of argument is used with the `paint()` method?

    (a) A `Graphics` object

    (b) A Boolean variable

    (c) None

2. Which method is handled right before an applet finishes running?

    (a) `decline()`

    (b) `destroy()`

    (c) `demise()`

3. Why can't all variables needed in an applet be created inside the `init()` method?

    (a) The scope of the variables would be limited to the method only.

    (b) Federal legislation prohibits it.

    (c) They can be created there without any problems.

Answers

1. a. The `Graphics` object keeps track of the behavior and attributes needed to display things on-screen in the applet window.

2. b.

3. a. Variables that are used in more than one method of a class should be created right after the class statement but before any methods begin.

Activities

You can apply your applet programming knowledge with the following activity:

☐ Create an applet that displays the values of an array in the applet window and adds one to some of the values each time the applet is repainted. Drag other windows atop the running version of this program to force it to require repainting. This exercise demonstrates how the `paint()` method is called for behind the scenes.

13

Hour 14

Creating a Threaded Applet

A computer term that is used often to describe the hectic pace of daily life is *multitasking*. (Another term is used more often around here, but the editors asked that it be omitted.) Multitasking means to do more than one thing at once—such as surfing the Web at your desk while participating in a conference call and using the Buttmaster exercise device to achieve more shapely shanks. The term comes from the world of operating systems, where a multitasking computer is one that can handle more than one program at a time.

One of the most sophisticated features of the Java language is the ability to write programs that can multitask. Under Java, each of the simultaneous tasks the computer handles is called a *thread* and the overall process is called *multithreading*. Threading is useful in animation and many other programs. This hour covers the subject of programming a threaded applet.

The following topics will be covered:

☐ Using an interface with a program

☐ Creating threads

☐ Starting and stopping threads

☐ Pausing a thread

☐ Loading a Web page from an applet program

☐ Catching errors

☐ Displaying an applet with other Web page elements

A Revolving-Link Applet

To provide more information on how applets are programmed, this hour is an extended workshop describing the design of a threaded applet. The program you'll be writing will rotate through a list of Web site titles and the addresses used to visit them. The following six Web sites will be listed:

☐ The JavaSoft Web site at `http://java.sun.com`

☐ The Gamelan Java directory at `http://www.gamelan.com`

☐ The JavaWorld Web magazine at `http://www.javaworld.com`

☐ This book's Web site at `http://www.prefect.com/java24`

☐ The Sams.net Publishing Developers' Solution Center at `http://www.mcp.com/sams`

☐ The Java Applet Ratings Service at `http://www.jars.com`

The title of each page and the Web address will be displayed in a continuous cycle. Users will be able to visit the currently displayed site by clicking anywhere on the applet with the mouse. This program operates over a period of time; information on each Web site must be shown long enough to be read, and the next site then will be shown. Because of this time element, threads are the best way to control the program.

Instead of entering this program into your word processor first and learning about it afterward, you'll get a chance to enter the full text of the `Revolve` applet at the end of the hour. Before then, each section of the program will be described.

The `class` Declaration

The first thing you need to do in this applet is to use `import` to make some classes available. The `Thread` class, which is part of the `java.lang` group of classes, comes with methods to start a thread, stop a thread, and pause a thread. All three of these methods will be useful in the `Revolve` applet.

The `java.awt` group of classes is needed because you'll be using one of them, `Graphics`, to display text on-screen. The `java.net` group will be used when you work with the Web addresses, and the `java.applet` group is needed when you tell the browser to load a new page.

14

Finally, the `java.awt.event` group is needed to respond to mouse clicks so that a user can visit one of the addresses shown.

Use the following `import` statements:

```
import java.applet.*;
import java.awt.*;
import java.awt.event.*;
import java.net.*;
```

JUST A MINUTE

> You might be wondering why the `java.lang` group of classes does not need to be imported. It automatically is available to all Java programs that you write and contains a lot of the classes you will use most often. The `String`, `Integer`, and `Math` classes are three examples of classes that belong to `java.lang`.

After you have used `import` to make some classes available, you're ready to begin the applet with the following statement:

```
public class Revolve extends Applet
    implements Runnable, ActionListener {
```

This statement creates the `Revolve` class as a subclass of the `Applet` class. It also uses a new statement called `implements`.

The `implements` statement enables this class to inherit some extra methods beyond those that were inherited from the `Applet` class. The `Runnable` and `ActionListener` classes are called *interfaces.* An interface is a special type of class that is only useful in conjunction with the `implements` statement. An interface extends the capabilities of a class. In this case, `Runnable` provides the behavior an applet needs in order to become a thread. By implementing the `Runnable` class, you will be able to use a `run()` method in this applet to make a thread begin running. The `ActionListener` interface enables the applet to respond to actions the user takes with the mouse. Implementing it enables the `actionPerformed()` method to be called when a mouse button is clicked.

Setting Up Variables

The first thing to do in the `Revolve` class is to create the variables and objects needed throughout the program. Create two arrays with six elements—an array of `String` objects called `pageTitle` and an array of `URL` objects called `pageLink`:

```
String[] pageTitle = new String[6];
URL[] pageLink = new URL[6];
```

14

The `pageTitle` array will store the titles of the six Web sites that will be displayed. The URL class of objects stores the value of a Web site address. URL has all the behavior and attributes that are needed to keep track of a Web address and use it to load the page with a Web browser. Both of these arrays are set up without any values at this point, so you'll have to provide them later.

The last two things to be created are an integer variable called `current` and a `Thread` object called `runner`:

```
int current = 0;
Thread runner;
```

The `current` variable will be used to keep track of which site is being displayed so that you can cycle through the sites. The `Thread` object `runner` represents the only thread this program runs. You will call methods of the `runner` object when you start, stop, and pause the operation of the applet.

Starting with `init()`

The `init()` method of an applet automatically is handled when the applet first starts to run. In this example, this method is used to assign values to the two arrays created for this applet, `pageTitle` and `pageLink`. It also is used to create a clickable button that will appear on the applet. The method consists of the following statements:

```
public void init() {
    Color background = new Color(255, 255, 204);
    setBackground(background);
    pageTitle[0] = "JavaSoft";
    pageLink[0] = getURL("http://java.sun.com");
    pageTitle[1] = "Gamelan";
    pageLink[1] = getURL("http://www.gamelan.com");
    pageTitle[2] = "JavaWorld";
    pageLink[2] = getURL("http://www.javaworld.com");
    pageTitle[3] = "Java 1.1 Programming in 24 Hours";
    pageLink[3] = getURL("http://www.prefect.com/java24");
    pageTitle[4] = "Sams.net Developers' Resource Center";
    pageLink[4] = getURL("http://www.mcp.com/sams");
    pageTitle[5] = "Java Applet Rating Service";
    pageLink[5] = getURL("http://www.jars.com");
    Button goButton = new Button("Go");
    goButton.addActionListener(this);
    add(goButton);
}
```

The first two statements of this method set up a background color for the applet. You'll learn how to do this during Hour 16, "Using Fonts and Color in Applets."

14

Strings are assigned to the six elements of the pageTitle array, which stores the title of each Web page. The elements of the pageLink array are assigned a value returned by the getURL() method, which you will be creating for this program.

The last three statements of the init() method are used to create a button that will appear on-screen when the applet runs. The button has the name goButton and is labeled with the text Go. The addActionListener(this); statement makes it possible for the program to respond when the user clicks the button. The add() statement adds the button to the applet's display area. Creating components like buttons and using them in programs will be explained in detail during Hour 19, "Building a Simple User Interface," and Hour 20, "Responding to User Events."

Catching Errors as You Set Up URLs

When you set up a URL object, you must make sure that the text used to set up the address is in a valid format. http://www.javasoft.com and http://www.gamelan.com are valid, but something such as http:www.javasoft.com would not be because of the missing // marks.

A special try-catch statement is used to catch errors inside the program instead of letting them cause it to stop running, as many errors do. The try statement lets your program try to do something that might cause an error. If an error does occur, the catch statement is used to catch the error before it brings the program to a crashing halt.

COFFEE BREAK

> If you're having trouble with the concept of try and catch statements, think of what it would be like to be one of Superman's best pals. Jimmy Olsen and Lois Lane can try all kinds of dangerous stunts without worrying as much about the consequences if they make an error. No narrow ledge or runaway locomotive is too risky an endeavor for them to attempt to navigate. If they try and fail, Superman will be there to catch them. No matter what you try in a Java program, you can create a catch statement that will catch errors.

The getURL() method takes a string of text as an argument. The string is checked to see whether it's a valid Web address, and if it is, the method returns that valid address. If it's erroneous, the method sends back a null value. The following is the getURL() method:

```
URL getURL(String urlText) {
    URL pageURL = null;
    try { pageURL = new URL(getDocumentBase(), urlText); }
    catch (MalformedURLException m) { }
    return pageURL;
}
```

14

The first line of this method includes three things, in this order:

☐ The type of object or variable that is returned by the method—a URL object in this case. If this is void, no information is returned by the method.

☐ The name of the method—getURL.

☐ The argument or arguments, if any, that this method takes—only one in this example, a String variable called urlText.

The try statement is followed by { and } marks. The program handles any statements between these marks, and if they generate any exception or error conditions, these will be sent to the catch statement.

The catch statement also has { and } marks as part of the statement. If catch is set up to catch an error from the try block statement, anything between the { and } marks will be handled. In this example, if a MalformedURLException error occurs during the try block of statements, any statements between the { and } marks after catch will be handled. Because there are no statements between { and } in this method, catch ignores any MalformedURLException errors that occur.

If the String variable sent to the method is a valid Web address, it will be sent back as a valid URL object. If not, null is returned. Because you were assigning values to six different URL objects in the pageURL array, the getURL() method makes this process easier to do.

Handling Screen Updates in the Paint() Method

The paint() method of any applet is handled when the screen needs to be updated. This situation can be caused by the Web browser or operating system outside of the applet if they obscure part of an applet window or change its dimensions in some way. The paint() method also can be manually called within an applet when the screen needs to be updated.

If you put a repaint(); statement in an applet, it forces the paint() method to be handled. This statement is a way you can tell the program that you have done something that requires a screen update. For example, if you are writing an animation program and you move an image from one place to another, you need to use repaint(); so that the image is shown in its new location.

The Revolve applet has a short paint() method:

```
public void paint(Graphics screen) {
    screen.drawString(pageTitle[current], 5, 60);
    screen.drawString("" + pageLink[current], 5, 80);
}
```

14

The two statements inside the method display lines of text on the screen at the (x,y) positions of (5, 60) and (5, 80). The first line that is displayed is an element of the pageTitle array. The second line that is displayed is the address of the URL object, which is stored in the pageLink array. The current variable is used to determine which elements of these arrays to display.

Starting the Thread

One of the objects created for this program is a Thread object called runner. In order for a thread to get started, a place is needed where the thread is given a value and told to begin running. In this applet, the runner thread will start whenever the start() method is handled and stop whenever stop() is handled.

The start() method of an applet is handled at two different times: Right after the init() method and every time the program is restarted after being stopped. An applet is stopped any time a user switches from the applet page to another Web page. It starts again when a user returns to the original page. The following is the start() method of the Revolve applet:

```
public void start() {
    if (runner == null) {
        runner = new Thread(this);
        runner.start();
    }
}
```

This method does only one thing: If the runner thread is not already started, it creates a new runner thread and starts it. The runner object equals null when it has not been started yet, so you can test for this condition with the if statement.

The statement runner = new Thread(this); creates a new Thread object with one argument—the this statement. Using this makes the applet itself the program that will run in the runner thread.

The runner.start(); statement causes the thread to begin running. When a thread begins, the run() method of that thread is handled. Because the runner thread is the applet itself, the run() method of the applet is handled.

Running the Thread

The run() method is where the main work of a thread takes place. It is comparable to the main() block statement of a Java application. In the Revolve applet, the following represents the run() method:

```
public void run() {
    while (true) {
        repaint();
```

14

```
            current++;
            if (current > 5)
                current = 0;
            try { Thread.sleep(10000); }
            catch (InterruptedException e) { }
        }
    }
```

All of the statements in this method are part of a while loop that has the Boolean value true as its condition. Because a while loop will continue looping as long as its condition equals true, while (true) will cause the loop to continue indefinitely. The only way the thread will stop is for the stop() method to be automatically called when the Web browser shuts down or the page containing the applet is replaced with another page.

The run() method first uses the repaint(); statement to cause the paint() method to be handled. Next, the value of the current variable increases by one, and if current exceeds 5, it is set to 0 again. The current variable is used in the paint() method to determine which Web site information to display. Changing current causes a different site to be displayed the next time paint() is handled.

This method includes another try-catch statement that handles an error that might occur. The Thread.sleep(10000); statement causes a thread to pause for 10,000 milliseconds. This statement causes the thread to wait long enough for users to read the name of the Web site and its address. The catch statement takes care of any InterruptedException errors that might occur while the Thread.sleep() statement is being handled. These errors would occur if something interrupted the thread while it was trying to sleep().

Stopping the Thread

The stop() method is handled any time the applet is stopped because the applet's page is exited, and it is the best place to stop the running thread. The stop() method for the Revolve applet contains the following statements:

```
public void stop() {
    if (runner != null) {
        runner.stop();
        runner = null;
    }
}
```

The if statement tests to see whether the runner object is equal to null. If it is, there isn't an active thread that needs to be stopped. Otherwise, the statement uses the stop() method of the runner object to stop that thread and sets runner equal to null.

14

Handling Mouse Clicks

Anything the user does with a mouse or keyboard in an applet is called an *event*, and the process of responding to events in a program is called *event-handling*. You'll learn all about events in Hour 20.

The last thing to take care of in the `Revolve` applet are mouse clicks. Whenever you click the Go button, the Web browser should open the Web site that is listed. This is done with a method called `actionPerformed()`. The `actionPerformed()` method is called whenever the button is clicked.

The following is the `actionPerformed()` method of the `Revolve` applet:

```
public void actionPerformed(ActionEvent evt) {
    runner.stop();
    AppletContext browser = getAppletContext();
    if (pageLink[current] != null)
        browser.showDocument(pageLink[current]);
}
```

The first thing that happens in this method is that the `runner` thread is stopped. The next two statements create a new `AppletContext` object called `browser` and check to see whether the currently displayed Web address is valid. If it is, the `showDocument` method of the `AppletContext` class is used to display a new Web page in the user's browser.

Workshop: Revolving Links

Now that all aspects of the `Revolve` applet have been described, you're ready to create the program and test it out. Run your word processor and create a new file called `Revolve.java`. Enter the text of Listing 14.1 and save the file when you're done.

Listing 14.1. The full text of `Revolve.java`.

```
 1: import java.applet.*;
 2: import java.awt.*;
 3: import java.awt.event.*;
 4: import java.net.*;
 5:
 6: public class Revolve extends Applet
 7:     implements Runnable, ActionListener {
 8:
 9:     String[] pageTitle = new String[6];
10:     URL[] pageLink = new URL[6];
11:     int current = 0;
12:     Thread runner;
13:
14:     public void init() {
```

14

continues

Listing 14.1. continued

```
15:            Color background = new Color(255, 255, 204);
16:            setBackground(background);
17:            pageTitle[0] = "JavaSoft";
18:            pageLink[0] = getURL("http://java.sun.com");
19:            pageTitle[1] = "Gamelan";
20:            pageLink[1] = getURL("http://www.gamelan.com");
21:            pageTitle[2] = "JavaWorld";
22:            pageLink[2] = getURL("http://www.javaworld.com");
23:            pageTitle[3] = "Java 1.1 Programming in 24 Hours";
24:            pageLink[3] = getURL("http://www.prefect.com/java24");
25:            pageTitle[4] = "Sams.net Developers' Resource Center";
26:            pageLink[4] = getURL("http://www.mcp.com/sams");
27:            pageTitle[5] = "Java Applet Rating Service";
28:            pageLink[5] = getURL("http://www.jars.com");
29:            Button goButton = new Button("Go");
30:            goButton.addActionListener(this);
31:            add(goButton);
32:        }
33:
34:    URL getURL(String urlText) {
35:        URL pageURL = null;
36:        try { pageURL = new URL(getDocumentBase(), urlText); }
37:        catch (MalformedURLException m) { }
38:        return pageURL;
39:    }
40:
41:    public void paint(Graphics screen) {
42:        screen.drawString(pageTitle[current], 5, 60);
43:        screen.drawString("" + pageLink[current], 5, 80);
44:    }
45:
46:    public void start() {
47:        if (runner == null) {
48:            runner = new Thread(this);
49:            runner.start();
50:        }
51:    }
52:
53:    public void run() {
54:        while (true) {
55:            repaint();
56:            current++;
57:            if (current > 5)
58:                current = 0;
59:            try { Thread.sleep(10000); }
60:            catch (InterruptedException e) { }
61:        }
62:    }
63:
64:    public void stop() {
65:        if (runner != null) {
66:            runner.stop();
67:            runner = null;
68:        }
```

14

```
69:    }
70:
71:    public void actionPerformed(ActionEvent evt) {
72:        runner.stop();
73:        AppletContext browser = getAppletContext();
74:        if (pageLink[current] != null)
75:            browser.showDocument(pageLink[current]);
76:    }
77: }
```

After you compile this program with the javac compiler tool, you need to create a Web page to put the applet on. Create a new file with your word processor and name it Revolve.html. Enter Listing 14.2 and save the file. Note that some HTML tags have been included so that you can see the applet in the way it might be presented on a real page.

Listing 14.2. The full text of Revolve.html.

```
1: <html>
2: <head>
3: <title>Homer's Home Page</title>
4: </head>
5: <body bgcolor="#C4C4C4">
6: <font face="Arial" size=3>
7: <table>
8: <tr>
9:
10: <td bgcolor="#FFCCFF" width=300 valign="TOP" align="CENTER">
11: <h2>Homer's Home Page</h2>
12: <p>Welcome to the cyberspace home of Homer! This page is under construction.
13: </td>
14:
15: <td bgcolor="#FFFFCC" width=200 valign="TOP" align="RIGHT">
16: <i><b>Some of my favorite links:</b></i>
17: <applet code="Revolve.class" height=100 width=200>
18: </applet>
19: <center>
20: <i>Click to visit</i>
21: </center>
22: </td>
23:
24: </tr>
25: </table>
26: </font>
27: </body>
28: </html>
```

When you're done, load this file into appletviewer. You can test the applet itself from this program, but you will not see the surrounding HTML or be able to load a new Web page when the Go button is clicked. These features require the use of a Web browser that is

14

equipped to handle Java 1.1 programs. Figure 14.1 shows the output of the Revolve applet in the appletviewer tool.

Figure 14.1.

A screen capture of the
Revolve *applet using*
appletviewer.

So that you can see how this applet would look on a Web browser, Figure 14.2 shows a modified version of Revolve using Netscape Navigator. This version uses no new features of Java 1.1, so it can be run on browsers that can handle Java 1.0.2 programs.

Figure 14.2.

A screen capture of a
modified Revolve
applet using Netscape
Navigator.

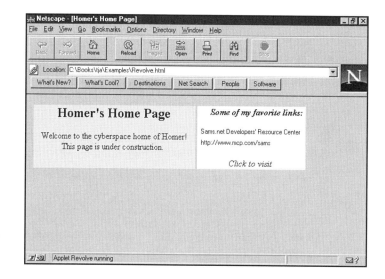

If you'd like to run this modified version using a Web browser, you can find it on this book's CD-ROM in the Win95nt4/Book/Source/Hour14 directory. Load the Web page OldRevolve.html into a Java-enabled browser.

Summary

Now that you have programmed applets and threads during the past two hours, you should be getting a better idea of the behind-the-scenes work that takes place in an applet. Many of the methods in these programs often are called automatically, such as paint().

14

With or without threads, writing applets requires an understanding of the methods that might be included in an applet and how they function. In the next several hours, you'll get more chances to see which methods are called automatically and how to use them in your own programs.

Even if you learned nothing else from this hour, you now have a new '90s term to describe your frenzied lifestyle. Use it in a few sentences to see if it grabs you:

- ☐ "Boy, I was really multithreading yesterday after Mom was indicted for mail fraud."
- ☐ "I multithreaded all through lunch, and it gave me gas."
- ☐ "Not tonight, dear, I'm multithreading."

Q&A

Q Why isn't `java.applet.Applet` needed in the `class` statement of the `Revolve` applet?

A It isn't needed because of the `import` statement that makes all of the `java.applet` classes available to the program. The only purpose of `import` is to make it easier to refer to classes in a program. If you don't use it, you have to use full class references such as `java.applet.Applet` instead of simply `Applet`. You could write all of your Java programs without using `import`, though it would make the source files more difficult to understand.

Q If the `Revolve` applet only has one thread, what's the point of using threads at all?

A Multithreading has benefits even it's really just single-threading. The reason is that you can start, stop, and pause a thread from within a program; you don't have the same kind of control without threads. Also, by making an applet a thread, even for a single-thread project, you make it easier to implement additional threads as needed later on.

Q Are there any reasons not to leave a pair of empty brackets after a `catch` statement, which causes errors to be disregarded?

A It depends on the type of error or exception that is being caught. In the `Revolve` applet, you know with both `catch` statements what the cause of an exception would be. Because of this knowledge, you can handle the error. In the `getURL()` method, the `MalformedURLException` would only be caused if the URL sent to the method is invalid.

14

Quiz

Set aside your threads (in the Java sense, not the nudity sense), and answer the following questions about multithreading in Java.

Questions

1. What class must be implemented for an applet to use threads?
   (a) `Runnable`
   (b) `Thread`
   (c) `Applet`

2. When a class has been set up as a thread, what method will be handled when the thread begins running?
   (a) `start()`
   (b) `run()`
   (c) `init()`

3. You're admiring the work of another programmer who has created an applet that handles four simultaneous tasks. What should you tell him?
   (a) "That's not half as exciting as the Eleanor Mondale screen saver I downloaded off the Web."
   (b) "You're the wind beneath my wings."
   (c) "Nice threads!"

Answers

1. a. `Runnable` must be used with the `implements` statement. `Thread` is used inside a multithreaded program, but it is not needed in the class statement that begins a program.

2. b. The `run()` statement is handled when the thread begins.

3. c. This compliment could be confusing if the programmer is well-dressed, but let's be honest—what are the chances of that?

14

Activities

If this long workshop hasn't left you feeling threadbare, expand your skills with the following activities:

☐ If you are comfortable with HTML, create your own home page that includes the Revolve applet and six of your own favorite Web sites. Use the applet along with other graphics and text on the page.

☐ Rewrite the Ouch applet from the previous hour to use threads and actually pause one second for each second that the national debt is increasing.

14

Hour 15

Sending Parameters to Applets

Now that you have had some experience writing computer programs, you might be feeling one of the strongest emotions of the programmer: compiler angst. Even though it takes no more than 15 seconds to compile most programs, that time can seem interminable when you're debugging a program. Write, Save, Compile, Aargh—an error! Write, Save, Compile, Aargh! Write, Save, Compile, Aargh!… As this vicious cycle repeats itself, it's easy to become world-weary as a program is compiled and recompiled.

One of the driving forces behind parameter use in Java applets is the fear and loathing of compilation. Parameters enable you to change elements of an applet without editing or recompiling anything. They also make the program more useful.

The following topics will be covered during this hour:

☐ Sending parameters to Java applets

☐ Receiving parameters in an applet program

☐ Checking for nonexistent parameters
☐ Converting parameters from one type to another
☐ Writing a program that uses parameters

Sending Parameters from a Web Page

Parameters are stored as part of the Web page that contains an applet. They are created using the HTML tag <PARAM> and its two attributes: NAME and VALUE. You can have more than one <PARAM> tag with an applet, but all of them must be between the opening <APPLET> tag and the closing </APPLET> tag. The following is an <APPLET> tag that includes several parameters:

```
<APPLET CODE="ScrollingHeadline.class" HEIGHT=50 WIDTH=400>
<PARAM NAME="Headline1" VALUE="Dewey defeats Truman">
<PARAM NAME="Headline2" VALUE="Stix nix hix pix">
<PARAM NAME="Headline3" VALUE="Man bites dog">
</APPLET>
```

This example could be used to send news headlines to an applet that scrolls them across the screen. Because news changes all the time, the only way to create a program of this kind is with parameters. No other solution would work; just imagine how long it would take to recompile a Java program every time a Dallas Cowboy ran afoul of the law.

You use the NAME attribute to give the parameter a name. This attribute is comparable to giving a variable a name. The VALUE attribute gives the named parameter a value.

Receiving Parameters in the Applet

You have to do something in your Java program to retrieve the parameters on the Web page or they will be ignored. The getParameter() method of the Applet class retrieves a parameter from a <PARAM> tag on a Web page. The parameter name, which is specified with the NAME attribute on the page, is used as an argument to getParameter(). The following is an example of getParameter() in action:

```
String display1 = getParameter("Headline1");
```

The getParameter() method returns all parameters as strings, so you have to convert them to other types as needed. If you want to use a parameter as an integer, you could use statements such as the following:

```
int speed;
String speedParam = getParameter("SPEED");
if (speedParam != null)
    speed = Integer.parseInt(speedParam);
```

15

This example sets the speed variable by using the speedParam string. You have to test for null strings before setting speed because the parseInt() method cannot work with a null string. When you try to retrieve a parameter with getParameter() that was not included on a Web page with the <PARAM> tag, it will be sent as null, which is the value of an empty string.

Workshop: Handling Parameters in an Applet

This hour's workshop project has little practical value, except perhaps as a taunting device. The ShowWeight applet takes a person's weight and displays it under several different units. The applet takes two parameters: a weight in pounds and the name of the person who weighs that amount. The weight is used to figure out the person's weight in ounces, kilograms, and metric tons, and all of these are displayed.

Create a new file with your word processor and give it the name ShowWeight.java. Enter Listing 15.1 into the file. Then save and compile the file.

Listing 15.1. The full text of ShowWeight.java.

```
 1: import java.awt.*;
 2:
 3: public class ShowWeight extends java.applet.Applet {
 4:     float lbs = (float)0;
 5:     float ozs;
 6:     float kgs;
 7:     float metricTons;
 8:     String name = "somebody";
 9:
10:     public void init() {
11:         String lbsValue = getParameter("weight");
12:         if (lbsValue != null) {
13:             Float lbsTemp = Float.valueOf(lbsValue);
14:             lbs = lbsTemp.floatValue();
15:         }
16:         String personValue = getParameter("person");
17:         if (personValue != null)
18:             name = personValue;
19:
20:         ozs = (float)(lbs * 16);
21:         kgs = (float)(lbs / 2.204623);
22:         metricTons = (float)(lbs / 2204.623);
23:     }
24:
25:     public void paint(Graphics screen) {
26:         screen.drawString("Studying the weight of " + name, 5, 30);
27:         screen.drawString("In pounds: " + lbs, 55, 50);
```

continues

Listing 15.1. continued

```
28:              screen.drawString("In ounces: " + ozs, 55, 70);
29:              screen.drawString("In kilograms: " + kgs, 55, 90);
30:              screen.drawString("In metric tons: " + metricTons, 55, 110);
31:        }
32:
33: }
```

The init() method is where the two parameters are loaded into the applet. Because they come from the Web page as strings, they must be converted into the form you need: a floating-point number for the lbs variable and a string for name. Converting a string to a floating-point number requires two steps: converting the string to a Float object and then converting that object to a variable of the type float.

JUST A MINUTE

As you learned with strings, objects and variables are treated differently in Java programs, and there are different things you can do with them. The reason there is a Float object and a float variable type is so you can use a floating-point number as either an object or a variable. The Float object class also has useful methods such as valueOf() and floatValue() that you can use to convert floating-point numbers into different types of variables.

Lines 20–22 are used to convert the lbs variable into different units of measure. Each of these statements has (float) in front of the conversion equation. This is used to convert the result of the equation into a floating-point number. You can use this structure to convert variables of one type to another. Put a variable type in parentheses in front of an equation that produces a result, and it will convert the result to that type.

The paint() method of the applet uses the drawString() method of the Graphics class to display a line of text on-screen. The paint() method has three arguments: the text to display and the x and y positions where the text should be shown.

Before you can test the ShowWeight applet, you need to create a Web page that contains the applet. Open up a new file on your word processor and name it ShowWeight.html. Enter Listing 15.2 and save it when you're done.

Listing 15.2. The full text of ShowWeight.html.

```
1: <applet code="ShowWeight.class" height=170 width=200>
2: <param name="person" value="Konishiki">
3: <param name="weight" value=605>
4: </applet>
```

Use the appletviewer tool to see the ShowWeight applet. This demonstration uses Konishiki as its example because the American-born sumo wrestling champion weighs in at more than 605 pounds, making him the largest of the bikini-wearing behemoths. You can substitute anyone whose weight is either exemplary or well-known. Figure 15.1 shows an example of output from the applet. As you can see, Konishiki's workout regimen doesn't include a lot of fat-free SnackWell's Devil's Food Cakes.

Figure 15.1.

The output of the ShowWeight *applet.*

To make the applet display a different name along with a different value for the "weight" parameter, all you have to change is the ShowWeight.html file. The applet itself will continue to work correctly.

Summary

If you visit a site such as Gamelan on the World Wide Web (http://www.gamelan.com), you'll see links to numerous applets that have been made available for public use, including some that offer the source file of the program. These applets often use parameters, especially for animation or scrolling text programs. During this hour you covered all aspects of parameter use in your applets. Parameters can greatly improve the usefulness and performance of applets.

Even if you're the paragon of programming patience and you can wait out the slowest compiler, you'll be using parameters in your Java applets. Like arguments for Java applications, parameters are a useful way to make one program perform in a variety of ways.

Q&A

Q Why can't parameters be used with Java applications?

A Parameters must be stored in some sort of document, such as a Web page. With a Java application that runs from the command line, there's nowhere to put them. However, you can specify arguments on the command line when you run the program, and these are brought in as strings also. Handling arguments in applications has many similarities to handling parameters in applets.

Q Does the name of a parameter on a Web page have to be capitalized exactly as it is shown as an argument to the getParameter() method?

A Like all HTML tags and attributes, the NAME and VALUE attributes of the <PARAM> tag do not have to be capitalized a specific way to work. The text "Speed" and "speed" and "SPEED" all refer to the same parameter.

Quiz

Test your knowledge of parameters with the following questions.

Questions

1. What's the name of the HTML tag that is used to send a parameter to a Java program?

   (a) <APPLET>

   (b) <VARIABLE>

   (c) <PARAM>

2. When the getParameter() method is used to load a parameter value into a program, what type of information is loaded?

   (a) a String variable

   (b) a different type depending on the parameter

   (c) an array of characters

3. If you try to load a parameter that is not included on the Web page that contains the applet, what will getParameter() do?

   (a) crash the program with an error

   (b) return the empty string null as a value

   (c) nothing

15

15

Answers

1. c. `<PARAM>` is the tag to send a parameter, and `<APPLET>` is the tag to load the applet itself.

2. a. All parameters are received by an applet as `String` variables. They have to be converted to another type of variable or object if you want to use them differently.

3. b. The `getParameter()` method must return some kind of value. The `null` value is used to signify the lack of a parameter that matches the argument of `getParameter()`.

Activities

If you're not overstuffed from the weighty subject of parameters, the following activities are suggested:

☐ Create an applet version of the `Repeat` application from Hour 8, "Repeating an Action with Loops," that takes the line to display over and over again as a parameter.

☐ Add a parameter to the `ShowWeight` applet that specifies the ideal weight of the person. Display how many weeks of dieting it would take them to reach it, given five pounds of weight loss per week.

Hour 16

Using Fonts and Color in Applets

A famous catchphrase from the television show *Saturday Night Live* during the 1980s was, "It's not how you feel, but how you look…and darling, you look MAH-ve-lous." The quote epitomized the philosophy of Fernando, comedian Billy Crystal's eternally tan and impeccably groomed celebrity. Regardless of what was going on in his life, as long as his hair was styled properly and he was dressed for the occasion, everything was copacetic. After all, though Fernando hadn't been in a hit movie since *Won Ton Ton, the Dog Who Saved Hollywood*, he still looked good. Correction: He looked MAH-ve-lous.

If you're interested in making your Java applets look MAH-ve-lous, you should know about the Font and Color classes. No self-respecting applet would be seen in public without them. With these classes, you can present text in several different fonts and sizes and change the colors of text, graphics, and other elements.

One of the principles of object-oriented programming is to make an object work for itself, and the Font and Color objects follow this rule. They store all the information that's needed to display a font or change a color, and they can handle other related tasks that are required. The following topics will be covered during this hour:

- Using fonts in your applets
- Setting a font's style and size
- Choosing a font
- Displaying colors in applets
- Using the color constants
- Setting up the background color
- Using RGB values to choose colors
- Using HSB values to choose colors
- Creating special text effects using colors

Using the Font Class

There are three things you need to know about a font in order to display it:

- The typeface of the font: Helvetica, Courier, Dialog, Times Roman, or others
- The style of the font: bold, italic, or plain
- The size of the font, in points

Before you can display text in a certain typeface, style, and point size, you need to create a Font object that holds this information. The following statement creates a 12-point Times Roman italic Font object:

```
Font currentFont = new Font("TimesRoman", Font.ITALIC, 12);
```

The typeface that you can select may vary depending on the system you're using. The current release of the Java Developer's Kit for Windows 95 includes Helvetica, Courier, Dialog, Dialog Input, and Times Roman.

You choose the style of the font by using one or more constant variables. Specifying the style as Font.PLAIN makes it nonbold and nonitalic, Font.BOLD makes it bold, and Font.ITALIC makes it italic. To combine bold and italic, use Font.BOLD+Font.ITALIC, as in the following code:

```
Font headlineFont = new Font("Courier", Font.BOLD+Font.ITALIC, 72);
```

16

The last argument specifies the point size of the font. To see a simple example of using fonts in an applet, open your word processor and create a new file called Fonts.java. Enter the text of Listing 16.1 and save the file.

Listing 16.1. The full text of Fonts.java.

```
 1: import java.awt.*;
 2:
 3: public class Fonts extends java.applet.Applet {
 4:
 5:     public void paint(Graphics screen) {
 6:         Font currentFont = new Font("TimesRoman", Font.PLAIN, 20);
 7:         screen.setFont(currentFont);
 8:         screen.drawString("If I've said it once, I've said it a thousand
 9:         times, darling,", 5, 50);
10:         currentFont = new Font("TimesRoman", Font.ITALIC, 40);
11:         screen.setFont(currentFont);
12:         screen.drawString("you look MAH-VE-LOUS", 5, 80);
13:     }
14: }
```

After you compile the file with the javac compiler tool, you need to create a Web page that contains the applet. Create a new file in your word processor called Fonts.html and enter the text of Listing 16.2.

Listing 16.2. The full text of Fonts.html.

```
1: <applet code="Fonts.class" height=125 width=450>
2: </applet>
```

Save this file and then load this page into the appletviewer tool by using the following command:

```
appletviewer Fonts.html
```

The output should resemble Figure 16.1.

Figure 16.1.

The output of the Fonts *applet.*

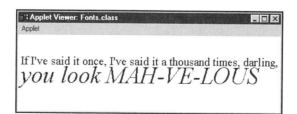

16

Using the `Color` Class

The simplest way to use a color in a Java program is to use one of the constant variables from the `Color` class. You can use the following constants: `black`, `blue`, `cyan`, `darkGray`, `gray`, `green`, `lightGray`, `magenta`, `orange`, `pink`, `red`, `white`, and `yellow`.

In an applet, you can set the background color of the applet window using these constants. The following is an example:

```
setBackground(Color.orange);
```

When you want to display text of a certain color or draw other graphics in different colors, you have to use a method that sets up the current color. You can do this from within the `paint()` method of an applet by using a `setColor()` method, as in the following:

```
public void paint(Graphics screen) {
    screen.setColor(Color.orange);
    screen.drawString("Go, Buccaneers!", 5, 50);
}
```

Unlike the `setBackground()` method, which is inherited directly from the `Applet` class, the `setColor()` method must be used on an object that can handle a color change. The preceding example shows the `setColor()` method of the `screen` object being used to change the current color of the applet window.

Other Ways to Choose Colors

To use a color not included in the 13 constant variables, you must specify the color's RGB or HSB values. RGB, which stands for Red Green Blue, defines a color by the amount of red, green, and blue that is present in the color. Each value ranges from 0, which means there is none of that color, to 255, which means the maximum amount of that color is present. Most graphics editing and drawing programs will identify a color's RGB values.

If you know a color's RGB values, you can use it to create a `Color` object. For example, an RGB value for dark red is 235 red, 50 green, and 50 blue, and an RGB value for light orange is 230 red, 220 green, and 0 blue. The following is an example of an applet that displays dark red text on a light orange background:

```
import java.awt.*;

public class GoBucs extends java.applet.Applet {

    public void init() {
        Color lightOrange = new Color(230, 220, 0);
        setBackground(lightOrange);
    }
```

 16

```
public void paint(Graphics screen) {
    Color darkRed = new Color(235, 50, 50);
    screen.setColor(darkRed);
    screen.drawString("Go, Buccaneers!", 5, 50);
}
}
```

COFFEE BREAK

Dark red on a light orange background isn't much more attractive on a Java applet than it is on the National Football League's Tampa Bay Buccaneers. Using RGB values enables you to select from more than 16.5 million possible combinations, although most computer monitors can only offer a close approximation for most of them. For guidance on whether light-light-light-semidark-midnight-blue goes well with medium-light-semidark-baby-green, purchase a copy of the upcoming *Teach Yourself Color Sense While Waiting in Line at This Bookstore* from Sams.net Publishing.

Another way to select a color in a Java program is the HSB system, which stands for Hue Saturation Brightness. Each of these is a floating-point number that ranges from 0.0 to 1.0. The HSB system isn't as commonly supported in graphics software, so you won't be using it as often in your programs as you use RGB values. However, one thing HSB values are convenient for is changing a color's brightness without changing anything else about the color. You'll see an example of this use and an example of using HSB values to choose a color in this hour's workshop.

Workshop: Displaying a Danger Message

You can use Java applets to present news headlines and other information in different ways. One special effect you might see on a Web page is text that fades to black. You also might see the reverse—text that brightens from black to white. This hour's workshop uses the Font and Color classes to create text that cycles in brightness from dark to bright. The text looks like an alert about impending danger, so the applet will be called Danger.

To make the applet more useful, the text of the warning will be set from a parameter on a Web page. The text that will be used in this example warns of a "Core breach in Sector 12," but you can substitute other threatening text of similar length.

COFFEE BREAK

If you're at a secure place in your life right now and can't think of anything suitably menacing, feel free to choose one of the following:

- ☐ "Mother-in-law wants to visit"
- ☐ "Boss approaching"
- ☐ "Dallas Cowboys scheduled to play here"
- ☐ "We have no bananas today"
- ☐ "No hamburger—cheeseburger"

Create a new file in your word processor called `Danger.java`. Each section of the applet will be described as you enter it. Begin with the following statements:

```
import java.awt.*;

public class Danger extends java.applet.Applet {
    String text = "No text has been specified";
    float hue = (float) 0.5;
    float saturation = (float) 0.8;
    float brightness = (float) 0.0;
    Font textFont = new Font("Dialog", Font.BOLD, 20);
    int textX;
```

The program begins like most applets that you will create. The `java.awt` classes, such as `Font`, `Color`, and `FontMetrics`, are made available for use in this program with the `import` statement. The `class` statement defines `Danger` as a subclass of the `Applet` class, as all applets must be.

The next several lines define variables and objects that will be used during the program. The string variable `text` is created with a default value, and it will be used to store the text that should be displayed on-screen. Three floating-point variables are used to store values for a color using its Hue Saturation Brightness (HSB) ratings. The `(float)` portion of each line converts the value that follows it into a floating-point number. This conversion must be done because the `hue`, `saturation`, and `brightness` variables must be of type `float`.

The text of the applet will be displayed in 20-point Dialog bold. In order to do this, you need to create a `Font` object to store that font's values. The `Font` object called `textFont` is created for this purpose. Finally, the integer variable `textX` will be used when you're centering text from left-to-right on the screen.

After inserting a blank line, continue entering the `Danger` program by entering the `init()` method of the applet:

```
public void init() {
    setBackground(Color.black);
    String paramName = getParameter("TEXT");
```

16

```
        if (paramName != null)
            text = paramName;
        FontMetrics fm = getFontMetrics(textFont);
        textX = size().width / 2 - fm.stringWidth(text) / 2;
    }
```

The init() method is handled once when the applet is first run, and then it is never handled again. It's a good place to set up some things that weren't set up when variables and objects were created. The first thing that happens in this method is the background of the applet is set to black by using the setBackground() method inherited by Danger from the Applet class.

Next, the parameter called TEXT is retrieved from the Web page that contains this applet. If no parameter is found, the default text stored in text will be displayed. Otherwise, the text specified by the parameter will be stored in text.

The FontMetrics class measures how wide a line of text will appear when it is displayed. Using the stringWidth() method of FontMetrics and the applet's size() method, you can center text on-screen. The textX variable stores the horizontal position where the text should be displayed.

Now continue by entering the paint() method of your class, which is called whenever the display on-screen needs to be updated. Leave a blank line after the init() method and enter the following:

```
public void paint(Graphics screen) {
    Color textColor = Color.getHSBColor(hue, saturation, brightness);
    screen.setColor(textColor);
    screen.setFont(textFont);
    screen.drawString(text, textX, 30);
    pause(250000);
    brightness += 0.05;
    if (brightness > 1) {
        brightness = (float) 0.0;
        pause(250000);
    }
    repaint();
}
```

The paint() method takes a Graphics object called screen as an argument. This object holds all the information needed to display something on-screen, and it has several methods you'll use.

The Color object called textColor is created using the HSB variables to select the color. The textColor object then becomes the current display color using the setColor() method of screen.

Using the drawString() method of screen, the variable text is displayed at the (x,y) position of textX and 30. The color of the text is the current display color. After the text has been displayed, a pause() method is called with an argument of 250,000. You'll see what this method does when you add it to your program.

In order for the text to change in brightness, you have to change the value of the brightness variable. The program increases the variable .05 (a 5 percent change), and if the variable has reached the maximum brightness of 1.0, it is reset to 0.0. Whenever brightness must be reset to 0.0, the program calls the pause() method.

The last thing that takes place in the paint() method is the repaint(); statement. You use this statement any time you need to redraw the screen because something has changed. Because the brightness variable has changed, you know there's a need to redisplay the text at the new brightness. The repaint() statement causes the paint() method to begin again.

The paint() method handles most of the work that takes place during the Danger applet. All you have left to add are two short methods called update() and pause(). Enter a blank line at the end of your program, and then continue with the following statements:

```
public void update(Graphics screen) {
    paint(screen);
}

void pause(int duration) {
    for (int pause = 0; pause < duration; pause++);
}

}
```

The update() method is one of the methods that normally works behind the scenes as an applet runs. It is handled any time the screen needs to be repainted or the repaint() statement is used. The update() method clears the screen and calls on paint() to do its work. However, clearing the screen when you're changing graphics or text often causes things to flicker badly in a Java program. In this code, you're overriding the update() method so it does not clear the screen at all, which will improve the quality of your applet's display. You'll learn more about this procedure during Hour 18, "Creating Animation."

The last thing in your applet is the pause() method, which takes an argument called duration. The method runs an empty for loop ranging from 0 to the value of duration. This loop causes the program to pause. The higher the value of duration, the longer the pause. When you are displaying changing graphics or text, you might need pauses of some kind to prevent things from changing too quickly. This pause() method is one way to create these pauses.

Save the Danger.java file, which should resemble Listing 16.3. The only difference might be in the way you have indented methods and other statements. That does not have to be changed in order for the program to run, but indentation and other spacing can make a program easier to understand.

Listing 16.3. The full text of Danger.java.

```
 1: import java.awt.*;
 2:
 3: public class Danger extends java.applet.Applet {
 4:     String text = "No text has been specified";
 5:     float hue = (float) 0.5;
 6:     float saturation = (float) 0.8;
 7:     float brightness = (float) 0.0;
 8:     Font textFont = new Font("Dialog", Font.BOLD, 20);
 9:     int textX;
10:
11:     public void init() {
12:         setBackground(Color.black);
13:         String paramName = getParameter("TEXT");
14:         if (paramName != null)
15:             text = paramName;
16:         FontMetrics fm = getFontMetrics(textFont);
17:         textX = size().width / 2 - fm.stringWidth(text) / 2;
18:     }
19:
20:     public void paint(Graphics screen) {
21:         Color textColor = Color.getHSBColor(hue, saturation, brightness);
22:         screen.setColor(textColor);
23:         screen.setFont(textFont);
24:         screen.drawString(text, textX, 30);
25:         pause(250000);
26:         brightness += 0.05;
27:         if (brightness > 1) {
28:             brightness = (float) 0.0;
29:             pause(250000);
30:         }
31:         repaint();
32:     }
33:
34:     public void update(Graphics screen) {
35:         paint(screen);
36:     }
37:
38:     void pause(int duration) {
39:         for (int pause = 0; pause < duration; pause++);
40:     }
41:
42: }
```

After compiling the file with the javac compiler tool, you need to create a Web page that contains the Danger applet. Create a new file with your word processor called Danger.html, and enter the text of Listing 16.4 into the file.

Listing 16.4. The full text of `Danger.html`.

```
1: <applet code="Danger.class" height=60 width=400>
2: <param name="TEXT" value="Core breach in Sector 12">
3: </applet>
```

You can change the value in Line 2 to any other menacing sounding text, as long as it is similar in size to `Core breach in Sector 12`. Use the `appletviewer` tool to view the Web page with the following command:

```
appletviewer Danger.html
```

Figure 16.2 shows the output of the `Danger` applet.

Figure 16.2.

A screen capture of the Danger *applet as it runs with the* appletviewer *tool.*

Summary

Now that you can use `Font` and `Color` objects in your programs to change the color scheme, you can no longer feign ignorance when it comes to designing an attractive applet. By using fonts and color instead of sticking to the familiar black text on a light gray background, you can draw more attention to elements of your programs and make them more compelling for users. You also, of course, can write programs that look MAH-ve-lous. It's what Fernando would want you to do.

Q&A

Q Is there a limit to the point size that can be used for text?

A The limiting factor is the height and width of your applet window or the part of an applet the text is supposed to be displayed in. Point sizes typically range from 9-point text for small lines that are readable to 48-point text for large headlines. Choosing the right size depends on the font typeface as well as the size, so it's largely a matter of trial and error.

16

Q What happens if a color defined in a Java program can't be displayed on the monitor of someone displaying the program? For example, if my monitor is set to display only 256 colors, what will occur if I choose one of the 16.5 million colors that isn't in those 256?

A When a monitor can't display a color selected with a `setColor()` or `setBackground()` method, it shows the closest existing color as a substitute. An example of this kind of substitution is the `Danger` applet, which runs differently depending on the number of colors that can be shown as the text cycles from black to light blue to white.

16

Quiz

Test whether your font and color skills are MAH-ve-lous by answering the following questions.

Questions

1. Which one of the following is *not* a constant used to select a color?
   (a) `Color.cyan`
   (b) `Color.teal`
   (c) `Color.magenta`

2. When you change the color of something and redraw it on an applet window, what must you do to make it visible?
   (a) Use the `drawColor()` method.
   (b) Use the `repaint()` statement.
   (c) Do nothing.

3. What do the initials HSB stand for?
   (a) Hue Saturation Brightness
   (b) Hue Shadows Balance
   (c) Lucy in the Sky with Diamonds

Answers

1. b.

2. b. The call to `repaint()` causes the `paint()` method to be manually called.

3. a. If c were the right answer, you could use colors that would only be visible years later during flashbacks.

Activities

To further explore the spectrum of possibilities when using fonts and color in your programs, do the following activities:

- [ ] Remove the update() method from the Danger applet to see what effect it has on the quality of the display.
- [ ] Add a way to specify the background of the Danger applet by sending parameters for the RGB values of the desired background color.

16

PART
V

Improving the Look of Your Programs

Hour

Hour 17

Working with Graphics

During the previous hour you had a chance to experience the joy of text by displaying strings in a variety of fonts and colors. Using these Java classes makes the programming language an enjoyable text aid, but at some point you probably were expecting more. There's more to life than text, and this hour is evidence of that. You'll get a chance to draw shapes of different colors in a program—everything from rectangles to ovals to lines.

The following subjects will be covered:

- ☐ The drawing methods of the Graphics class
- ☐ Drawing lines
- ☐ Drawing rectangles, rounded rectangles, and 3-D rectangles
- ☐ Drawing polygons
- ☐ Drawing ovals
- ☐ Drawing with different colors
- ☐ Drawing filled and unfilled shapes

Using Graphics in an Applet

This isn't meant as a knock to those of us who enjoy displaying arrays, incrementing variables, or using a constructor method, but let's face it—many subjects in a programming language such as Java tend to be dry. It's hard to impress your non-programming acquaintances with the way your do-while loop determines which method to use in a mathematical application. Dates don't get nearly as excited as you do when a switch-case block statement handles a variety of different circumstances correctly. Nobody ever attracted a mate because they use the conditional operator (using conditioner, on the other hand…). Graphics programming is the exception to this general rule. When you write a program that does something interesting with graphics, it's a way to have fun with a programming language and impress relatives, friends, strangers, and prospective employers.

Drawing things such as lines and polygons is as easy in a Java applet as displaying text. You use a method of the Graphics class inside the paint() method of the program. The Graphics class stores information required to display something on-screen. The most common use of the class is to create an object that represents the applet window. This Graphics object is often called screen, and its methods are used to draw text with a command such as the following:

```
screen.drawString("Draw, pardner!", 15, 40);
```

This statement causes the text Draw, pardner! to be displayed at the (x,y) coordinates of (15,40).

All of the shape- and line-drawing methods work using the same (x,y) coordinate system as text. The (0,0) coordinate is at the upper-left corner of the applet window. x values go up as you head to the right, and y values go up as you head downward. You can determine the maximum (x,y) value that you can use in an applet with the following statements:

```
int maxXValue = size().width;
int maxYValue = size().height;
```

Drawing Lines and Shapes

Figure 17.1 shows JavaMan, an illustration composed of all the different things you'll be learning to draw during this hour:

- Lines: JavaMan's arm and fingers are lines.
- Rounded rectangles: The border of the illustration is a rectangle with rounded corners.
- Rectangles: JavaMan's torso is composed of a filled gray rectangle covered with 100 unfilled rectangles. His mouth is another rectangle.

17

☐ Ovals: JavaMan's eyes are ovals.

☐ Polygons: JavaMan's hat is a polygon.

Figure 17.1.

JavaMan, a figure composed of Java polygons and lines.

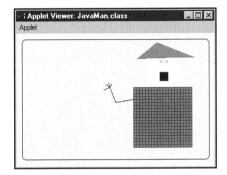

With the exception of lines, all of the shapes you can draw can be filled or unfilled. A filled shape is drawn with the current color completely filling the space taken up by the shape. Unfilled shapes just draw a border with the current color. The rounded rectangle around Figure 17.1 is an example of an unfilled shape. Only the border of the rectangle is drawn. JavaMan's hat is a filled shape because the entire hat is filled in with the same color.

Before you create an applet to draw JavaMan, each of the drawing methods will be described. The screen object will be used as the Graphics object throughout this section, and it's the object used as an argument to the paint() method of an applet.

Drawing Lines

To draw a line, a statement such as the following is used:

```
screen.drawLine(200,110,170,115);
```

This statement draws a line beginning at the (x,y) coordinate of (200,110) and ending at (170,115). All lines in Java are one pixel in width, so you have to draw several lines side by side if you want to draw a thick line.

Drawing Rectangles

Rectangles can be filled or unfilled, and they can have rounded corners or square ones. The following statement draws an unfilled rectangle with square corners:

```
screen.drawRect(245,65,20,10);
```

This statement draws a rectangle with its upper-left corner at the (x,y) coordinate of (245,65). The width of the rectangle is 20 and the height is 10. These dimensions are expressed in pixels, the same unit of measure used for coordinates.

If you want to make the rectangle filled in, use the `fillRect()` method instead of `drawRect()`. The arguments are the same:

```
screen.fillRect(245,65,20,10);
```

You can draw rectangles with rounded corners instead of square ones by using the `drawRoundRect()` and `fillRoundRect()` methods. As you might expect, you use the `drawRoundRect()` to draw an unfilled rectangle, and you use the `fillRoundRect()` method to draw a filled rectangle. These methods have two extra arguments at the end that specify the distance from the corner to begin making it round. The following statement draws an unfilled, rounded rectangle:

```
screen.drawRoundRect(10,10,size().width-20, size().height-20, 15, 15);
```

This rectangle has its upper-left corner at the (10,10) coordinate. The last two arguments to `drawRoundRect()` specify that the corner should begin rounding 15 pixels away from the corner at (10,10). As with other rectangle methods, the third and fourth arguments specify how wide and tall the rectangle should be. In this case, `size().width` and `size().height` are used so that the rectangle can use the size of the applet window as a way to determine how large the rectangle should be.

Drawing Ovals and Circles

To draw ovals and circles, use the `drawOval()` and `fillOval()` methods. You can draw a circle by specifying the same width and height values, as in the following:

```
screen.fillOval(245,45,5,5);
```

This statement draws an oval at (245,45) with a height and width of 5. Changing one of the height or width coordinates to a different value would make the shape an oval instead of a circle.

Drawing Polygons

Polygons are the most complicated shape to draw because they have a varying number of points. To set up the points, all of the x coordinates of the polygon are put into an array of integers. All of the y coordinates are then put into another array, in the same order. The `drawPolygon()` and `fillPolygon()` methods are used with the arrays and the number of points as arguments:

17

```
int[] xPoints = { 205, 305, 240 };
int[] yPoints = { 43, 40, 15 };
int points = 3;
screen.fillPolygon(xPoints, yPoints, points);
```

You can use the `fillPolygon()` method to draw the entire polygon with the same color or use `drawPolygon()` to only draw the polygon's outline. All polygons are completed automatically by making the last point join up with the first point. In this example, (240,15) will connect to (205,43).

Another way to draw polygons is to use a `Polygon` object to hold all of the point values, as in the following:

```
int[] yellowX = { 64, 126, 136, 74, 64 };
int[] yellowY = { 228, 176, 184, 240, 228 };
yellow = new Polygon(yellowX, yellowY, 5);
screen.fillPolygon(xPositions, yPositions, points);
```

Polygons do not have to meet in a point, however; you can use `drawPolyline()` to draw partial polygons. This is done by specifying two integer arrays containing all of the points and the number of points, as in the following:

```
int[] xPoints = { 205, 305, 240 };
int[] yPoints = { 43, 40, 15 };
int points = 3;
screen.drawPolyline(xPoints, yPoints, points);
```

Unlike `drawPolygon()` and `fillPolygon()`, this method does not connect the first and last lines.

Creating JavaMan

To put all of these shapes together, load your word processor and create a new file called `JavaMan.java`. Enter Listing 17.1 into the file and save it when you're done.

Listing 17.1. The full text of `JavaMan.java`.

```
 1: import java.awt.*;
 2:
 3: public class JavaMan extends java.applet.Applet {
 4:
 5:     public void init() {
 6:         setBackground(Color.yellow);
 7:     }
 8:
 9:     public void paint(Graphics screen) {
10:
11:         screen.setColor(Color.black);
```

continues

Listing 17.1. continued

```
12:                           screen.drawRoundRect(10,10,size().width-20,
13:                           size().height-20,15,15);
14:
15:          screen.setColor(Color.gray);
16:          screen.fillRect(200,90,100,100);
17:
18:          screen.setColor(Color.blue);
19:                  for (int x = 200; x < 300; x += 5)
20:              for (int y = 90; y < 190; y += 5)
21:                  screen.drawRect(x,y,5,5);
22:
23:          screen.setColor(Color.black);
24:          screen.drawLine(200,110,170,115);
25:          screen.drawLine(170,115,160,90);
26:          screen.drawLine(160,90,150,94);
27:          screen.drawLine(160,90,153,85);
28:          screen.drawLine(160,90,158,83);
29:          screen.drawLine(160,90,163,84);
30:
31:          screen.setColor(Color.white);
32:          screen.fillOval(220,30,60,60);
33:
34:          screen.setColor(Color.green);
35:          screen.fillOval(245,45,5,5);
36:          screen.fillOval(255,45,5,5);
37:
38:          screen.setColor(Color.black);
39:          screen.fillRect(245,65,15,15);
40:
41:          screen.setColor(Color.magenta);
42:          int[] xPoints = { 205, 305, 240, 205 };
43:          int[] yPoints = { 43, 40, 15, 43 };
44:          int points = 4;
45:          screen.fillPolygon(xPoints, yPoints, points);
46:      }
47: }
```

After compiling the program successfully, create a new file in your word processor called JavaMan.html. Enter Listing 17.2 into the file.

Listing 17.2. The full text of JavaMan.html.

```
1: <applet code="JavaMan.class" height=220 width=340>
2: </applet>
```

When you use appletviewer or a Java-capable Web browser to view this applet, you will discover why I chose computer book writing as a profession over illustration. If you're using appletviewer, resize the window a few times to see how the rounded black border changes.

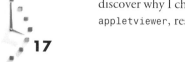

17

Workshop: Drawing Attention to Something

To draw this hour to a close, you'll create an applet that uses a polygon, several polylines, a rounded rectangle, and three ovals. The finished product ought to be a familiar face.

Load your word processor and create a new file called Drawing.java. Enter the full text of Listing 17.3, and then save and compile the file when you're done.

Listing 17.3. The full text of Drawing.java.

```
 1: import java.awt.*;
 2:
 3: public class Drawing extends java.applet.Applet {
 4:     Polygon hair;
 5:
 6:     public void init() {
 7:         int[] hairX = { 125, 131, 156, 217, 270, 314, 244, 233,
 8:             196, 162, 147, 153, 180, 189, 125 };
 9:         int[] hairY = { 314, 122, 75, 57, 96, 287, 319, 118,
10:             87, 92, 133, 203, 231, 258, 314 };
11:         hair = new Polygon(hairX, hairY, 15);
12:
13:         setBackground(Color.lightGray);
14:     }
15:
16:     public void paint(Graphics screen) {
17:         screen.setColor(Color.white);
18:         screen.fillRoundRect(147,84,103,74,23,23);
19:         screen.fillOval(147,94,103,132);
20:
21:         screen.setColor(Color.black);
22:         screen.fillPolygon(hair);
23:
24:         int[] eyebrow1X = { 151, 168, 174, 171, 178, 193 };
25:         int[] eyebrow1Y = { 145, 140, 148, 184, 191, 188 };
26:         screen.drawPolyline(eyebrow1X, eyebrow1Y, 6);
27:
28:         int[] eyebrow2X = { 188, 197, 213, 223 };
29:         int[] eyebrow2Y = { 146, 141, 142, 146 };
30:         screen.drawPolyline(eyebrow2X, eyebrow2Y, 4);
31:
32:         int[] mouthX = { 166, 185, 200 };
33:         int[] mouthY = { 199, 200, 197 };
34:         screen.drawPolyline(mouthX, mouthY, 3);
35:
36:         screen.fillOval(161,148,10,3);
37:         screen.fillOval(202,145,12,5);
38:     }
39: }
```

17

The Drawing applet includes two methods, init() and paint(), and a single Polygon object as the only variable. The Polygon object is used to store all the information that's needed to draw a polygon.

The polygon is drawn by setting up an array of integers with the x coordinates of each point on the polygon. Next, another array of integers is set up with the y coordinates of each point. When both of these are set up, the following statement is used:

```
hair = new Polygon(hairX, hairY, 15);
```

The first two arguments to the Polygon constructor method are the integer arrays—hairX and hairY. The last argument is the number of points in the polygon.

Once you have created a polygon in this manner, you can use the drawPolygon() or fillPolygon() methods of the Graphics class to draw it. This action takes place in the paint() method of the applet because you need a Graphics object that indicates where the polygon should be drawn. An object called screen is used:

```
screen.fillPolygon(hair);
```

The fillPolygon() method draws a polygon that is filled in with the current color. If you do not want the polygon to be filled in, you can use the drawPolyline() method with two integer arrays instead.

You select colors with the setColor() method of the Graphics class. Constants from the Color class such as Color.red and Color.green are used as arguments to the setColor() method. The following statement in the paint() method sets the current color to black:

```
screen.setColor(Color.black);
```

In addition to the polygons, three ovals are drawn in the Drawing applet. The following is one of the statements used to draw an oval:

```
screen.fillOval(161,148,10,3);
```

The first two parameters to the fillOval() method are the (x,y) coordinates where the oval should be drawn. The last two parameters are the width and height of the oval.

After you have compiled Drawing.java successfully, open a new file in your word processor to create a the Web page to put the applet on. Create a new file called Drawing.html and enter Listing 17.4 into the file.

Listing 17.4. The full text of Drawing.html.

```
<applet code="Drawing.class" height=340 width=280>
</applet>
```

17

After saving the file, view the applet with the appletviewer tool or a Web browser. Figure 17.2 shows what the finished product should look like.

Figure 17.2.

The output of the Drawing *applet.*

If the long black hair, moony expression, and stoned smile aren't enough of a visual clue, this applet attempts to draw the Mona Lisa using a few polygons and lines. Leonardo da Vinci didn't have the chance to use Java drawing commands when he created the real Mona Lisa in 1503–1506, so he used paint instead. His results were pretty impressive too, but it took him considerably longer than an hour to finish his version.

COFFEE BREAK

The Louvre, the home of the *Mona Lisa*, has an extensive Web site at the following address:

http://mistral.culture.fr/louvre/

A picture of the Mona Lisa is displayed under the title *La Joconde (Monna Lisa)* at the following address:

http://mistral.culture.fr/louvre/anglais/musee/collec/monna.htm

Summary

Drawing something using the polygons and other shapes available with Java might seem like more trouble than it's worth, especially when you can load image files such as .GIF files and

.JPG files, as you'll see in the next hour. However, graphics depicted with polygons have two advantages over graphics that are loaded from image files:

☐ Speed: Even a small graphic, such as an icon, would take longer to load and display than a series of polygons.

☐ Scaling: You can change the size of an entire image that uses polygons simply by changing the values to create it. For example, you could add a function to the Drawing class that doubles the values for every (x,y) point in the arrays before you display anything, and it would result in an image twice as large. Polygon images scale much more quickly than image files do and produce better results.

There are many instances where it makes more sense to use graphics files in your programs, but polygons can be a useful option.

Q&A

Q Why does the JavaMan image flicker when I resize the applet window?

A The reason for this flicker is that the screen is automatically cleared each time the screen must be repainted. This happens in a method called update() that normally works behind the scenes. You can override this method in your programs to prevent the flickering problem, as you will see during the next hour.

Q Ovals and circles don't have corners. What are the (x,y) coordinates specified with the fillOval() and drawOval() method?

A The (x,y) coordinates represent the smallest x value and smallest y value of the oval or circle. If you drew an invisible rectangle around it, the upper-left corner of the rectangle would be the x and y coordinates used as arguments to the method.

Quiz

Test whether your Java graphics skills are taking shape by answering the following questions.

Questions

1. What method is used to change the current color before you draw something in a program?

(a) shiftColor()

(b) setColor()

(c) Could you repeat the question?

17

2. If you want to use the height and width of an applet window to determine how big something should be drawn, what can you use?

   (a) A ruler and a friend who's good at math

   (b) `getHeight()` and `getWidth()`

   (c) `size().height` and `size().width`

3. What personal failing did this book's author admit to during this hour?

   (a) poor grooming

   (b) poor drawing ability

   (c) codependency

Answers

1. b. You can use the `setBackground()` method to set the background color of an applet, and you can use the `setColor()` method of the `Graphics` class to select the current color.

2. c.

3. b. JavaMan represents one of the high points of my illustrative career.

Activities

To draw upon your vast storehouse of graphical skills, do the following activities:

☐ Create a method that can multiply every integer in an array by some kind of common factor. You can use this method in the `Drawing` applet to change the points in a polygon to make it bigger or smaller before it is created.

☐ Add parameters to the `JavaMan` applet to control the colors used on the background, body, and hat.

Hour 18

Creating Animation

Like the final voyage of the S.S. Minnow, the trip through the visual side of Java programming is a three-hour tour. At this point, you have learned how to use text, fonts, color, lines, and polygons in your Java applets. Any adversity you have experienced should have been minor, at least in comparison to the castaways of *Gilligan's Island*. At this point in the tour, passengers were asking the Skipper if hurricane-force winds were a scheduled part of the itinerary.

This third hour shows how to display image files in the `.GIF` and `.JPG` formats in your applets and some tricks to use when presenting these images in an animation. The following topics will be covered:

- [ ] Using `Image` objects to hold image files
- [ ] Putting a series of images into an array
- [ ] Cycling through an image array to produce animation
- [ ] Using the `update()` method to reduce flickering problems
- [ ] Using the `drawImage()` command
- [ ] Drawing to an off-screen workspace
- [ ] Why double-buffering improves animation results
- [ ] Establishing rules for the movement of an image

Creating an Animated Logo Applet

Computer animation at its most basic consists of drawing an image at a specific place, moving the location of the image, and telling the computer to redraw the image at its new location. Many animations on Web pages are a series of image files, usually .GIF or .JPG files, that are displayed in the same place in a certain order. You can do this to simulate motion or to create some other effect.

The first program that you will be writing today uses a series of image files for an animated logo. Several details about the animation will be customizable with parameters, so you can replace any images of your own for those provided for this example. Create a new file in your word processor called Animate.java. Enter Listing 18.1 into the file, and remember to save the file when you're done entering the text.

Listing 18.1. The full text of Animate.java.

```
 1: import java.awt.*;
 2:
 3: public class Animate extends java.applet.Applet implements Runnable {
 4:
 5:     Image[] picture = new Image[6];
 6:     int totalPictures = 0;
 7:     int current = 0;
 8:     Thread runner;
 9:     int pause = 500;
10:
11:     public void init() {
12:         for (int i = 0; i < 6; i++) {
13:             String imageText = null;
14:             imageText = getParameter("image"+i);
15:             if (imageText != null) {
16:                 totalPictures++;
17:                 picture[i] = getImage(getCodeBase(), imageText);
18:             } else
19:                 break;
20:         }
21:         String pauseText = null;
22:         pauseText = getParameter("pause");
23:         if (pauseText != null) {
24:             pause = Integer.parseInt(pauseText);
25:         }
26:     }
27:
28:     public void paint(Graphics screen) {
29:         screen.drawImage(picture[current],0,0,this);
30:     }
31:
```

```
32:     public void start() {
33:         if (runner == null) {
34:             runner = new Thread(this);
35:             runner.start();
36:         }
37:     }
38:
39:     public void run() {
40:         while (true) {
41:             repaint();
42:             current++;
43:             if (current >= totalPictures)
44:                 current = 0;
45:             try { Thread.sleep(pause); }
46:             catch (InterruptedException e) { }
47:         }
48:     }
49:
50:     public void stop() {
51:         if (runner != null) {
52:             runner.stop();
53:             runner = null;
54:         }
55:     }
56:
57:     public void update(Graphics screen) {
58:         paint(screen);
59:     }
60: }
```

This program uses the same threaded applet structure that you used during Hour 14, "Creating a Threaded Applet." Threads are often used during animation programming because they give you the ability to control the timing of the animation. The Thread.sleep() method is an effective way to determine how long each image should be displayed before the next image is shown.

The Animate applet retrieves images as parameters on a Web page. The parameters should have names starting at "image0" and ending at the last image of the animation, such as "image3" in this hour's example. The maximum number of images that can be displayed by this applet is 6, but you could raise this number by making changes to Lines 5 and 12.

The totalPicture integer variable determines how many different images will be displayed in an animation. If fewer than 6 image files have been specified by parameters, the Animate applet will determine this during the init() method when imageText equals null after Line 14.

The speed of the animation is specified by a pause parameter. Because all parameters from a Web page are received as strings, the Integer.parseInt() method is needed to convert the text into an integer. The pause variable keeps track of the number of milliseconds to pause after displaying each image in an animation.

Preventing Flickering Animation

As with most threaded programs, the run() method contains the main part of the program. A while (true) statement in Line 40 causes Lines 41–46 to loop as long as the program is not stopped by someone leaving the Web page.

The first thing that happens in the run() method is a repaint(); statement. This statement causes the update() method and paint() method to be handled, in that order, so that the screen can be updated. Use repaint() any time you know something has changed and the display needs to be changed to bring it up to date. In this case, every time the Animate loop goes around once, a different image should be shown.

The update() method contains only one statement, paint(screen);. The reason to use this method is that it overrides the behavior that update() normally performs. If you did not override update() in the Animate program, it would clear the screen before calling on the paint() method. This action causes flickering animation problems that have been mentioned in previous hours.

Loading and Displaying Images

The paint() method is simple in this applet: It draws an image on-screen with the drawImage() method. The drawImage() method displays a current Image object at the (x, y) position specified. The following is another example of a drawImage() statement:

```
screen.drawImage(turtlePicture, 10, 25, this);
```

This statement displays the Image object called turtlePicture at the (x, y) coordinates of (10, 25). The this statement sent as the fourth argument to drawImage() enables the program to use a class called ImageObserver. This class tracks when an image is being loaded and when it is finished. The Applet class contains behavior that works behind the scenes to take care of this process, so all you have to do is specify this as an argument to drawImage() and some other methods related to image display. The rest is taken care of for you.

The preceding example assumed that an `Image` object called `turtlePicture` had been created and loaded with a valid image. The way to load an image in an applet is to use the `getImage()` method. This method takes two arguments, the Web address or directory that contains the image file and the file name of the image.

The first argument is taken care of with the `getCodeBase()` method, which is part of the `Applet` class. This method returns the location of the applet itself, so if you put your images in the same directory as the applet's class file, you can use `getCodeBase()`. The second argument should be a `.GIF` file or `.JPG` file to load. The following statement loads the `turtlePicture` object with a file called `Mertle.gif`:

```
Image turtlePicture = getImage(getCodeBase(), "Mertle.gif");
```

Storing a Group of Related Images

In the `Animate` applet, images are loaded into an array of `Image` objects called `pictures`. The `pictures` array is set up to handle six elements in Line 5 of the program, so you can have `Image` objects ranging from `picture[0]` to `picture[5]`. The following statement in the applet's `paint()` method displays the current image:

```
screen.drawImage(picture[current],0,0,this);
```

The `current` variable is used in the applet to keep track of which image to display in the `paint()` method. It has an initial value of 0, so the first image to be displayed is the one stored in `picture[0]`. After each call to the `repaint()` statement in Line 41 of the `run()` method, the `current` variable is incremented by one in Line 42.

The `totalPictures` variable is an integer that keeps track of how many images should be displayed. It is set when images are loaded from parameters off the Web page. When `current` equals `totalPictures`, it is set back to 0. As a result, `current` cycles through each image of the animation, and then begins again at the first image.

Sending Parameters to the Applet

Becaus the `Animate` applet relies on parameters to specify the image files it should display, you need to create a Web page containing these file names before you can test the program. After saving and compiling the `Animate.java` file, open up a new file in your word processor and call it `Animate.html`. Enter Listing 18.2 into that file, and save it when you're done.

Listing 18.2. The full text of `Animate.html`.

```
1: <applet code="Animate.class" width=230 height=166>
2: <param name="image0" value="sams0.gif">
3: <param name="image1" value="sams1.gif">
4: <param name="image2" value="sams2.gif">
5: <param name="image3" value="sams3.gif">
6: <param name="pause" value="400">
7: </applet>
```

This file specifies four image files: `sams0.gif`, `sams1.gif`, `sams2.gif`, and `sams3.gif`. These files are listed as the values for the parameters `image0` through `image3`. You can find the files used in this example on this book's CD-ROM in the directory `Win95nt4/Book/Source/Hour18`. They also can be downloaded from the book's official Web site at the following address:

`http://www.prefect.com/java24`

Look for the `Hour 18's graphics` link that's available on the main page of the site. You also can specify any of your own `.GIF` or `.JPG` files if desired. Whichever files you choose should be placed in the same directory as the `Animate.class` and `Animate.html` files. With the `"pause"` parameter, you can specify how long the program should pause after each image is displayed.

JUST A MINUTE

You might be wondering why the files and the parameters are given names that start numbering with 0 instead of 1. This is done because the first element of an array in a Java program is numbered 0. Putting an `image0` called `sams0.gif` into `pictures[0]` makes it easier to know where these images are being stored.

Once the files have been put in the right place, you're ready to try out the `Animate` applet. Type the following command to use the `appletviewer` to view the page:

`appletviewer Animate.html`

Figure 18.1 shows the four images of the animation that was provided for this book.

18

Figure 18.1.
Four shots of the
Animate *applet as*
it runs.

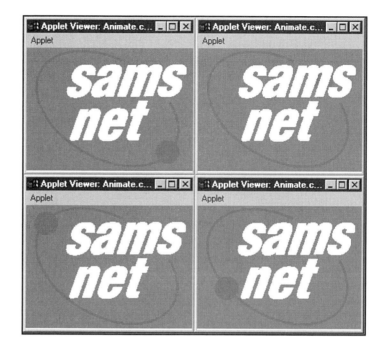

Although this is a simple animation program, hundreds of applets on the Web use similar functionality to present a series of image files as an animation. Presenting a sequence of image files through Java is similar to the animated .GIF files that are becoming more commonplace on Web pages. Although Java applets are often slower to load than these .GIF files, applets can provide more control of the animation and allow for more complicated effects.

Workshop: Follow the Bouncing Ball

This hour's workshop is an animation that definitely couldn't be replicated with an animated .GIF file or any other non-programming alternative. You'll write a program that bounces a tennis ball around the screen in lazy arcs, caroming off the sides of the applet window. Though a few laws of physics will be broken along the way, you'll learn one way to move an image file around the screen.

Create a new file in your word processor called Bounce.java, and enter the text of Listing 18.3 into it. Save and compile the file when you're done.

Listing 18.3. The full text of `Bounce.java`.

```
 1: import java.awt.*;
 2:
 3: public class Bounce extends java.applet.Applet implements Runnable {
 4:
 5:     Image ball;
 6:     float current = (float) 0;
 7:     Thread runner;
 8:     int xPosition = 10;
 9:     int xMove = 1;
10:     int yPosition = -1;
11:     int ballHeight = 102;
12:     int ballWidth = 111;
13:     int height;
14:     Image workspace;
15:     Graphics offscreen;
16:
17:     public void init() {
18:         workspace = createImage(size().width, size().height);
19:         offscreen = workspace.getGraphics();
20:         setBackground(Color.white);
21:         ball = getImage(getCodeBase(), "tennis.jpg");
22:     }
23:
24:     public void paint(Graphics screen) {
25:         height = size().height - ballHeight;
26:         if (yPosition == -1)
27:             yPosition = height;
28:         offscreen.setColor(Color.white);
29:         offscreen.fillRect(0,0,size().width,size().height);
30:         offscreen.drawImage(ball,
31:             (int) xPosition,
32:             (int) yPosition,
33:             this);
34:         screen.drawImage(workspace, 0, 0, this);
35:     }
36:
37:     public void start() {
38:         if (runner == null) {
39:             runner = new Thread(this);
40:             runner.start();
41:         }
42:     }
43:
44:     public void run() {
45:         while (true) {
46:             repaint();
47:             current += (float) 0.1;
48:             if (current > 3)
```

```
49:                    current = (float) 0;
50:                xPosition += xMove;
51:                if (xPosition > (size().width - 111))
52:                    xMove *= -1;
53:                if (xPosition < 1)
54:                    xMove *= -1;
55:                double bounce = Math.sin(current) * height;
56:                yPosition = (int) (height - bounce);
57:                try { Thread.sleep(200); }
58:                catch (InterruptedException e) { }
59:            }
60:        }
61:
62:    public void stop() {
63:        if (runner != null) {
64:            runner.stop();
65:            runner = null;
66:        }
67:    }
68:
69:    public void update(Graphics screen) {
70:        paint(screen);
71:    }
72: }
```

Before you dive into the discussion of what's taking place in this applet, you should see what it does. Create a new file in your word processor called Bounce.html and enter Listing 18.4 into it.

Listing 18.4. The full text of Bounce.html.

```
1: <applet code="Bounce.class" width=500 height=300>
2: </applet>
```

After saving this file, you need to get a copy of the tennis.jpg file and put it in the same directory as Bounce.class and Bounce.html. This file is available from the same place as the Sams.net logo image files: the /Win95nt4/Source/Hour18 directory of the CD-ROM and the book's Web site at http://www.prefect.com/java24. Once you have copied tennis.jpg into the right place, use appletviewer or a Java-enabled Web browser to display this program. Figure 18.2 shows the Bounce applet running on Netscape Navigator.

Figure 18.2.

The Bounce *applet running on a Web page loaded by Netscape Navigator.*

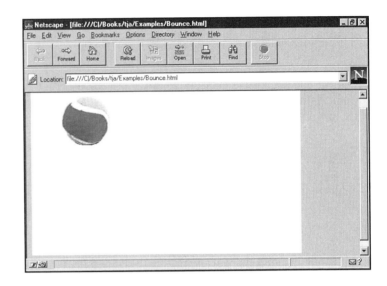

This applet displays a .JPG file of a tennis ball bouncing back and forth. It hits a point at the bottom edge of the applet window and rebounds upward close to the top edge of the window. When the ball hits the right or left edge of the window, it bounces in the opposite direction. If you're using appletviewer to try the applet out, resize the window by making the right and left edges smaller. The Bounce applet can keep track of your actions.

The Bounce applet is a relatively simple example of how to animate an image file using Java. It consists of the following steps:

☐ Draw the ball at its current location.

☐ Move the ball according to the rules that have been established for how the ball should move.

☐ Check whether the rules need to be changed based on the ball's new location.

☐ Repeat.

Drawing the Image

The Bounce applet has the same basic structure as the Animate applet. It's a threaded program with start(), stop(), and run() methods to control the operation of the thread. There are also update() and paint() methods to display information on-screen.

18

The `Image` object called `ball` is loaded with the `tennis.jpg` image in the `init()` method. Several variables are used in the applet to keep track of the ball's location and its current rate of movement:

☐ `xPosition`: This variable is the x coordinate where the ball should be drawn. This coordinate begins as 10.

☐ `xMove`: This variable is the amount that the ball should move along the x axis after every screen update. This amount starts out as 1, but it will change to -1 when the ball hits the right edge of the applet window. It changes back and forth from -1 to 1 every time it hits an edge, and this change is handled by Lines 51–54.

☐ `yPosition`: This variable is the y coordinate where the ball should be drawn. This coordinate is initially set to -1, which is a signal to the `paint()` method that the `yPosition` needs to be set up before the ball can be drawn for the first time. The `yPosition` value varies from a point near the bottom of the applet window to the top edge.

☐ `current`: This floating-point number starts at 0 and increases by 0.1 each time the ball is redrawn. When it reaches 3, it is set back to 0 again. The `current` variable is used with a mathematical sine function to determine how high the ball bounces. Sine waves are a good way to approximate the movements of a bouncing ball, and the `Math.sin()` method enables a sine value to be used in conjunction with animation. The tennis ball is traveling half a sine wave each time it goes from the ground to the top of the window and back.

The movement rules that you establish for an animation applet will vary depending on what you're trying to show. The `Bounce` applet uses the `Math.sin()` method to create the slow arcs traveled by the ball.

Drawing to a Hidden Screen

The `paint()` method uses a technique called double-buffering to make the animation display more smoothly. *Double-buffering* is drawing everything off-screen to a storage place that's the same size as the program's display area and copying it to the display only when all drawing is done. The advantage to using double-buffering is that it reduces flickering and other things that might be seen while the `paint()` method is drawing things on-screen.

Because all drawing in an applet is done to a `Graphics` object that represents the applet window, you have to create an additional `Graphics` object for the off-screen area. You also must create an `Image` object to hold everything that's being drawn to the hidden area. Lines 14–15 create an `Image` object called `workspace` and a `Graphics` object called `offscreen`. These objects are set up in the `init()` method. Line 18 uses the `createImage()` method to set up `workspace` as an empty image the size and width of the applet window. Line 19 associates the `offscreen` object with the `workspace` image, using the `getGraphics()` method of the `Image` class.

The key to double-buffering is to draw everything to the off-screen area in the `paint()` method. To do this, use the `offscreen` object for all display methods instead of the `screen` object. Each of these methods will update the `workspace` image with the things that are being displayed.

When all drawing has been done and you know the off-screen area looks the way the screen should look, draw that entire off-screen image to the applet window by using a statement such as the one on Line 34:

```
screen.drawImage(workspace, 0, 0, this);
```

Because `workspace` is an `Image` object with the same dimensions as the applet window, you can use (0,0) as its coordinates, and it will fill the display area.

When you are drawing only one image to the screen during each update, as you did in the `Animate` applet, there's no reason to use double-buffering. However, if the animation involves more than one thing to draw, you will get better results by drawing to an off-screen area and then copying the whole thing to the screen at one time.

The `Bounce` applet requires an off-screen area because it clears the screen right before drawing the tennis ball during each update. The screen is cleared by drawing a filled white rectangle the size of the applet window. This rectangle is needed to remove the image of the ball in its last position before the new position is drawn.

Summary

Using the classes that come with the Java language, you can produce some interesting animated graphics and games. A lot of graphics functionality is built-in and can be used in short programs like those written during this hour.

Because Java is an interpreted language, its programs run at speeds slower than compiled languages such as C can achieve. This makes it more of a challenge to produce animated graphics at acceptable speeds. However, many applets on display on World Wide Web pages showcase Java's graphics capabilities.

What you have learned about graphics and animation should keep you from running adrift if you venture into uncharted waters like Java game programming and other visually inventive projects. Java animation programming is quite a challenge, but it could be worse. The Professor on *Gilligan's Island* had nothing to work with but coconuts and palm fronds, and he produced a washing machine.

Q&A

Q Does a threaded animation program have to use `Thread.sleep()` to pause, or can you omit it to produce the fastest possible animation?

A You have to put some kind of pause in place in an animation program, or the program will crash or behave erratically. Your applet is running as part of a bigger program, the Web browser or `appletviewer`, and that program won't be able to keep up with constant `repaint()` requests without the pause. Part of the process of animation design in Java is finding the right display speed that all applet-running environments can handle.

Q What happens if you draw something such as an image to coordinates that aren't within the applet window?

A Methods that draw something to a coordinate will continue to draw it even if none of it is visible within the area shown by the applet window. To see this in action, reduce the height of the `Bounce` applet as it runs in the `appletviewer` tool. The tennis ball will drop below the window and bounce back upwards into the window.

Quiz

Animate yourself as much as you can muster and answer the following questions to test your skills.

Questions

1. Where is the (0,0) coordinate on an applet window?

    (a) In the off-screen double-buffering area

    (b) The exact center of the window

    (c) The upper-left corner of the applet window

2. What thing did you *not* learn during this hour?

    (a) How to use `Graphics` and `Image` objects to create an off-screen workspace

    (b) How to override the `update()` method to reduce animation flickering

    (c) Why Thurston Howell III and his wife Lovey packed so much clothing for a three-hour tour

3. In a threaded animation applet, where should you handle most of the movement of an image?

    (a) The `run()` method

    (b) The `init()` method

    (c) The `update()` method

Answers

1. c. The x value increases as you head to the right, and the y value increases as you head downward.

2. c. If the tiny ship had not been so weighted down with smoking jackets and evening gowns, the Skipper and Gilligan might have been able to outrun the storm.

3. a. Some movement might be handled by statements in the `paint()` method, but most of it will take place in `run()` or a method called from within `run()`.

Activities

Before you're stranded and the subject of graphics is abandoned, picture yourself doing the following activities:

☐ Change the `Bounce` applet so that the ball loses 10 percent of its bouncing strength each time it hits the ground. You can do this by changing the `height` variable at a certain time within the `run()` method.

☐ Create an animation applet where the object or objects you move wrap around the edges of the applet window, coming back through the opposite side.

Hour 19

Building a Simple User Interface

Because of the popularity of Microsoft Windows and Apple Macintosh systems, computer users have come to expect certain things from their software. It should use a graphical user interface, be controllable with a mouse, and work like a lot of their other programs do. These expectations are a far cry from the heyday of MS-DOS and other command-line systems, when the user interface varied greatly with each program you used and point-and-click was something photographers did.

Today's programs that use a graphical user interface and mouse control are called *windowing software*. Although you've been using a command-line interface to write Java programs, you can create windowing programs using a group of classes called the Abstract Windowing Toolkit (AWT). You'll learn how to create a windowing program during this hour.

The following topics will be covered:

- ☐ Using user interface components such as buttons
- ☐ Putting components on-screen

☐ Putting components onto other components

☐ Using layout managers to organize an interface

☐ Organizing components into a grid

☐ Using labels, text fields, and other components

☐ Testing an interface

The Abstract Windowing Toolkit

Because Java is a cross-platform language that enables you to write programs for many different operating systems, its windowing software must be flexible. Instead of catering only to the Microsoft Windows-style of windowing or the Apple Macintosh version, it must handle both, along with other platforms. The Abstract Windowing Toolkit gets its name because it is a set of classes intended to work with any platform that runs Java programs. This approach was needed so that programmers could offer their applets on the World Wide Web, which is used by people on dozens of different types of computers, operating systems, and Web browsers.

The Toolkit classes include everything you need to write programs that use a GUI (pronounced *gooey*). If you think a GUI is the brother of Huey, Louie, and Dewey, know that the acronym stands for *graphical user interface*. With Java's windowing toolkit, you can create a GUI that includes all of the following:

☐ Buttons, check boxes, labels, and other simple components

☐ Text fields and more complex components

☐ Dialog boxes and other windows

☐ Pull-down menus

☐ Applets that offer these interface components

The Toolkit also includes classes that you have been using up to this point to offer fonts, color, and graphics in your programs. Another element of the Toolkit you'll be learning about during Hour 20, "Responding to User Events," is how the Toolkit can be used to receive mouse clicks and other user input.

Using Components

To use components such as buttons and text fields in a Java program, you create a component object and use the add() method to add it to an existing component. For example, a Button component is a clickable button with a label that describes what clicking the button will do. One of the most basic ways to use a component such as a button is to add it to an applet. You

19

can add a button to an applet with two statements, one to create the Button object and one to add it to the applet itself. The following short Java applet will do this:

```java
import java.awt.*;

public class ShowButton extends java.applet.Applet {
    Button panicButton = new Button("Panic");

    public void init() {
        add(panicButton);
    }
}
```

The panicButton object is created as an object variable so that you can use it in all methods of the applet program. The argument used with new Button specifies the label of the button. The add(panicButton); statement adds the Button component to the ShowButton applet. Figure 19.1 shows what the output of this program would be.

Figure 19.1.

A Button *component.*

Each of the user components available as part of the Abstract Windowing Toolkit can be added in this manner.

JUST A MINUTE

Because so many different things must be introduced during this hour, the full source code used to create each figure is not listed here. You can find full versions of each program on the book's CD-ROM in the Win95nt4/Book/Source/Hour19 directory or on this book's Web site at http://www.prefect.com/java24. Choose the Hour 19's programs link from the front page.

Labels and Text Fields

A Label component displays a string that cannot be modified by the user. These components get their name from their usefulness as a way to label other components in an interface. They often are used to identify text fields. A TextField component is an area where a user can enter a single line of text. You can set up the width of the box when you create the text field.

The following statements create a `Label` component and `TextField` object and add them to an applet:

```
Label eMailLabel = new Label("E-mail address: ", Label.RIGHT);
TextField eMailAddress = new TextField(25);
add(eMailLabel);
add(eMailAddress);
```

Figure 19.2 shows this label and text field side-by-side. Both of the statements in this example use an argument to configure how the component should look. The `eMailLabel` label is set up with the text `E-mail address:` and a `Label.RIGHT` argument. This last value indicates that the label should appear flush right. `Label.LEFT` aligns the label text flush left, and `Label.CENTER` centers it. The argument used with `TextField` indicates that the text field should be approximately 25 characters wide. You also can specify default text that will appear in the text field with a statement such as the following:

```
TextField state = newTextField("TX", 2);
```

This statement would create a `TextField` object that is two characters wide and has the text `TX` in the field.

Figure 19.2.

`Label` *and* `TextField`
components.

Check Boxes

A `Checkbox` component is a box next to a line of text that can be checked or unchecked by the user. The following statements create a `Checkbox` object and add it to an applet:

```
Checkbox jumboSize = new Checkbox("Jumbo Size");
add(jumboSize);
```

The argument to the `Checkbox()` constructor method indicates the text to be displayed alongside the box. If you wanted the box to be checked, you could use the following statement instead:

```
Checkbox jumboSize = new Checkbox("Jumbo Size", true);
```

A `Checkbox` can be presented singly or as part of a group. In a group of check boxes, only one can be checked at a time. To make a `Checkbox` object part of a group, you have to create a `CheckboxGroup` object. Consider the following:

```
CheckboxGroup meals = new CheckboxGroup();
Checkbox frogLegs = new Checkbox("Frog Leg Grande", true, meals);
Checkbox fishTacos = new Checkbox("Fish Taco Platter", false, meals);
Checkbox emuNuggets = new Checkbox("Emu Nuggets", false, meals);
```

19

```
add(frogLegs);
add(fishTacos);
add(emuNuggets);
```

This code creates three check boxes that are all grouped under the `CheckboxGroup` object called `meals`. The `Frog Leg Grande` box is checked initially, but if the user checked one of the other meal boxes, the check next to `Frog Leg Grande` would disappear automatically. Figure 19.3 shows the different check boxes from this section.

Figure 19.3.

`Checkbox` *components.*

Choice Lists

A `Choice` component is a pop-up list of choices from which a single choice can be made. It serves a similar purpose to a group of check boxes, except that only one of the selections is visible unless the pop-up list is being displayed.

To create a `Choice` object, you have to add each of the choices after creating the object, as in the following example:

```
Choice profession = new Choice();
profession.add("Butcher");
profession.add("Baker");
profession.add("Candlestick maker");
profession.add("Fletcher");
profession.add("Fighter");
profession.add("Technical writer");
add(profession);
```

This example creates a single `Choice` component that provides six choices for the user to select from. When one is selected, it appears in the display of the component. Figure 19.4 shows this example while the pop-up list of choices is being displayed.

Figure 19.4.

A Choice *component.*

Text Areas

A TextArea component is a text field that enables the user to enter more than one line of text. You can specify the width and height of the component. For example, the following statements create a TextArea component with an approximate width of 50 characters and a height of 10 lines and then add the component to an applet:

```
TextArea comments = new TextArea("", 10, 50);
add(comments);
```

You can specify a string in the TextArea() constructor method to be displayed in the text area. You can use the newline character \n to send text to the next line, as in the following:

```
TextArea desire = new TextArea("I should have been a pair\nof ragged claws.",
10, 25);
```

If the user enters text that extends beyond the component's area, scrollbars will become active on the sides of the component, as shown in Figure 19.5. This TextArea is 10 lines tall and approximately 50 characters wide.

Figure 19.5.

A TextArea *component.*

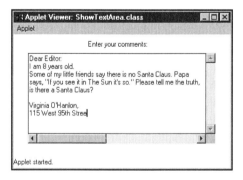

19

Using Layout Managers

The last of the components you'll learn to create during this hour are Panel objects. Panel objects are part of of a broader category of objects known as *containers*. Panel objects don't display anything. Instead, they are used to contain other components. The purpose of Panel objects is to subdivide a display area into different groups of components. When the display is divided into sections, you can use different rules for how each section is displayed on-screen.

You can create a Panel object and add it to an applet with the following statements:

```
Panel topRow = new Panel();
add(topRow);
```

When you place components onto an applet or some other kind of container, the way they are organized on-screen is highly variable. The layout of buttons, text fields, and other components can be affected by the following things:

- The size of the applet window
- The size of other components and containers
- The layout manager that is being used

There are several layout managers that you can use to affect how components are shown. The default manager is the FlowLayout class, which is what has been used for all of the examples shown up to this point. Under FlowLayout, components are dropped onto an area in the same way words are organized on a printed page—from left to right, and on to the next line when there's no more space.

To set up an applet to work under FlowLayout, create a FlowLayout object and then use it as an argument to the setLayout() method:

```
FlowLayout topLayout = new FlowLayout();
setLayout(topLayout);
```

You also can set up a layout manager to work within a specific container, such as a Panel object. You can do this by using the setLayout() method of that container object. The following statements create a Panel object called inputArea and set it up to use FlowLayout as its layout manager:

```
Panel inputArea = new Panel();
FlowLayout inputLayout = new FlowLayout();
inputArea.setLayout(inputLayout);
```

To give you an idea of how the different layout managers work, a simple applet will be shown under each of the classes. The Crisis applet has a graphical user interface with five buttons. Load your word processor and open up a new file called Crisis.java. Enter Listing 19.1, and save the file when you're done.

19

Listing 19.1. The full text of `Crisis.java`.

```
 1: import java.awt.*;
 2:
 3: public class Crisis extends java.applet.Applet {
 4:     Button panicButton = new Button("Panic");
 5:     Button dontPanicButton = new Button("Don't Panic");
 6:     Button blameButton = new Button("Blame Others");
 7:     Button mediaButton = new Button("Notify the Media");
 8:     Button saveButton = new Button("Save Yourself");
 9:
10:     public void init() {
11:         add(panicButton);
12:         add(dontPanicButton);
13:         add(blameButton);
14:         add(mediaButton);
15:         add(saveButton);
16:     }
17: }
```

After saving the source file `Crisis.java`, you need to create a simple Web page that will display this applet. Create a new file called `Crisis.html` and enter Listing 19.2.

Listing 19.2. The full text of `Crisis.html`.

```
1: <applet code="Crisis.class" height=228 width=308>
2: </applet>
```

Save the Web page, and then compile the `Crisis.java` file with the `javac` compiler tool. This applet does not specify a layout manager to use, so the rules default to `FlowLayout`. Use `appletviewer` to load the Web page, and you should see something resembling Figure 19.6.

The `FlowLayout` class uses the dimensions of its container as the only guideline for how to lay out components. Resize the window of `appletviewer` as it is, showing the `Crisis` applet. Make the window twice as wide, and you'll see all of the `Button` components now are shown on the same line. Java programs that use the Abstract Windowing Toolkit often will behave differently when their display area is resized.

19

Figure 19.6.
The Crisis *applet with all of its components laid out under the* FlowLayout *class.*

The GridLayout **Manager**

The GridLayout class organizes all components in a container into a specific number of rows and columns. All components are allocated the same amount of space in the display area. To see the Crisis applet with a grid layout, load the file Crisis.java back into your word processor and edit the init() method. Right after the public void init() { statement, add the following statements:

```
GridLayout crisisLayout = new GridLayout(2, 3);
setLayout(crisisLayout);
```

Save and compile the new version of Crisis.java and load the Crisis.html Web page back into appletviewer. The output should resemble Figure 19.7.

Figure 19.7.
The Crisis *applet with all of its components laid out under the* GridLayout *class.*

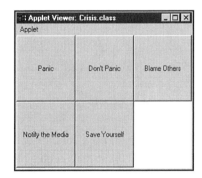

19

GridLayout places all components as they are added into a place on a grid. Components are added from left to right until a row is full, and then the leftmost column of the next grid is filled.

The BorderLayout **Manager**

The last layout manager left to experiment with is the BorderLayout class. Return to the Crisis.java file in your word processor, and replace the init() method with the following statements:

```
public void init() {
    BorderLayout crisisLayout = new BorderLayout();
    setLayout(crisisLayout);
    add(panicButton, "North");
    add(dontPanicButton, "South");
    add(blameButton, "East");
    add(mediaButton, "West");
    add(saveButton, "Center");
}
```

After you save the change and recompile the Crisis applet, the page you load with the appletviewer should resemble Figure 19.8.

Figure 19.8.

The Crisis *applet with all of its components laid out under the* BorderLayout *class.*

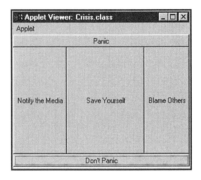

The BorderLayout manager arranges components into five areas: four denoted by compass directions and one for the center area. When you add a component under this layout, the add() method includes a second argument to specify where the component should be placed. The strings "North", "South", "East", "West", and "Center" are used for this argument.

Like the GridLayout class, BorderLayout devotes all available space to the components. The component placed in the center is given all space that isn't needed for the four border components, so it usually is the largest.

Workshop: Laying Out an Applet

The layout managers that you have seen thus far were applied to an entire applet; the setLayout() method of the applet was used, and all components followed the same rules. This setup can be suitable for some programs, but as you try to develop a graphical user interface

19

with the Abstract Windowing Toolkit, you often will find that none of the layout managers fits. One way around this problem is to use a group of Panel objects as containers to hold different parts of the applet window. You can set up different layout rules for each of these parts by using the setLayout() methods of each Panel object.

This hour's workshop will be to develop a full interface for the program that you will write during the next hour, "Responding to User Events." The program is a Lotto number cruncher that will assess a user's chance of winning one of the multimillion-dollar Lotto contests in the span of a lifetime. This chance will be determined by running random six-number Lotto drawings again and again until the user's numbers turn up as a big winner. Figure 19.9 shows the GUI that you will be developing for the applet.

Figure 19.9.

The LottoGUI *applet.*

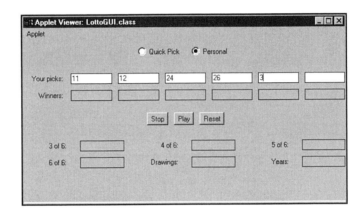

Create a new file in your word processor called LottoGUI.java. Enter Listing 19.3, and save the file when you're done.

Listing 19.3. The full text of LottoGUI.java.

```
 1: import java.awt.*;
 2:
 3: public class LottoGUI extends java.applet.Applet {
 4:     // set up row 1
 5:     Panel row1 = new Panel();
 6:     CheckboxGroup option = new CheckboxGroup();
 7:     Checkbox quickpick = new Checkbox("Quick Pick", option, true);
 8:     Checkbox personal = new Checkbox("Personal",option, false);
 9:     // set up row 2
10:     Panel row2 = new Panel();
11:     Label numbersLabel = new Label("Your picks: ", Label.RIGHT);
12:     TextField[] numbers = new TextField[6];
13:     Label winnersLabel = new Label("Winners: ", Label.RIGHT);
14:     TextField[] winners = new TextField[6];
```

continues

Listing 19.3. continued

```
15:        // set up row 3
16:        Panel row3 = new Panel();
17:        Button stop = new Button("Stop");
18:        Button play = new Button("Play");
19:        Button reset = new Button("Reset");
20:        // set up row 4
21:        Panel row4 = new Panel();
22:        Label got3Label = new Label("3 of 6: ", Label.RIGHT);
23:        TextField got3 = new TextField();
24:        Label got4Label = new Label("4 of 6: ", Label.RIGHT);
25:        TextField got4 = new TextField();
26:        Label got5Label = new Label("5 of 6: ", Label.RIGHT);
27:        TextField got5 = new TextField();
28:        Label got6Label = new Label("6 of 6: ", Label.RIGHT);
29:        TextField got6 = new TextField(10);
30:        Label drawingsLabel = new Label("Drawings: ", Label.RIGHT);
31:        TextField drawings = new TextField();
32:        Label yearsLabel = new Label("Years: ", Label.RIGHT);
33:        TextField years = new TextField();
34:
35:        public void init() {
36:            GridLayout appletLayout = new GridLayout(5, 1, 10, 10);
37:            setLayout(appletLayout);
38:
39:            FlowLayout layout1 = new FlowLayout(FlowLayout.CENTER, 10, 10);
40:            row1.setLayout(layout1);
41:            row1.add(quickpick);
42:            row1.add(personal);
43:            add(row1);
44:
45:            GridLayout layout2 = new GridLayout(2, 7, 10, 10);
46:            row2.setLayout(layout2);
47:            row2.setLayout(layout2);
48:            row2.add(numbersLabel);
49:            for (int i = 0; i < 6; i++) {
50:                numbers[i] = new TextField();
51:                row2.add(numbers[i]);
52:            }
53:            row2.add(winnersLabel);
54:            for (int i = 0; i < 6; i++) {
55:                winners[i] = new TextField();
56:                winners[i].setEditable(false);
57:                row2.add(winners[i]);
58:            }
59:            add(row2);
60:
61:            FlowLayout layout3 = new FlowLayout(FlowLayout.CENTER, 10, 10);
62:            row3.setLayout(layout3);
63:            row3.add(stop);
64:            row3.add(play);
65:            row3.add(reset);
66:            add(row3);
67:
```

19

```
68:            GridLayout layout4 = new GridLayout(2, 3, 20, 10);
69:            row4.setLayout(layout4);
70:            row4.add(got3Label);
71:            got3.setEditable(false);
72:            row4.add(got3);
73:            row4.add(got4Label);
74:            got4.setEditable(false);
75:            row4.add(got4);
76:            row4.add(got5Label);
77:            got5.setEditable(false);
78:            row4.add(got5);
79:            row4.add(got6Label);
80:            got6.setEditable(false);
81:            row4.add(got6);
82:            row4.add(drawingsLabel);
83:            drawings.setEditable(false);
84:            row4.add(drawings);
85:            row4.add(yearsLabel);
86:            years.setEditable(false);
87:            row4.add(years);
88:            add(row4);
89:        }
90: }
```

Compile this file with the javac compiler tool, and return to your word processor to create a Web page for this applet. Create a new file called LottoGUI.html and enter Listing 19.4. Save the file when you're done.

Listing 19.4. The full text of LottoGUI.html.

```
1: <html>
2: <head>
3: <title>Lotto Madness</title>
4: </head>
5: <body bgcolor="#4b4b4b">
6: <applet code="LottoGUI.class" width=550 height=270>
7: </applet>
8: </body>
9: </html>
```

Try this Web page out with the appletviewer tool, and you'll get a chance to see how the LottoGUI applet will work. Even though you haven't added any statements that make the program do anything yet, you can make sure that the graphical interface does what you need it to do.

This applet uses several different layout managers. If you look carefully at each of the components, you might be able to determine which manager is in use in the different areas of the program. To get a clearer picture of how the applet is laid out, take a look at Figure

19.10. The interface is divided into five horizontal rows. Each of these rows is a `Panel` object, and the overall layout manager of the applet organizes these rows into a `GridLayout` of five rows and one column.

Figure 19.10.

The way the `LottoGUI` *class is organized.*

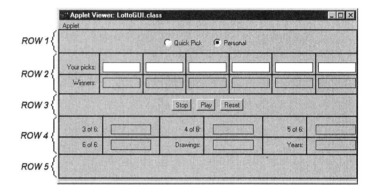

Within the rows, different layout managers are used to determine how the components should appear. Rows 1 and 3 use `FlowLayout` objects. Line 39 of the program shows how these objects are created:

```
FlowLayout layout1 = new FlowLayout(FlowLayout.CENTER, 10, 10);
```

Three arguments are used with the `FlowLayout()` constructor method. The first argument, `FlowLayout.CENTER`, indicates that the components should be centered within their container—the horizontal `Panel` they are placed on. The last two components specify the width and height each component should be moved away from other components. Using a width of 10 pixels and a height of 10 pixels puts a small amount of extra distance between the components.

Row 2 of the applet is laid out into a grid that is two rows tall and seven columns wide. The `GridLayout()` constructor also specifies that components should be set apart from other components by 10 pixels in each direction. Lines 45 and 46 set up this grid:

```
GridLayout layout2 = new GridLayout(2, 7, 10, 10);
row2.setLayout(layout2);
```

Row 4 uses `GridLayout` to arrange components into a grid that is two rows tall and six columns wide.

The `LottoGUI` applet uses several of the components described during this hour. Lines 4–33 are used to set up objects for all of the components that make up the interface. The statements are organized by row. First, a `Panel` object for the row is created, and then each component that will go on the row is set up. This code creates all of the components and containers, but they will not be displayed unless an `add()` method is used to put them onto the display area.

19

In Lines 36–88, the components are added. Lines 39–43 are indicative of the entire `init()` method:

```
FlowLayout layout1 = new FlowLayout(FlowLayout.CENTER, 10, 10);
row1.setLayout(layout1);
row1.add(quickpick);
row1.add(personal);
add(row1);
```

After a layout manager object is created, it is used with the `setLayout()` method of the row's `Panel` object—`row1` in this case. Once the layout has been specified, components are added to the `Panel` object by using its `add()` method. Once all of the components have been placed, the entire `row1` object is added to the applet window using its own `add()` method.

Summary

Users have come to expect a point-and-click, visual environment for the programs that they run. This expectation makes creating software more of a challenge, but Java puts these capabilities into your hands with the windowing toolkit. The Abstract Windowing Toolkit provides all the classes you will need to provide a working, useful GUI in the tradition of Windows and Macintosh software—regardless of what kind of setup you're running Java programs on.

During the next hour, you'll learn more about the function of a graphical user interface. You'll get a chance to see the `LottoGUI` interface in use as it churns through lottery drawings and tallies up winners.

Q&A

Q **Why are some of the text fields in the `LottoGUI` applet shaded in gray while others are white?**

A The `setEditable()` method has been used on the gray fields to make them impossible to edit. The default behavior of a text field is to enable users to change the value of the text field by clicking within its borders and typing any desired changes. However, some fields are intended to display information rather than take input from the user. The `setEditable()` method prevents users from changing a field that they should not modify.

Q **Can more than one line of text be displayed on a `Label` object?**

A No, labels are limited to a single line of text. You cannot use newline characters (`'\n'`) as you might with a `TextArea` object to create default text that is more than one line long.

Quiz

If your brain hasn't been turned into a GUI mush with this hour's toil, test your skills by answering the following questions.

Questions

1. Which user component is used as a container to hold other components?

   (a) `TupperWare`

   (b) `Panel`

   (c) `Choice`

2. Which of the following must be done first within a container?

   (a) Establish a layout manager

   (b) Add components

   (c) Doesn't matter

3. Where does the `BorderLayout` class get its name?

   (a) The border of each component

   (b) The way components are organized along the borders of a container

   (c) Sheer capriciousness on the part of Java's developers

Answers

1. b.

2. a. You must specify the layout manager before the components so that you can add them in the correct way.

3. b. The border position of components must be specified as they are added to a container with the use of directional strings such as "East" and "West."

Activities

To interface further with the subject of GUI design, undertake the following activity:

☐ Create a modified version of the `Crisis` applet with the `panic` and `dontPanic` objects organized under one layout manager and the remaining three buttons under another.

19

Hour 20

Responding to User Events

The graphical user interface that you developed during the past hour can run on its own without any changes. Buttons can be clicked, text fields filled with text, and the applet window can be resized with wild abandon. Sooner or later, however, even the least discriminating user is going to be left wanting more. The graphical user interface that a program offers has to cause things to happen when a mouse click or keyboard entry occurs. Text areas and other components must be updated to show what's happening as the program runs.

These things are possible when your Java program can respond to user events. An *event* is something that happens when a program runs, and user events are things that a user causes by using the mouse, keyboard, or another input device. Responding to user events often is called *event-handling*, and it's the activity you'll be learning about during this hour.

The following topics will be covered:

- ☐ Making your programs aware of events
- ☐ Setting up a component so it can cause events
- ☐ Components that can be ignored
- ☐ Where events end up in a program
- ☐ Storing information in the interface
- ☐ Using numeric variables with text fields

Getting Your Programs to Listen

Responding to user events in a Java program requires the use of one or more `EventListener` interfaces. As you might recall from using the `Runnable` interface for multithreaded programs, interfaces are special classes that enable a class of objects to inherit behavior that it would not be able to use otherwise. Adding an `EventListener` interface involves two things right away. First, because the listening classes are part of the `java.awt.event` group of classes, you must make them available with the following statement:

```
import java.awt.event.*;
```

Secondly, the class must use the `implements` statement to declare that it will be using one or more listening interfaces. The following statement creates a class that uses `ActionListener`, an interface used with buttons and other components:

```
public class Graph extends java.applet.Applet implements ActionListener {
```

The `EventListener` interfaces enable a component of a graphical user interface to generate user events. Without one of the listeners in place, a component cannot do anything that can be heard by other parts of a program. A program must include a listener interface for each type of component it wants to listen to. To have the program respond to a mouse click on a button or the Enter key being pressed in a text field, you must include the `ActionListener` interface. To respond to the use of a choice list or check boxes, the `ItemListener` interface is needed. When you require more than one interface, separate their names with commas after the `implements` statement. The following is an example:

```
public class Graph3D extends java.applet.Applet implements ActionListener,
MouseListener {
```

20

Setting Up Components to Be Heard

Once you have implemented the interface that is needed for a particular component, you have to set up that component so that it generates user events. A good example to consider is the use of Button objects as components. When you use a button in an interface, something has to happen in response to the click of the button. Otherwise, the button's not needed for the interface at all.

The program that needs to respond to the button click should use the ActionListener interface. The name of the interface comes from calling a button click or the press of the Enter key an action event, because it signifies that some kind of action should be taken. To make a Button object generate an event, use the addActionListener() method, as in the following:

```
Button fireTorpedoes = new Button("Fire torpedoes");
fireTorpedoes.addActionListener(this);
```

This code creates the fireTorpedoes object and then calls that object's addActionListener() method. The this statement indicates that the current class of objects will receive the user event and handle it as needed.

Handling User Events

When a user event is generated by a component that has a listener, a method will be called automatically. The method must be found in the class that was specified when the listener was attached to the component. For instance, in the example of the fireTorpedoes object, the method must be located in the same program because the this statement was used.

Each listener has different methods that are called to receive their events. The ActionListener interface sends events to a class called actionPerformed(). The following is a short example of an actionPerformed() method:

```
void public actionPerformed(ActionEvent evt) {
    // method goes here
}
```

All action events sent in the program will go to this method. If only one component in a program can possibly send action events, you can put statements in this method to handle the event. If more than one component can send these events, you need to use the object that is sent to the method.

In this case, an ActionEvent object is sent to the actionPerformed() method. There are several different classes of objects that represent the user events that can be sent in a program. These classes have methods you can use to determine which component caused the event to happen. In the actionPerformed() method, if the ActionEvent object is named evt, you can identify the component with the following statement:

```
String cmd = evt.getActionCommand();
```

20

The `getActionCommand()` method sends back a string. If the component is a button, the string will be the label that is on the button. If it's a text field, the string will be the text entered in the field. The `getSource()` method sends back the object that caused the event.

You could use the following `actionPerformed()` method to receive events from three components: a `Button` object called `start`, a `TextField` called `speed`, and another `TextField` called `viscosity`:

```
void public actionPerformed(ActionEvent evt) {
    Object source = evt.getSource();
    if (source == speed) {
        // speed field caused event
    } else if (source == viscosity) {
        // viscosity caused event
    } else
        // start caused event
```

You can use the `getSource()` method with all types of user events to identify the specific object that caused the event.

Check Box and Choice Events

Choice lists and check boxes require the `ItemListener` interface. To make one of these components generate events, use the `addItemListener()` method. For example, the following statements create a check box called `superSize` and cause it to send out user events when selected or deselected:

```
Checkbox superSize = new Checkbox("Super Size", true);
superSize.addItemListener(this);
```

These events are received by the `itemStateChanged()` method, which takes an `ItemEvent` object as an argument. To see which object caused the event, you can use the `getItem()` method.

To determine whether a check box is selected or deselected, use the `getStateChange()` method with the constants `ItemEvent.SELECTED` and `ItemEvent.DESELECTED`. The following is an example for an `ItemEvent` object called `item`:

```
int status = item.getStateChange();
if (status == ItemEvent.SELECTED)
    // item was selected
```

To determine the value that has been selected in a `Choice` object, use `getItem()` and convert that value to a string, as in the following:

```
Object which = item.getItem();
String answer = (String) which;
```

20

Other Text Field Events

If you want to check on a text field or text area after its value has been changed, use the TextListener interface. The addTextListener() method makes a text component actively generate user events, and the textValueChanged() method receives the events. The following example receives events from TextField objects called address and zipCode:

```
public void textValueChanged(TextEvent txt) {
    Object source = txt.getSource();
    if (source == address)
        String newAddress = address.getText();
    } else
        String newZipCode = zipCode.getText();
}
```

The getText() method is used with text components to retrieve their values. The setText() method can set the value of a text field or text area.

Enabling and Disabling Components

You may have seen a component in a program that appears shaded instead of its normal appearance. This shading indicates that users cannot do anything to the component because it is disabled. Disabling and enabling components as a program runs is done with the setEnabled() method of the component. A Boolean value is sent as an argument to the method, so setEnabled(true) enables a component for use, and setEnabled(false) disables a component.

This method is an effective way to prevent a component from sending a user event when it shouldn't. For example, if you're writing a Java applet that takes a user's address in text fields, you might want to disable a Continue button until all of the fields have some kind of value.

Workshop: A Little Lotto Madness

For more examples of how event-handling works in the context of a Java program, you will finish the Lotto applet that you began during Hour 19, "Building a Simple User Interface." The name of the applet will be changed from LottoGUI to LottoMadness to reflect its status as a program. The purpose of this applet is to assess the user's chances of winning a six-number Lotto drawing in a lifetime. Figure 20.1 shows a screen capture of the program as it continues to run.

Instead of using probability to figure out this problem, the computer will take a more anecdotal approach: It will conduct drawing after drawing after drawing until you win. Because the 6-out-of-6 win is extremely unlikely, the program also will report on any combination of three, four, or five winning numbers.

20

The interface that you created includes 12 text fields for Lotto numbers and two check boxes labeled Quick Pick and Personal. Six of the text fields are disabled from input; they will be used to display the winning numbers of each drawing. The other six text fields are for the user's choice of numbers. If the user wants to select six numbers manually, he should select the Personal check box. If he selects the Quick Pick box instead, six random numbers will appear in the text fields.

Figure 20.1.

The LottoMadness
applet continues to run.

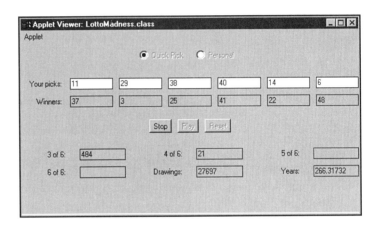

Three buttons control the activity of the program: Stop, Play, and Reset. When the Play button is pressed, the program starts a thread called playing and generates Lotto drawings as fast as it can. Pressing the Stop button stops the thread, and pressing Reset clears all fields so the user can start the number-crunching all over again.

The LottoMadness applet implements three interfaces: ActionListener, ItemListener, and Runnable. The first two are needed to listen to user events generated by the buttons and check boxes on the applet. The program does not need to listen to any events related to the text fields, because they will be used strictly to store the user's choice of numbers. The user interface handles this function automatically.

Listing 20.1 shows the full text of the LottoMadness applet. The shaded lines in the listing were unchanged from LottoGUI.java. The unshaded statements are what must be added to respond to user events and run the Lotto drawings.

Making this program aware of user events for some components requires only a few additions. The class statement in Lines 4–6 is changed to use the interfaces. Lines 46–51 add the listeners that are needed for the two check boxes and three button components. One line is added to the program in the init() method where components are placed on the user interface. In Line 77, the stop object is disabled with the setEnabled(false) method. Because no drawings are taking place when the program begins running, the Stop button should not be usable at that point.

20

The following methods are used in the program to accomplish specific tasks:

☐ Lines 146–156: The `clearAllFields()` method causes all text fields in the applet to be emptied out. This method is handled when the Reset button is pressed.

☐ Lines 159–162: The `addOneToField()` method converts a text field to an integer, increments it by one, and converts it back into a text field. Because all text fields are stored as strings, you have to take special steps to use some of them as numbers.

☐ Lines 165–169: The `numberGone()` method takes three arguments—a single number from a Lotto drawing, an array that holds several `TextField` objects, and a `count` integer. This method makes sure that each number in a drawing hasn't been selected already in the same drawing.

☐ Lines 172–178: The `matchedOne()` method takes two arguments—a `TextField` object and an array of six `TextField` objects. This method checks to see whether one of the user's numbers is a winner.

The `actionPerformed()` method of the applet receives the action events caused when the user presses Stop, Play, or Reset. The `getActionCommand()` method retrieves the label of the button, which is used to determine which component was pressed. Pressing the Play button causes four components to be disabled so that they do not interfere with the drawings as they are taking place. Pressing Stop reverses this by enabling every component except for the Stop button.

The `itemStateChanged()` method receives the user events caused when one of the check boxes is selected. The `getItem()` method sends back an `Object`, which is converted to a string to determine the label of the check box.

One last thing to note about the `LottoMadness` applet is the lack of variables used to keep track of things like the number of drawings, winning counts, and Lotto number text fields. This element of user interface programming differs from other types of programs. You can use the interface to store values and display them automatically.

Load the original `LottoGUI.java` program into your word processor and save the file under the new name `LottoMadness.java`. After changing the `class` statement to reflect the new name of the program and the interfaces it will use, insert all of the non-shaded lines from Listing 20.1 and save the file.

20

Listing 20.1. The full text of `LottoMadness.java`.

```
1: import java.awt.*;
2: import java.awt.event.*;
3:
4: public class LottoMadness extends java.applet.Applet
```

continues

Listing 20.1. continued

```
 5:     implements ItemListener, ActionListener,
 6:     Runnable {
 7:
 8:     Thread playing;
 9:
10:     // set up row 1
11:     Panel row1 = new Panel();
12:     CheckboxGroup option = new CheckboxGroup();
13:     Checkbox quickpick = new Checkbox("Quick Pick", option, false);
14:     Checkbox personal = new Checkbox("Personal",option, true);
15:     // set up row 2
16:     Panel row2 = new Panel();
17:     Label numbersLabel = new Label("Your picks: ", Label.RIGHT);
18:     TextField[] numbers = new TextField[6];
19:     Label winnersLabel = new Label("Winners: ", Label.RIGHT);
20:     TextField[] winners = new TextField[6];
21:     // set up row 3
22:     Panel row3 = new Panel();
23:     Button stop = new Button("Stop");
24:     Button play = new Button("Play");
25:     Button reset = new Button("Reset");
26:     // set up row 4
27:     Panel row4 = new Panel();
28:     Label got3Label = new Label("3 of 6: ", Label.RIGHT);
29:     TextField got3 = new TextField();
30:     Label got4Label = new Label("4 of 6: ", Label.RIGHT);
31:     TextField got4 = new TextField();
32:     Label got5Label = new Label("5 of 6: ", Label.RIGHT);
33:     TextField got5 = new TextField();
34:     Label got6Label = new Label("6 of 6: ", Label.RIGHT);
35:     TextField got6 = new TextField(10);
36:     Label drawingsLabel = new Label("Drawings: ", Label.RIGHT);
37:     TextField drawings = new TextField();
38:     Label yearsLabel = new Label("Years: ", Label.RIGHT);
39:     TextField years = new TextField();
40:
41:     public void init() {
42:         setBackground(Color.lightGray);
43:         GridLayout appletLayout = new GridLayout(5, 1, 10, 10);
44:         setLayout(appletLayout);
45:
46:         // Add listeners
47:         quickpick.addItemListener(this);
48:         personal.addItemListener(this);
49:         stop.addActionListener(this);
50:         play.addActionListener(this);
51:         reset.addActionListener(this);
52:
53:         FlowLayout layout1 = new FlowLayout(FlowLayout.CENTER, 10, 10);
54:         row1.setLayout(layout1);
55:         row1.add(quickpick);
56:         row1.add(personal);
57:         add(row1);
58:
```

20

```
59:          GridLayout layout2 = new GridLayout(2, 7, 10, 10);
60:          row2.setLayout(layout2);
61:          row2.setLayout(layout2);
62:          row2.add(numbersLabel);
63:          for (int i = 0; i < 6; i++) {
64:              numbers[i] = new TextField();
65:              row2.add(numbers[i]);
66:          }
67:          row2.add(winnersLabel);
68:          for (int i = 0; i < 6; i++) {
69:              winners[i] = new TextField();
70:              winners[i].setEditable(false);
71:              row2.add(winners[i]);
72:          }
73:          add(row2);
74:
75:          FlowLayout layout3 = new FlowLayout(FlowLayout.CENTER, 10, 10);
76:          row3.setLayout(layout3);
77:          stop.setEnabled(false);
78:          row3.add(stop);
79:          row3.add(play);
80:          row3.add(reset);
81:          add(row3);
82:
83:          GridLayout layout4 = new GridLayout(2, 3, 20, 10);
84:          row4.setLayout(layout4);
85:          row4.add(got3Label);
86:          got3.setEditable(false);
87:          row4.add(got3);
88:          row4.add(got4Label);
89:          got4.setEditable(false);
90:          row4.add(got4);
91:          row4.add(got5Label);
92:          got5.setEditable(false);
93:          row4.add(got5);
94:          row4.add(got6Label);
95:          got6.setEditable(false);
96:          row4.add(got6);
97:          row4.add(drawingsLabel);
98:          drawings.setEditable(false);
99:          row4.add(drawings);
100:         row4.add(yearsLabel);
101:         years.setEditable(false);
102:         row4.add(years);
103:         add(row4);
104:      }
105:
106:     public void actionPerformed(ActionEvent event) {
107:         String command = event.getActionCommand();
108:         if (command == "Reset")
109:             clearAllFields();
110:         if (command == "Play") {
111:             playing = new Thread(this);
112:             playing.start();
113:             play.setEnabled(false);
```

continues

Listing 20.1. continued

```
114:              stop.setEnabled(true);
115:              reset.setEnabled(false);
116:              quickpick.setEnabled(false);
117:              personal.setEnabled(false);
118:          }
119:          if (command == "Stop") {
120:              playing.stop();
121:              stop.setEnabled(false);
122:              play.setEnabled(true);
123:              reset.setEnabled(true);
124:              quickpick.setEnabled(true);
125:              personal.setEnabled(true);
126:          }
127:
128:      }
129:
130:      public void itemStateChanged(ItemEvent event) {
131:          String command = (String) event.getItem();
132:          if (command == "Quick Pick") {
133:              for (int i = 0; i < 6; i++) {
134:                  int pick;
135:                  do {
136:                      pick = (int)Math.floor(Math.random() * 50 + 1);
137:                  } while (numberGone(pick, numbers, i));
138:                  numbers[i].setText("" + pick);
139:              }
140:          } else {
141:              for (int i = 0; i < 6; i++)
142:                  numbers[i].setText(null);
143:          }
144:      }
145:
146:      void clearAllFields() {
147:          for (int i = 0; i < 6; i++) {
148:              numbers[i].setText(null);
149:              winners[i].setText(null);
150:          }
151:          got3.setText(null);
152:          got4.setText(null);
153:          got5.setText(null);
154:          got6.setText(null);
155:          drawings.setText(null);
156:          years.setText(null);
157:      }
158:
159:      void addOneToField(TextField field) {
160:          int num = Integer.parseInt("0" + field.getText());
161:          num++;
162:          field.setText("" + num);
163:      }
164:
165:      boolean numberGone(int num, TextField[] pastNums, int count) {
166:          for (int i = 0; i < count; i++)
```

```
167:                    if (Integer.parseInt(pastNums[i].getText()) == num)
168:                        return true;
169:            return false;
170:        }
171:
172:        boolean matchedOne(TextField win, TextField[] allPicks) {
173:            for (int i = 0; i < 6; i++) {
174:                String winText = win.getText();
175:                if ( winText.equals( allPicks[i].getText() ) )
176:                    return true;
177:            }
178:            return false;
179:        }
180:
181:        public void run() {
182:            while (true) {
183:                addOneToField(drawings);
184:                int draw = Integer.parseInt(drawings.getText());
185:                float numYears = (float)draw / 104;
186:                years.setText("" + numYears);
187:
188:                int matches = 0;
189:                for (int i = 0; i < 6; i++) {
190:                    int ball;
191:                    do {
192:                        ball = (int)Math.floor(Math.random() * 50 + 1);
193:                    } while (numberGone(ball, winners, i));
194:                    winners[i].setText("" + ball);
195:                    if (matchedOne(winners[i], numbers))
196:                        matches++;
197:                }
198:                switch (matches) {
199:                    case 3:
200:                        addOneToField(got3);
201:                        break;
202:                    case 4:
203:                        addOneToField(got4);
204:                        break;
205:                    case 5:
206:                        addOneToField(got5);
207:                        break;
208:                    case 6:
209:                        addOneToField(got6);
210:                        stop.setEnabled(false);
211:                        play.setEnabled(true);
212:                        playing.stop();
213:                }
215:            }
216:        }
218: }
```

After saving the LottoMadness.java file, load the file LottoGUI.html into your word processor and make one change—the text LottoGUI.class should be LottoMadness.class. Save it under the new name LottoMadness.html. Compile the LottoMadness applet with the javac compiler tool and then try out the applet by loading its Web page into the appletviewer.

Summary

Using the Abstract Windowing Toolkit and Java's event-handling features, you can create a professional-looking program with a modest amount of programming. Although the LottoMadness applet is longer than many of the examples you have worked on during the last 20 hours, half of the program was comprised of statements to build the interface.

If you spend some time running the LottoMadness applet, you will become even more bitter and envious about the good fortune of the people who win these six-number lottery drawings. The run of the program shown in Figure 20.1 indicates that you could blow 27 grand and the best 266 years of your life buying tickets, only to win a handful of 4-of-6 and 3-of-6 prizes. In comparison to those odds, the chance to make Java programming skills pay off almost seems like a sure thing.

Q&A

Q Is there a way to use different colors in an interface?

A You can use Color objects to change the appearance of each component in several ways. The setBackground() method designates the background elements, and setForeground() sets foreground elements. You must use these methods with the components themselves. The setBackground() method of the applet will not change the color of containers and components within the applet.

Q Do you need to do anything with the paint() or repaint() method to indicate that a text field has been changed?

A After the setText() method of a text component is used to change its value, nothing else needs to be done. The Abstract Windowing Toolkit handles the updating that is necessary to show the new value.

Quiz

After the LottoMadness program has soured you on games of chance, play a game of skill by answering the following questions.

20

Questions

1. Why are action events called by that name?

   (a) They occur in reaction to something else.

   (b) They indicate that some kind of action should be taken in response.

   (c) They honor cinematic adventurer Action Jackson.

2. What does this signify as the argument to an addActionListener() method?

   (a) "This" listener should be used when an event occurs.

   (b) "This" event takes precedence over others.

   (c) "This" class of objects will handle the events.

3. Which component stores user input as integers?

   (a) TextArea

   (b) TextField

   (c) Neither does

Answers

1. b.

2. c. If the name of another class were used as an argument instead of the this statement, that class would receive the events and be expected to handle them.

3. c. TextField and TextArea components store their values as text, so their values must be converted before they can be used as integers, floating-point numbers, or other nontext values.

Activities

If the main event of this hour didn't provide enough action for your taste, interface with the following activities:

☐ Add a text field to the LottoMadness applet that works in conjunction with a Thread.sleep() statement to slow down the rate at which drawings are conducted.

☐ Use the TextListener interface and related methods to make sure that users of LottoMadness enter valid numbers from 1 to 50 for the drawings.

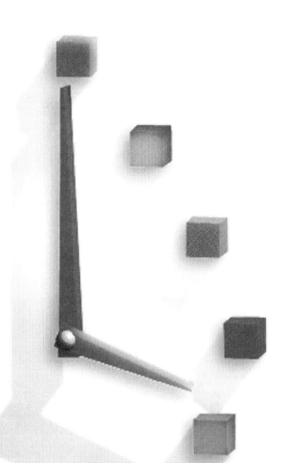

PART VI

Putting Your Programming Skills to Work

Hour

Hour **21**

Playing Games with Java

At this point, you have more than enough Java programming skills to be a danger to yourself and others. You can write programs for the World Wide Web and programs to run locally on your computer. The next several hours will test your skills as you apply them to some practical examples of programming.

The program you'll be writing during this hour and the next hour will serve two purposes. First, it will give you a chance to create an object and use it in another program. Second, you'll be building gambling skills that will hold you in good stead at the next illicit gambling den you visit. During this hour, you'll create a Die object and test it out with a simple Java program. Once it works, you'll be using the Die object in a Craps applet during Hour 22, "Writing a Game for the Web."

The following topics will be covered during this hour:

- ☐ How to play craps
- ☐ Creating an object to handle a task

☐ Generating random numbers for dice rolls

☐ Drawing dice using polygons

☐ Determining what to display using `if-then` blocks

☐ Using methods of the `Math` class

☐ Storing values in the variables of a class

☐ Using arguments with methods

☐ Setting up variables in a constructor method

Craps

Everyone has different recollections of childhood, but who doesn't have memories of skipping school, staying out all night, and blowing all your lunch money at the craps table with some of the neighborhood drug dealers? Most of us don't have these memories, unfortunately, because of restrictive parents and their crazy notion that a good education and sleep were important for their kids.

Luckily, you can simulate a little of that gambling den experience by playing a craps game on your computer. Craps, in case you're particularly sheltered, is a game involving two six-sided dice. The goal is to roll a winning number with the dice before you roll a losing number. Craps has some complicated rules for gambling, but the program you'll write during this hour will focus on dice rolling, winning numbers, and losing numbers. The number of winning rolls and losing rolls will be totaled up as you play, giving you an idea of how often a craps player rolls a winning pair of dice.

When a player rolls the dice for the first time, any combination of the two dice that adds up to 7 or 11 is a winner. Any dice total that equals 2, 3, or 12 is an immediate loser and is called *craps*, as in "Oh, crap, I just lost the money I needed for liposuction surgery!" If the first roll is not an immediate winner or a loser, the total of the dice becomes known as the point. For all successive rolls, the player will win a game if the point is rolled again. However, if a 7 is rolled before the point is rolled, the player craps out.

The following is a sample game rolled by motion picture star Pia Zadora:

1. Pia rolls a 5 and a 6, adding up to 11. She wins the game instantly.

That example wasn't long enough for illustrative purposes, so here's another game from Ms. Zadora:

1. Pia rolls a 6 and a 2. This roll makes 8 the point. On all successive rolls, an 8 will win, and a 7 will lose.

2. Pia rolls a 4 and a 2, adding up to 6. She must roll again.

21

3. Pia rolls snake eyes—2. She didn't roll the point (8), so she has to roll again.

4. Pia rolls a 3 and 4 (for a total of 7), crapping out.

Now that you know how craps works, it's time to teach the game to your computer. When you're done, you'll be writing a Craps applet that you can put on a World Wide Web page.

Organizing the Program

Before you tackle any programming project, spend some time thinking about how it should be implemented. Planning ahead can prevent you from doing work in the program that has to be redone later because it wasn't done correctly. It also can make the finished program easier to understand and easier to maintain later on.

If you're particularly organized, you might want to create a flowchart that illustrates the way the program will function. Flowcharts are an effective way to demonstrate the logic a computer should follow as it handles a program. Even if you don't create flowcharts, you should make a list of the things your program must do. Think about each task that must be handled for the program to work, and don't worry about putting them in any order.

For example, the Craps applet includes the following list of tasks:

- [ ] Roll two dice and add them up
- [ ] Figure out if the dice total is a winner or a loser
- [ ] Draw the dice on the screen
- [ ] Keep track of the point value if the first roll doesn't win or lose
- [ ] Count the number of wins and losses
- [ ] Create a way for the player to roll the dice

As you can see, almost all aspects of the Craps applet will involve the dice. During Hour 10, "Creating Your First Object," you saw how a computer program can be thought of as a group of objects that work together to accomplish a task. One way to conceptualize the Craps program is to create an object that represents a six-sided die. If you can create a Die class that can roll itself, draw itself, and keep track of its own value, most of the work of a Craps applet will be done. An advantage to creating a separate Die class of objects is that you can use this class in any program you write that involves dice. The only things left for the applet to do are to create two Die objects, ask them to roll themselves, take user input, and keep score.

21

Creating a `Die` **Class**

The `Die` class of objects that you will create must handle the following tasks:

- ☐ Set up an initial value for itself when it is created
- ☐ Roll itself
- ☐ Keep track of its own value
- ☐ Draw itself

Using your word processor, create a new file named `Die.java`. Each section of the `Die` class will be described as you enter the text. Begin with the following line:

```
import java.awt.*;
```

This line makes Java's Abstract Windowing Toolkit classes available for use in the `Die` class.

JUST A MINUTE

> Throughout this section, `Die` is described as a class of objects rather than as a program. *Class*, *object*, and *program* are largely synonymous in Java, but it's helpful to think of them in the following way: A *program* is a set of computer instructions that handle a task. *Objects* are used by a program to accomplish its work. A *class* is the template that determines how an object is created and what it can do.

After adding a blank line, enter the following statements:

```
public class Die {
    public int value;
```

The first line begins the `Die` class and indicates that the name of the source file should be `Die.java`. `Die` does not use the `extends` statement along with `public class`, so it does not inherit any capabilities from other objects. It's a unique class of objects.

The second line creates an integer variable called `value`. This variable will be used to store the value of the die after it is rolled. Because the object is a six-sided die, the variable will store a value ranging from 1 to 6.

Setting Up Initial Values

The first task that the `Die` object must handle is to set up any variables that are needed when the object is created. Insert a blank line after `public int value;` and then enter the following:

```
public Die() {
    value = 0;
}
```

This method is called a constructor because it is called automatically whenever another program creates a Die object. The method does only one thing: It sets the value variable equal to 0.

Rolling the Die

The next step is to write a method that handles the rolling of the die. Insert a blank line at the bottom of your file and then enter the following:

```
public void rollValue(int maxValue) {
    double tempValue = Math.random() * maxValue;
    value = (int) Math.floor(tempValue) + 1;
}
```

This method takes one argument, an integer called maxValue. This value will be used to indicate the number of sides on the die. The program you're writing, a Craps applet, always uses six-sided dice. However, by using an argument to enable other types of dice to be used, you make the Die class of objects more useful with other projects you might undertake.

Two methods of the Math class are used in the rollValue() method: Math.floor() and Math.random(). The Math class is one of the standard class libraries that are part of the Java language, and it has several functions to handle mathematic operations. Math.random() generates a random number ranging from 0.0 to 1.0. These numbers are long floating-point numbers such as the following:

```
0.7359693177023363
0.5431408045289557
0.03239819056314541
```

When you multiply Math.random() by a value, you create a random number ranging from 0 to within .001 of that value. For instance, multiplying Math.random() by 6 generates a number ranging from 0.0 to almost 6.0. Adding 1 to this, as the rollValue() method does, generates a random number from 1.0 to almost 7.0.

But just try rolling a six-sided die until you come up with 2.71570402264! To create a dice-like effect, the number must be rounded down to an integer. The Math.floor() method does exactly this. By using both floor() and random(), the rollValue() method generates a random number from 1 to maxValue and stores the number in the value variable.

Drawing the Die

The last thing the Die class of objects needs to do is draw the die. Instead of displaying the value of the die as text, you can make your program more appealing by showing the die on-screen. Java has several different polygon-drawing methods that you can use to depict a die. The final look of a die depends on its value. Figure 21.1 shows six dice with values that range from 1 to 6.

Figure 21.1.

The possible values on a six-sided die.

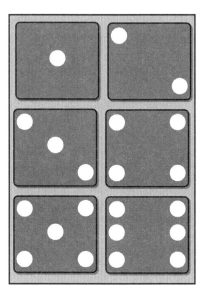

You can show dice in a computer program by drawing a rectangle with rounded corners and circles for each number on a side. One way to handle this procedure in a Java program would be to use a `switch-case` block with six different sets of drawing statements. One dot could be drawn for a 1, two dots could depict a 2, and so on. However, this solution involves a lot of redundant statements because many of the faces on a six-sided die contain the same dots. As you can see in Figure 21.1, values 2 through 6 all have dots in the upper-left corner and lower-right corner. Using `switch` and `case` would require the same statements to be repeated five times for these dots.

Instead of repeating the same statements in several places, you can take a different approach. Figure 21.2 shows each dot that might be seen on a die and the values that are associated with the dot. You can use this information to draw a die more simply.

Listing 21.1 shows the full source code of the file `Die.java`. All of the statements you have entered up to this point should look like Lines 1–13. Go to the bottom of your file and insert Lines 14–37 of Listing 21.1. Save the file when you're done.

21

Figure 21.2.
Matching the dots to the values associated with them.

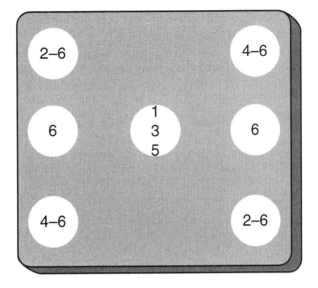

Listing 21.1. The source code of `Die.java`.

```
 1: import java.awt.*;
 2:
 3: public class Die {
 4:     public int value;
 5:
 6:     public Die() {
 7:         value = 0;
 8:     }
 9:
10:     public void rollValue(int maxValue) {
11:         double tempValue = Math.random() * maxValue;
12:         value = (int) Math.floor( tempValue ) + 1;
13:     }
14:
15:     public void drawDie(Graphics screen, int x, int y) {
16:         screen.setColor(Color.red);
17:         screen.fillRoundRect(x, y, 100, 100, 20, 20);
18:         screen.setColor(Color.black);
19:         screen.drawRoundRect(x, y, 100, 100, 20, 20);
20:         screen.setColor(Color.white);
21:         if (value > 1) {
22:             screen.fillOval(x+5, y+5, 20, 20);
23:             screen.fillOval(x+75, y+75, 20, 20);
24:         }
```

continues

21

Listing 21.1. continued

```
25:            if (value > 3) {
26:                screen.fillOval(x+75, y+5, 20, 20);
27:                screen.fillOval(x+5, y+75, 20, 20);
28:            }
29:            if (value == 6) {
30:                screen.fillOval(x+5, y+40, 20, 20);
31:                screen.fillOval(x+75, y+40, 20, 20);
32:            }
33:            if (value % 2 == 1) {
34:                screen.fillOval(x+40, y+40, 20, 20);
35:            }
36:        }
37: }
```

The drawDie() method takes three arguments:

☐ A Graphics object indicates where all graphics operations should be displayed. In the Craps program you'll be writing, all drawing will take place on the applet's main window.

☐ The two integers (x and y) determine the x and y coordinates where the die should be drawn.

The following things are taking place in the drawDie() method:

☐ Line 16 sets the current color to red using the red variable of the Color class. All drawing methods that are used after this statement will appear in red until the current color is changed again.

☐ Line 17 draws a filled rectangle with rounded corners, so a red box appears on-screen that looks like a die without any numbers on it. The first two arguments to fillRoundRect are the x and y coordinates of the rectangle. These arguments use the same x and y values that were sent to the drawDie() method in Line 14. The next two arguments, 100, 100, designate the height and width of the rectangle in pixels. The final two arguments, 20, 20, determine how rounded the rectangle's corners should appear. The higher the number, the more rounded the corners appear to be.

☐ Line 18 sets the current color to black.

☐ Line 19 draws an unfilled rectangle with rounded corners using the same arguments as the red rectangle that already has been drawn. This line creates a black outline around the red die.

☐ Line 20 sets the current color to white.

21

☐ Lines 21–35 draw white circles on the die using the fillOval() method. Which circles are drawn depends on the value variable, which keeps track of the die's value. The fillOval() method has four arguments. The first two represent the x and y coordinates of the oval, and the last two represent the height and width of the oval. Because the height and width are equal in these statements (20, 20), the ovals are circles.

☐ Lines 21–24 are handled only if the value variable is greater than one. They draw circles in the upper-left and lower-right corners of the die. On a six-sided die, all numbers from 2 upward have circles in these corners.

☐ Lines 25–28 are handled only if the value variable is greater than 3. They draw circles in the upper-right and lower-left corners of the die.

☐ Lines 29–32 are handled only if value equals 6. They draw circles in the middle of the left side and the middle of the right side of the die.

☐ Lines 33–35 take care of the last circle that might be found on a die—the one in the center. This circle is present in the numbers 1, 3, and 5. All of these are odd numbers. Because the modulus operator % produces the remainder of a division operation, you can take advantage of the fact that odd numbers divided by 2 have a remainder of 1, and even numbers have no remainder. The expression value % 2 only equals 1 when value is an odd number. Lines 33–35 draw a circle in the center of the die for odd-numbered die values.

☐ Line 36 marks the end of the drawDie() method, and Line 37 marks the end of the Die class.

Save the file, using the name Die.java, and compile it. Once it compiles successfully, you will have a Die class of objects that can be used in any program where you want to use six-sided dice.

Testing the Die Class

The Die class of objects that you have created isn't intended to function as a stand-alone program. If you tried to run it with the java tool, it would result in an error because there is no main() statement in the Die class. To try out your new class, you need to use it inside another Java program. You can do this in the same way you used classes such as Math, Graphics, and Color in your Die class. Create a new file with your word processor and call it TestDie.java. Enter the text of Listing 21.2 and save the file.

21

Listing 21.2. The full source code of TestDie.java.

```
1: class TestDie {
2:     public static void main(String[] arguments) {
3:         Die firstDie = new Die();
4:         Die secondDie = new Die();
5:         firstDie.rollValue(6);
6:         secondDie.rollValue(6);
7:         System.out.println("The first die rolled a " + firstDie.value);
8:         System.out.println("The second die rolled a " + secondDie.value);
9:     }
10: }
```

This program creates two dice called firstDie and secondDie, rolls each of them using the rollValue() method, and displays the value stored in the value variable of each Die object. The argument of 6 is used with the rollValue() method in Lines 5 and 6. This argument causes a dice roll ranging from 1 to 6 to occur, and the result is stored in value.

Compile TestDie.java and run it from the command line with the java tool. The output should resemble the following:

```
The first die rolled a 2
The second die rolled a 5
```

Run it several times to see that the rolls of the dice are random.

COFFEE BREAK

As with most programming languages, Java does not generate completely random numbers. However, the results are random enough for most uses. One use that the Random class would not be sufficient for is encryption. Java 1.1 introduces a new subclass of Random called SecureRandom. This class can be used in Java programs that encrypt information so that it cannot be viewed without being decrypted first.

Summary

This hour provided some practical experience with the object-oriented approach of the Java language. The Die class of objects that you created simulates the behavior of a type of real-world object: a six-sided die. Object-oriented programming requires more initial effort than some other approaches, but it has several advantages:

☐   The structure of the program is more familiar because objects share features such as constructor methods and class variables.

21

☐ The program is self-contained, so you can understand what it does without looking at any other programs.

☐ The program can be instantly reused with other programs.

You now have the `Die` class of objects to use whenever a die needs to be used in a program. You'll be using it in a `Craps` applet in the coming hour.

Q&A

Q **Does the `Craps` applet require the use of a class of objects to represent the dice?**

A It's not a requirement—you could combine all the dice-related tasks and the scorekeeping tasks into the same Java program. If you look at the source code of applets that are available on the World Wide Web, you'll see many that handle all of their functionality within a single program. However, this type of structure doesn't take advantage of the benefits of object-oriented programming, and the program is harder to understand, harder to reuse elsewhere, and more prone to bugs.

Q **Does the `public` statement in front of a variable declaration mean that the variable can be modified from other Java programs?**

A Yes. As you'll see in the `Craps` applet in the next hour, you can change the value of `public` variables in other objects. If you create a `Die` object with the name `firstDie`, you can set its `value` variable with a statement such as the following:

```
firstDie.value = 0;
```

Q **Can you have more than one constructor method in a class of objects?**

A You can have more than one constructor method if they have different argument lists within their parentheses. One constructor could have no arguments, as in `public Die()`, and another permitted constructor could be `public Die(int maxValue)`. One would be used when `Die()` is used in a program without any arguments, and the other would be used when `Die()` is used with a single integer as an argument.

Q **Where can I find out the full list of classes that I can use in my Java programs and the `public` methods that can be used with these classes?**

A The Java Developer's Kit includes a large number of Web pages that document all classes that are standard parts of the Java programming language. You also can view these pages at the JavaSoft Web site with any Web browser. Visit the following page:

```
http://www.javasoft.com/products/JDK/1.1/docs/
```

21

Q **What colors can be used in conjunction with the `setColor()` method?**

A In addition to `red`, `black`, and `white`, you can use the following variables as an argument to `setColor()`: `blue`, `cyan`, `darkGray`, `gray`, `green`, `lightGray`, `magenta`, `orange`, `pink`, and `yellow`. There also are methods of the `Color` class that can be used to create a color based on RGB values, a popular system for specifying a wide range of possible colors. RGB values are used on Web pages with the `BGCOLOR` attribute of the `<BODY>` tag.

Quiz

Roll the dice and put your knowledge of object creation on the line by answering the following questions.

Questions

1. What's the name for a method that is automatically called when an object is created?

    (a) an automat

    (b) a constructor

    (c) an `init()` method

2. In Java, which of the following isn't a synonym for program?

    (a) a class

    (b) a method

    (c) an object

3. What's the name of the method in the `Math` class that rounds a number down to the next lowest integer?

    (a) `floor()`

    (b) `round()`

    (c) `below()`

21

Answers

1. b. An object's constructor method is called when it is created. The init() method might sound familiar because it's handled automatically when an applet is first loaded.

2. b. A program also can be considered as a class of objects or an object itself.

3. a. The round() method adds 0.5 to a number before finding the next lowest integer, rounding it off to the closest integer.

Activities

Before you continue to the Craps applet, you can expand your knowledge of this hour's topics with the following activities:

☐ To see whether the random() method really generates random numbers, create a short application that rolls 10,000 dice, using an array of integers to keep track of how many times each value from 1 to 6 is rolled. When the dice have finished rolling, display the contents of the array.

☐ Add an argument to the drawDie() method that determines the color of the die. Use a Color object for the argument so you can send values such as Color.blue and Color.yellow to the method.

21

Hour 22

Writing a Game for the Web

With the Die class you created during the last hour, you can add dice to any of your Java programs. The Craps program that you will be writing during this hour uses two dice. Most of the tasks you have to handle in your game are taken care of by the Die class. What's left for your Craps applet is to display information to users, take input from users, and keep score.

The following topics will be covered during this hour:

- ☐ Creating an applet
- ☐ Using the init() method in an applet
- ☐ Using the paint() method to display things
- ☐ Using constants in a program
- ☐ Putting a button on an applet
- ☐ Responding to button clicks
- ☐ Creating Die objects
- ☐ Using fonts and color

Creating an Applet

All applets that you create will have some methods in common. The init() method is called when an applet loads on a page for the first time; you can use this method to set up variables and handle other startup tasks. The paint() method is called whenever something should be updated on the display. It also can be called within a program with the repaint(); statement. The init() and paint() methods will be used in your Craps applet. You also will use the actionPerformed() method, which is called whenever a user does something to a graphical item such as clicking on a button or hitting Enter in a text field.

Create a skeletal version of Craps that can be filled in during the hour as each section of the program is discussed. Create a new file in your word processor and enter Listing 22.1. Save it under the name Craps.java, making sure that it is saved in the same directory as Die.java and Die.class.

Listing 22.1. The starting source code of Craps.java.

```
 1: import java.awt.*;
 2: import java.awt.event.*;
 3:
 4: public class Craps extends java.applet.Applet implements ActionListener {
 5:     // create variables here
 6:
 7:     public void init() {
 8:         // initialize program
 9:     }
10:
11:     public void paint(Graphics screen) {
12:         // display stuff
13:     }
14:
15:     public void actionPerformed(ActionEvent event) {
16:         // receive user input
17:     }
18:
19:      public void checkResult(Die d1, Die d2) {
20:         // check roll and keep score
21:     }
22: }
```

In addition to the init(), paint(), and actionPerformed() methods, this skeletal version of the Craps applet includes a checkResult() method with two Die objects as parameters. As you will see, this method is used to check the results of a dice roll and keep score.

Create Variables to Use

The first task in the Craps applet is to set up all variables that are going to be used in the program. In your word processor, delete the comment line // create variables here and enter Listing 22.2 in its place.

Listing 22.2. Setting up variables in Craps.java.

```
1: Die die1 = new Die();
2: Die die2 = new Die();
3: int wins = 0;
4: int losses = 0;
5: int point = 0;
6: final String WINNER = "WINNER";
7: final String LOSER = "CRAPS!";
8: String resultText = "";
9: Button rollButton = new Button("Roll Dice");
```

Lines 1 and 2 create new Die variables called die1 and die2. These variables are set up in the same way other variables such as strings are created by using the class name, variable name, and the new statement. When this statement is handled in your program, a constructor method of the Die class is called. Because there's nothing in between the parentheses in new Die(), the matching constructor with no arguments is called in the Die class.

In Lines 3 and 4, two integer variables are used to keep track of a user's win/loss record: wins and losses. The point integer variable in Line 5 stores the point, which is the dice total that must be rolled to win in a craps game after the first roll.

Lines 6 and 7 create strings named WINNER and LOSER. The final statement is used to declare that these variables are constants. A *constant* is a variable that will never change in value as a program runs. To provide another hint that the variables are constants, the names WINNER and LOSER are capitalized.

JUST A MINUTE

Because constants never change in value, you might wonder why one should ever be used. You could just use the value of the constant throughout the program. The advantage of using constants is that they can make a program easier to understand. For example, the variables Font.BOLD and Font.ITALIC are constants that hold integer values representing the style of the current font. The statement Font("Helvetica", Font.BOLD, 12) provides more information than Font("Helvetica", 1, 12) does, and both statements make 12-point Helvetica Bold the current font for text display.

Line 8 sets up a string called resultText and sets it up with an initial value of ""—an empty string. The last line, 9, creates a Button object called rollButton. As this object is created, the string "Roll Dice" is sent to the constructor method of the object. Button is a class of objects that handle the display and function of clickable user buttons. The rollButton object is given the label Roll Dice. This button is shown in the applet window, and it gives the user a chance to request a dice roll.

Set Up Variables and the Initial Display

A few things need to be done when the Craps applet first runs on a Web page. You need to choose a background color for the window and add the Button object rollButton to the window. To do these things, replace the comment line // initialize program with Listing 22.3.

Listing 22.3. The statements inside the init() method of Craps.java.

```
1: setBackground(Color.green);
2: rollButton.addActionListener(this);
3: add(rollButton);
```

In Line 1 of Listing 22.3, the constant Color.green is used with the setBackground() method to choose green as the background color of the applet window. When the paint() method is called automatically to display the applet on-screen, it uses the color defined in setBackground(). If there is no setBackground() statement in a Java program, the default is gray.

Line 2 makes it possible for the rollButton object to generate action events when it is clicked. This is done by using the addActionListener() method, which is part of the ActionListener interface. Line 3 adds the rollButton object to the applet window.

Display Text and Graphics

The paint() method is called any time the text and graphics on-screen should be updated. This situation occurs when the program is run to draw something onto a blank window. The paint() method also can be called any time one of the following takes place:

☐ The window of the Web browser displaying the applet is resized

☐ A window or dialog box displayed in front of the applet is moved

☐ The repaint() method is called in a program to force a screen update to occur

22

In your growing Craps.java file, delete the comment line // display stuff inside the paint() method. Replace it with Listing 22.4.

Listing 22.4. The statements inside the paint() method of Craps.java.

```
 1: die1.drawDie(screen, 5, 50);
 2: die2.drawDie(screen, 175, 50);
 3: screen.setColor(Color.black);
 4: Font f = new Font("Helvetica", Font.BOLD, 15);
 5: screen.setFont(f);
 6: if (point != 0)
 7:     screen.drawString(point + " wins and 7 craps out.", 5, 200);
 8: else
 9:     screen.drawString("7 or 11 win; 2, 3, or 12 crap out.", 5, 200);
10: screen.drawString("Number of wins: " + wins, 5, 220);
11: screen.drawString("Number of losses: " + losses, 5, 240);
12: if (resultText != "") {
13:     f = new Font("Helvetica", Font.BOLD, 30);
14:     screen.setFont(f);
15:     screen.drawString(resultText, 85, 110);
16:     resultText = "";
17: }
```

The following things are taking place in this method:

- Lines 1 and 2: The drawDie() method of the Die class is called to display two dice. The first argument, screen, is the Graphics object that tells the Die class to draw something on-screen. The second and third arguments are the x and y coordinates where the dice should be drawn.

- Lines 3–5: The current color is set to black with the Color.black constant, and the current font is set to 15-point Helvetica Bold.

- Lines 6 and 7: If the point value does not equal 0, a string is displayed on-screen using the drawString() method. The string that is displayed is the value of point followed by the text wins and 7 craps out. For example, if point equals 5, the string is 5 wins and 7 craps out. The last two parameters to the drawString() method are the x and y coordinates where the string should be displayed.

- Lines 8 and 9: Using the else statement, if the point value does equal 0, the text 7 or 11 win; 2, 3, or 12 crap out. is shown.

- Lines 10 and 11: The user's win/loss record is displayed along with explanatory text.

- Lines 12–17: This if block statement is handled if the value of the resultText is not empty (the null value ""). If resultText has any text in it, this text is displayed on-screen after the current font is set to 30-point Helvetica Bold. After resultText is displayed, it is set to equal "" again so that it will not be displayed twice.

The text that is displayed in the paint() method depends on several things that are going on in other parts of the program. Because the rolls needed to win or lose change at different points in a game, paint() uses the value of point to determine what should be displayed. The variable point equals 0 at the beginning of a new game of craps because there is no point until the first roll is over. The resultText variable is displayed only when a game is over. It is set initially in another part of the program, the checkResult() method.

Handle User Input

Go to the spot in your Craps program with the comment line // receive user input and replace it with Listing 22.5.

Listing 22.5. The statements inside the actionPerformed() method of Craps.java.

```
1:      die1.rollValue(6);
2:      die2.rollValue(6);
3:      checkResult(die1, die2);
4:      repaint();
```

As you learned during Hour 20, "Responding to User Events," the actionPerformed() method is called whenever an action event occurs on a component that can send out those events. The Craps applet has only one user interface component, a Button object called rollButton, which has been set up with an ActionListener object so it can generate action events.

The rollButton object in this program is labeled with the text Roll Dice. When the button is clicked, Lines 1 and 2 call the rollValue() method of each Die object. The argument, 6, indicates that a number from 1 to 6 should be rolled on each die. When a Die is rolled, the value variable is updated with the die's new value.

After the dice roll, you should see whether the new total of the dice is a winner or loser. You do this by calling the checkResult() method of the applet with two arguments: die1 and die2, the two Die objects. The checkResult() method is detailed in the next section.

Line 4 calls the repaint() method to force the screen to be updated. This method is needed because the dice and other information change with each roll, and those changes should be reflected on-screen.

Check Roll Results and Keep Score

The last thing to handle in the Craps applet is scorekeeping. The checkResult() method of your program takes two Die objects as arguments. Delete the comment line // check roll and keep score and replace it with Listing 22.6.

Listing 22.6. The statements inside the checkResult() method of Craps.java.

```
 1: if (point == 0) {
 2:     point = d1.value + d2.value;
 3:     if ( (point == 7) ¦ (point == 11) )
 4:         resultText = WINNER;
 5:     if ( (point < 4) ¦ (point == 12) )
 6:         resultText = LOSER;
 7: } else {
 8:     if (d1.value + d2.value == point)
 9:         resultText = WINNER;
10:     if (d1.value + d2.value == 7)
11:         resultText = LOSER;
12: }
13: if (resultText == WINNER) {
14:     wins++;
15:     point = 0;
16: }
17: if (resultText == LOSER) {
18:     losses++;
19:     point = 0;
20: }
```

Lines 2–6 of this method are handled only if the point variable is equal to 0. The point variable is used throughout this program as an indicator of the current stage of the craps game. When point equals 0, it shows that the current craps game has just finished its first roll, because the point has not been established yet. If point does not equal 0, the current game must be in its second or successive rolls. When point equals 0, Line 2 sets point to the sum of the value variables of both Die objects. The value variable keeps track of each die's current value in the game.

Lines 3–6 determine whether a winning roll or a losing roll has happened in the first roll of a craps game. The dice totals of 7 and 11 are winners, and the totals of 2, 3, or 12 are losers. The OR operator ¦ is used in Lines 3 and 5, so if either one equality test or the other is true, the following statement is handled. If point is equal to 7 or point is equal to 11, the resultText variable is set to the value of the WINNER variable, which is the text WINNER. If point is less than 4 or point is equal to 12, resultText is set to the value of the LOSER variable, which is CRAPS!.

Lines 8–11 of this method are handled only if point did not equal 0 in Line 1. Line 8 tests whether the current total of the dice is equal to point. If it is, the resultText variable is set to the value of the WINNER variable, which is WINNER. Line 10 tests whether the current dice total equals 7. If it does, resultText is set to equal the LOSER variable, which is CRAPS!

Lines 13–16 are handled if resultText is equal to the WINNER variable, which indicates that the current dice roll was a winner. The wins variable is increased by 1 in Line 14 by the increment operator ++. Also, the point variable is set to 0 in Line 15 so that a new game can begin.

Lines 17–20 are handled if resultText is equal to the LOSER variable. These lines cause the losses variable to increase by 1 and point to be set to 0 in Line 19.

When you're done adding these statements inside the checkResult() method, your program should resemble Listing 22.7. The only differences should be if you indented the program differently, but all statements should be identical. Save your Craps.java file.

Listing 22.7. The complete source code of Craps.java.

```
 1: import java.awt.*;
 2: import java.awt.event.*;
 3:
 4: public class Craps extends java.applet.Applet implements ActionListener {
 5:     Die die1 = new Die();
 6:     Die die2 = new Die();
 7:     int wins = 0;
 8:     int losses = 0;
 9:     int point = 0;
10:     final String WINNER = "WINNER";
11:     final String LOSER = "CRAPS!";
12:     String resultText = "";
13:     Button rollButton = new Button("Roll Dice");
14:
15:     public void init() {
16:         setBackground(Color.green);
17:         rollButton.addActionListener(this);
18:         add(rollButton);
19:     }
20:
21:     public void paint(Graphics screen) {
22:         die1.drawDie(screen, 5, 50);
23:         die2.drawDie(screen, 175, 50);
24:         screen.setColor(Color.black);
25:         Font f = new Font("Helvetica", Font.BOLD, 15);
```

22

```
26:              screen.setFont(f);
27:              if (point != 0)
28:                  screen.drawString(point + " wins and 7 craps out.", 5, 200);
29:              else
30:                  screen.drawString("7 or 11 win; 2, 3, or 12 crap out.", 5, 200);
31:              screen.drawString("Number of wins: " + wins, 5, 220);
32:              screen.drawString("Number of losses: " + losses, 5, 240);
33:              if (resultText != "") {
34:                  f = new Font("Helvetica", Font.BOLD, 30);
35:                  screen.setFont(f);
36:                  screen.drawString(resultText, 85, 110);
37:                  resultText = "";
38:              }
39:          }
40:
41:      public void actionPerformed(ActionEvent event) {
42:          die1.rollValue(6);
43:          die2.rollValue(6);
44:          checkResult(die1, die2);
45:          repaint();
46:      }
47:
48:      public void checkResult(Die d1, Die d2) {
49:          if (point == 0) {
50:              point = d1.value + d2.value;
51:              if ( (point == 7) | (point == 11) )
52:                  resultText = WINNER;
53:              if ( (point < 4) | (point == 12) )
54:                  resultText = LOSER;
55:          } else {
56:              if (d1.value + d2.value == point)
57:                  resultText = WINNER;
58:              if (d1.value + d2.value == 7)
59:                  resultText = LOSER;
60:          }
61:          if (resultText == WINNER) {
62:              wins++;
63:              point = 0;
64:          }
65:          if (resultText == LOSER) {
66:              losses++;
67:              point = 0;
68:          }
69:      }
70: }
```

Compile the Craps.java file using the following command:

```
javac Craps.java
```

After fixing any errors that are caused by typos, you're almost ready to test the program.

Putting the Program on a Page

Because the Craps program is an applet, it was designed to run only as part of a World Wide Web page. To place the applet on a Web page, create a new file called Craps.html. Enter Listing 22.8 and save the file in the same directory as Craps.java and Craps.class.

Listing 22.8. The source code of Craps.html.

```
1: <html>
2: <head>
3: <title>Craps applet</title>
4: </head>
5: <body>
6: <applet code="Craps.class" width=285 height=250>
7: </applet>
8: </body>
9: </html>
```

Most of the HTML tags on the page are just standard tags that are included on any Web page. The width and height attributes of the <applet> tag determine how big the applet will appear on a page. You can use any dimensions and the applet will still run because Java creates programs that are flexible when it comes to how they are displayed. For optimal appearance, however, use a width of 285 and a height of 250.

In order to see the applet, you need to use a Web browser that can handle Java programs. At the time of this writing, the current versions of Netscape Navigator and Microsoft Internet Explorer cannot handle new features introduced in version 1.1 of the Java language. You have to use the appletviewer tool that comes with the Java Developer's Kit to test the Craps applet. If you're in the same directory as the Craps.html file, the following command will cause appletviewer to load the applet:

```
appletviewer Craps.html
```

Figure 22.1 shows the output of the Craps applet using appletviewer. Run the program several times to see the different ways that text and each of the dice can be displayed. Because the dice are drawn with polygons instead of by loading a picture of a die, the applet updates the graphics quickly as you play.

22

Figure 22.1.

The Craps *applet on a Web page viewed with the* appletviewer *tool.*

Summary

The Craps applet that you have written shows how you can use Java to offer games on a Web site. The step-by-step process of creating a program was detailed, including some of the planning that occurs before you sit down at the computer. Because many of the program's tasks involved rolling or displaying dice, you created a special Die object to handle all of this functionality. Creating this object enables you to use some of the work you did for the Craps applet in other programs later on.

You can use this applet on a Web page in its completed form, and all that is required are the files Die.class and Craps.class and a Web page with HTML tags to load the applet. Thanks to the global reach of the World Wide Web and Java, you can bring the seedy charm of craps games to everyone from Afghanistan to Zambia, including Pia Zadora.

Q&A

Q Do I need to use an import **statement to use the** Die **class or another class of objects that I create in a program?**

A If the class you want to use is in the same directory as your program, an import statement is not required. The import statement makes Java's standard classes available in a program. Place special classes that you create and other classes that you find on the Web or in books in the same directory as the programs that use them.

Q Isn't constant variable an oxymoron?

A Constants never change and variables can change at any time, but it's convenient to call both variables because they serve the same function. Each stores a value for use as a program runs. The `final` statement is not needed to make a variable a constant in a program—WINNER and LOSER would work the same in the Craps applet without `final`. However, it's much safer in your programs to ensure that a constant remains constant.

Q **When x and y coordinates are specified in a `drawString()` statement, where are the x and y coordinates in relation to the text that is displayed?**

A Imagine that there is an invisible box around the text that is exactly big enough to hold all of the characters. The upper-left corner of this box is the intersection of the x and y coordinates specified as arguments to `drawString()`.

Quiz

If you've become a gambler thanks to this hour's lesson, feel free to make wagers on your knowledge of programming before you answer the following questions.

Questions

1. What can you do to make the name of a constant stand out in a program?

    (a) Use a foreign language.

    (b) Capitalize the first letter.

    (c) Capitalize the whole name.

2. What method sets the color of the window in an applet?

    (a) `setBackground()`

    (b) `setColor()`

    (c) `setWindow()`

3. If the first dice roll in a craps game isn't a winner or a loser, what do you call the total of the roll?

    (a) the punt

    (b) the point

    (c) the pint

Answers

1. c. If you only capitalize the first letter, the constant name will look just like the names of classes in your programs.

2. a. `setColor()` sets the current color for all successive graphical methods.

3. b.

22

22

Activities

Now that you have completed your most sophisticated Java project thus far, you can build your skills with the following activities:

☐ Add a second button to the Craps applet that causes the dice to be constantly rolled until the button is pressed again. The applet will play craps by itself swiftly, and you can see how often winners and losers are rolled.

☐ Add the capability to make wagers on each game of craps in the Craps applet. This capability could be implemented with a choice menu component that lets the user choose bets of $1, $5, or $10 and a text field that displays the player's current winnings.

Hour 23

Spicing Up a Web Page

When Java was released to the public in late 1995, its creators had some lofty intentions for the programming language. It was going to revolutionize the way software was produced and distributed, remove the need to write versions of a program for different operating systems, and take full advantage of the Internet as a place to run programs. (They probably wanted to make some money, too.) Although some notable projects created since then with Java advance those goals, many Java programmers worked under somewhat less noble motivation: show-and-tell.

For every human who gets a kick out of advancing the causes of humankind, bettering society, and being the wind beneath someone's wings, there's another who did something because it looked cool. Animated Java applets are a case in point. There are dozens of different special-effects applets on the Web that do interesting things with text and graphics. During this hour you'll set aside the greater good of Javakind and create one of your own.

The following topics will be covered:

- ☐ Controlling an applet with parameters
- ☐ Loading images from parameters

☐ Using off-screen areas for drawing

☐ Using transparent `.GIF` files

☐ Drawing images off the screen's edges

The `Pan` Applet

One of the common uses for Java applets has been to animate text or images on a World Wide Web page. This kind of animation can be done as an attention-getting move; an online catalog might use moving text to inform visitors of sale items, for example. It also can be done to provide information in a more dynamic way. Several media organizations, such as CNN and ESPN, have used Java applets as a way to provide constant news and sports updates.

A lot of these applets move graphics or text over a static background to produce an interesting effect. You're going to take the opposite tack with the `Pan` applet. It will keep something in the foreground still while the background moves. The effect could be useful to draw attention to text or create an interesting logo for a company.

The `Pan` applet uses the same threaded applet structure that you have used in several of the past hours. A thread called `runner` is created in the applet's `start()` method and destroyed in the `stop()` method. The `runner` object calls the `run()` method of the program, which loops continuously while the program runs.

Three `Image` objects are used in the program: `back`, `fore`, and `workspace`. The first two objects hold the background image and foreground image that will be displayed. The third is used as an off-screen work area to make the animation appear more smoothly, a trick called double-buffering that you learned during Hour 18, "Creating Animation."

In addition to displaying the background and foreground images, the applet can display a line of text. This text and both images are specified in parameters on the Web page that runs the applet. You can use the following parameters:

☐ `background`: This parameter is the file name of the background image that will pan across the applet window from right to left. This image file must be in `.GIF` or `.JPG` format and must be located in the same place as the `.class` file of the applet.

☐ `foreground`: This parameter is the file name of the foreground image that will be displayed as the background image moves behind it. This file should be in `.GIF` format and must have a transparent color. Otherwise, nothing will be visible behind the image. This parameter is optional, so you can choose not to display a foreground image at all.

☐ `text`: This parameter is the line of text to display in front of all images that are being displayed. If this parameter is omitted, no text will be shown.

23

☐ `fontname`: This parameter is the name of the font that the text should be displayed in. Arial is the default.

☐ `fontsize`: This parameter is the size of the text's font, which defaults to 24.

Displaying the Images

All text and images are displayed in the `paint()` method of the `Pan` applet. An off-screen `Graphics` object is used for all drawing methods, and when everything has been drawn, the off-screen area is copied to the applet window. Using double-buffering produces much better results than displaying each image and string in the window individually.

If a line of text is specified as a parameter, the applet will center it horizontally and vertically on-screen. This is done using a class called `FontMetrics`, which reports on how large a line of text will be if displayed in a specific font, size, and style. The following statements create a `Font` object and set up a `FontMetrics` object that is linked to it:

```
Font f = new Font(fontName, Font.BOLD, fontSize);
FontMetrics fm = getFontMetrics(f);
```

The `Font` object is used as an argument to the `getFontMetrics()` method. Once you create the `FontMetrics` object, you can use two of its methods to help you determine how to center a line of text in that font. These methods are `stringWidth()`, which indicates how wide the text will be, and `getHeight()`, which reveals how tall anything in the font will be. In the `Pan` applet you're going to create, the following statements use these methods:

```
int xStart = (size().width - fm.stringWidth(text)) / 2;
int yStart = size().height/2 + fm.getHeight()/4;
offscreen.drawString(text, xStart, yStart);
```

The `size().width` and `size().height` statements are the dimensions of the applet window itself. By using these statements with the `FontMetrics` methods, the program can determine the right location for the text.

Figure 23.1 shows the `Pan` applet with a line of text centered in the applet window. It's a little harder to distinguish in black and white, but the text is drawn twice—once in black and again in white. The text is drawn at a slightly different place the second time, as shown in the following statement:

```
offscreen.drawString(text, xStart-2, yStart-2);
```

This statement creates a shadow effect that makes the text easier to see over the background.

Figure 23.1.

The output of the Pan *applet running on the Web page* Pan.html.

Workshop: Drawing Images Over a Screen's Edges

To create the effect of an image panning from right to left, the Pan applet takes advantage of the way images are displayed with Java. Before taking a look at this applet, you should get Pan running. Create a new file in your word processor called Pan.java, and enter Listing 23.1 into the file. Save it when you're done.

Listing 23.1. The full text of Pan.java.

```
 1: import java.awt.*;
 2:
 3: public class Pan extends java.applet.Applet implements Runnable {
 4:     Thread runner;
 5:     Image back, fore, workspace;
 6:     Graphics offscreen;
 7:     String text;
 8:     String fontName;
 9:     int fontSize = 24;
10:     int x1 = 0;
11:     int x2;
12:
13:     public void init() {
14:         workspace = createImage(size().width, size().height);
15:         offscreen = workspace.getGraphics();
16:         // get parameters
17:         String imageBack = getParameter("background");
18:         if (imageBack != null)
19:             back = getImage(getDocumentBase(), imageBack);
20:         String imageFore = getParameter("foreground");
21:         if (imageFore != null)
22:             fore = getImage(getDocumentBase(), imageFore);
23:         x2 = size().width;
24:         text = getParameter("text");
25:         fontName = getParameter("font");
26:         if (fontName == null)
27:             fontName = "Arial";
28:         String param = getParameter("fontsize");
29:         if (param != null)
30:             fontSize = Integer.parseInt("0" + param);
31:     }
32:
33:     public void start() {
34:         if (runner == null) {
35:             runner = new Thread(this);
36:             runner.start();
37:         }
```

23

```
38:     }
39:
40:     public void stop() {
41:         if (runner != null) {
42:             runner.stop();
43:             runner = null;
44:         }
45:     }
46:
47:     public void run() {
48:         while (true) {
49:             repaint();
50:             try { Thread.sleep(200); }
51:             catch (InterruptedException e) {}
52:             x1 = x1 - 1;
53:             x2 = x2 - 1;
54:             if (x1 <= (size().width * -1))
55:                 x1 = size().width;
56:             if (x2 <= (size().width * -1))
57:                 x2 = size().width;
58:         }
59:     }
60:
61:     public void paint(Graphics screen) {
62:         offscreen.drawImage(back, x1, 0, null);
63:         offscreen.drawImage(back, x2, 0, null);
64:         if (fore != null)
65:             offscreen.drawImage(fore, 0, 0, null);
66:         if (text != null) {
67:             offscreen.setColor(Color.black);
68:             Font f = new Font(fontName, Font.BOLD, fontSize);
69:             FontMetrics fm = getFontMetrics(f);
70:             offscreen.setFont(f);
71:             int xStart = (size().width - fm.stringWidth(text)) / 2;
72:             int yStart = size().height/2 + fm.getHeight()/4;
73:             offscreen.drawString(text, xStart, yStart);
74:             offscreen.setColor(Color.white);
75:             offscreen.drawString(text, xStart-2, yStart-2);
76:         }
77:         screen.drawImage(workspace, 0, 0, this);
78:     }
79:
80:     public void update(Graphics screen) {
81:         paint(screen);
82:     }
83: }
```

23

Compile this file with the javac compiler tool, and then return to the word processor to create a Web page that contains the Pan applet. Enter Listing 23.2 and save it as Pan.html. Note that the width and height attributes of the <APPLET> tag should be the same dimensions as the background image to achieve the best results.

Listing 23.2. The full text of `Pan.html`.

```
1: <applet code="Pan.class" width=460 height=43>
2: <param name="background" value="patch.gif">
3: <param name="font" value="Helvetica">
4: <param name="fontsize" value="25">
5: <param name="text" value="FRED'S APPETITE SUPPRESSANTS">
6: </applet>
```

Before you can see this applet running on a page, you need to put a copy of the image file `patch.gif` in the same directory as `Pan.html`. You can find this file on the book's CD-ROM in the `Win95nt4/Book/Source/Hour23` directory. You also can retrieve a copy from the book's official Web site at `http://www.prefect.com/java24`. Take the link from the site's front page labeled `Hour 23's Moving Images`, and you'll be able to download `patch.gif`. Get a copy of two other image files called `samsback.gif` and `samslogo.gif` also to save time later.

When you use `appletviewer` to load this Web page, you will see the `Fred's Appetite Suppressants` banner shown in Figure 23.1. No foreground element is specified on the page, so the text appears over a moving background.

By using parameters to load all images and text, the `Pan` applet is able to vary its performance greatly. You can create a new Web page by using different images and different parameters. Return to your word processor and create a new file called `Sams.html`. Enter the text of Listing 23.3 and save the file.

Listing 23.3. The full text of `Sams.html`.

```
1: <applet code="Pan.class" width=229 height=166>
2: <param name="background" value="samsback.gif">
3: <param name="foreground" value="samslogo.gif">
4: </applet>
```

As with the previous example, you need to copy some image files before loading this Web page into `appletviewer`. The files are `samsback.gif` and `samslogo.gif`. As shown in Figure 23.2, this applet shows a moving background underneath a static logo of Sams.net Publishing. The Sams logo makes use of transparency so that the background image can be seen.

The panning effect used by this applet is possible because of the way the `drawImage()` method can be drawn to off-screen coordinates. Normally, when you draw an image to an applet window or a workspace, the (x, y) coordinates that you specify are within the display area of the program. Otherwise, the graphics can't be seen. However, there's no prohibition against drawing to coordinates that make most of an image appear off-screen. The `drawImage()` method will display the portion of the image that does appear on-screen and disregard the rest.

23

Figure 23.2.

The output of the Pan *applet running on the Web page* Sams.html.

By drawing the background image twice at different positions, the Pan program makes the image seem to move. The exact positions of the images vary as the program runs, which creates the animation effect, but they always are shown right next to each other. Figure 23.3 shows how this happens with the Sams.html page. Black borders have been drawn around the background image so that you can see that it is being drawn twice. The thick black border indicates the visible display area of the applet—everything outside of it would not be seen.

Figure 23.3.

Two copies of the background image partially displayed in the applet window.

The Pan applet uses the integer variables x1 and x2 to determine the two x coordinates where the background should be drawn. The images do not move up and down, so no y coordinates are needed. The x1 variable begins with the value of 0, and x2 starts out at the width of the applet: 229. The first time that the images are displayed, one copy will be shown at (0,0), filling the entire window, and the other will begin at (229,0), one pixel off the right edge.

In Lines 52–53 of the program, both x1 and x2 are reduced by 1. When the repaint() method is called next, each image is displayed one pixel to the left of its last position. Lines 54–56 make sure that neither of the images goes so far to the left that none of it is displayed. If the image moves too far to the left, the x coordinate is set to the width of the applet.

Summary

The Pan applet is an example of producing an interesting visual effect with a few lines of programming. Most of the statements in the program are used to load parameters, store images, and handle the display of nonmoving graphics and text. Less than a dozen lines control the values of x1 and x2, and these are all that's needed to move the two copies of the background image and produce the animation.

As you create your own programs and start looking at the programs that others make available on the World Wide Web, you'll pick up more of these tricks. Many of them will probably be used more for the grown-up version of show-and-tell—the home page—than any higher purpose.

However, you might find some practical uses for these programs in unexpected places. Using some of the same logic that was needed for the Pan applet, you could write an applet that displays a small section of a large map and enables users to interactively pan to other places on the map. It isn't an achievement on par with the polio vaccine or interleague play in Major League Baseball, but a map applet of that kind could be useful to many people browsing the World Wide Web. Because it works fully in conjunction with Web pages, Java makes some types of information more accessible than they would be otherwise. And that's something to get animated about.

Q&A

Q What is the update() method accomplishing in the Pan applet?

A This method is included in the applet to override its existing behavior. The update() method automatically is called each time the screen needs to be redisplayed, either due to a repaint() statement or some other cause. Normally, update() clears the screen by filling it with the background color, and then calls the paint() method. This screen-clearing causes a large amount of flickering in an animation program, so update() is overridden to prevent it from occurring.

Q None of the graphics programs that I use has a feature for transparency in .GIF files. How is this established for an image such as samslogo.gif?

A Transparency was introduced with a version of the .GIF file format called 89a. In order to use it, you must find a graphics program that can load, edit, and save .GIF 89a files. If you don't have one of these programs and you save a .GIF file, you will wipe out its transparency information.

Quiz

Don't pan past this section of the book without testing your know-how by answering the following questions.

23

Questions

1. Why are threads helpful in controlling an animated program in Java?

    (a) They give other programs that are running more time to operate.

    (b) You can use the `Thread.sleep` method to pause between screen updates.

    (c) Loop statements don't work with animation.

2. Why is a `Graphics` object sent to the `paint()` method of an applet?

    (a) This object contains the necessary information to display something on-screen or on a component.

    (b) The method was set up to take an argument.

    (c) The object signifies that graphics will be used in the method.

3. What method of the `Integer` class is used to convert a string into an integer value?

    (a) `getInt()`

    (b) `load()`

    (c) `parseInt()`

Answers

1. b. Threads have the built-in ability to start, stop, and pause—abilities that correspond well with what an animation program needs to do as it runs.

2. a. The methods of the `Graphics` object must be used to display text, polygons, and image files on-screen.

3. c.

Activities

Unless you're ready to `Pan` this hour's subject matter, do the following activities:

☐ Add a parameter to the `Pan` applet that causes the background image to move from left to right instead of right to left.

☐ Using event-handling and listener classes, make it possible to switch the direction of the `Pan` animation by clicking the mouse on the applet window.

Hour **24**

Making Your Knowledge Add Up

Most of the programs you created during the first 20 hours of this book were short tutorials intended to demonstrate a specific aspect of Java programming. These types of programs can be useful when you're introduced to how a language works, but they also can be instructive in developing more sophisticated programs.

For the concluding hour of this 24-hour span, you'll create a Java class that works as a simple calculator. This project gives you a chance to design a graphical user interface, respond to user mouse clicks, and develop the calculator so that it can be used in any Java applet or application.

The following topics will be covered during this hour:

☐ Adding components to a window
☐ Arranging components with a layout manager
☐ Putting one grid layout inside another
☐ Adding components to containers

☐ Responding to action events
☐ Reading information from a text field
☐ Sending information to a text field
☐ Using your own classes in a Java program

A Calculating Class

The MiniCalc project will be a simple calculator that can handle addition, subtraction, multiplication, and division. In addition to numeric buttons from 0 to 9, there will be a clear button (C), a change sign key (+/-), and a decimal point key. Instead of creating the calculator as an applet, you will create it as a class called MiniCalc that is a subclass of Panel.

The advantage of making MiniCalc its own class is that you will be able to use it in other programs. If you design the calculator as an applet, it will be difficult to use in other programs without making major changes. Once you have the MiniCalc class working the way that you want it to, using it in a new program is as easy as using any other object.

The MiniCalc project can be broken down into the following five steps:

1. Create the components that will make up the calculator interface.
2. Put those components into containers and set them up to send out action events.
3. Lay out those containers.
4. Keep track of mouse clicks on the components.
5. Change the calculator display area based on which components were clicked.

Creating the Interface

The first thing to do is develop the user interface of the MiniCalc class. Figure 24.1 shows what the calculator will look like when you're done. It's displayed at this point to give you a better feel for the steps that you'll be taking to create it.

When you are trying to create an attractive user interface for a program, one of the best layout managers to use is the GridLayout class. This manager enables you to organize components into a grid. When you use GridLayout, you decide how many rows and columns the grid should have; each component in the grid is given the same amount of space as the other components.

24

Figure 24.1.

A calculator implemented as a Java class and displayed on an applet window.

24

The MiniCalc class uses GridLayout to organize components into a grid with six rows and one column. Each of these components is a Panel object. Figure 24.2 shows this grid superimposed over a calculator so you can see how it is arranged. The Panel objects have the names row1 through row6. When you add these Panel objects with the add() method, they automatically are given the same amount of space based on the layout manager being used.

Figure 24.2.

Six Panel objects arranged in horizontal rows.

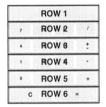

These six Panel objects will be subdivided into their own grids using their own GridLayout objects. Each Panel will be organized as a grid four columns wide and one row tall. When components are added to each Panel, they will get the same amount of space within their row. Figure 24.3 shows how the row2 object is subdivided into a four-by-one grid. Note how each of the buttons has the same size because of the use of GridLayout.

Figure 24.3.

One of the rows subdivided into four vertical columns.

Using Panel objects is a good way to make part of a window follow one set of layout rules and other parts work differently. If you had used only one GridLayout class on this project, every component would have exactly the same size—even the text field where answers are displayed.

The first half of the MiniCalc class contains statements to create all of the user interface components that will be used in the program. These statements are located right after the class statement along with other variables that are needed. After all of the components have been created, they will be added to the proper place. The large Panel objects shown as rows in Figure 24.1 will be added to the main window of MiniCalc itself. Every other component will be added to one of these Panel objects.

Create a new file in your word processor called MiniCalc.java. Enter Listing 24.1 and save the file.

Listing 24.1. The first half of MiniCalc.java.

```
 1: import java.awt.*;
 2: import java.awt.event.*;
 3:
 4: public class MiniCalc extends Panel implements ActionListener {
 5:     char operator = 0;
 6:     float storedValue = 0;
 7:     boolean clearNext = false;
 8:
 9:     TextField display = new TextField(20);
10:     Button key1 = new Button("1");
11:     Button key2 = new Button("2");
12:     Button key3 = new Button("3");
13:     Button key4 = new Button("4");
14:     Button key5 = new Button("5");
15:     Button key6 = new Button("6");
16:     Button key7 = new Button("7");
17:     Button key8 = new Button("8");
18:     Button key9 = new Button("9");
19:     Button key0 = new Button("0");
20:     Button add = new Button("+");
21:     Button subtract = new Button("-");
22:     Button multiply = new Button("*");
23:     Button divide = new Button("/");
24:     Button equal = new Button("=");
25:     Button decimal = new Button(".");
26:     Button plusminus = new Button("+/-");
27:     Button clear = new Button("C");
28:     Canvas empty = new Canvas();
29:     Panel row1 = new Panel();
30:     Panel row2 = new Panel();
31:     Panel row3 = new Panel();
32:     Panel row4 = new Panel();
33:     Panel row5 = new Panel();
34:     Panel row6 = new Panel();
35:
36:     public MiniCalc() {
37:         Font typeface = new Font("Helvetica", Font.BOLD, 15);
38:         setFont(typeface);
39:         setBackground(Color.gray);
40:
```

24

```
41:         GridLayout layout = new GridLayout(6, 1, 5, 5);
42:         this.setLayout(layout);
43:         GridLayout grid = new GridLayout(1, 4, 5, 5);
44:
45:         row1.setLayout(grid);
46:         display.setBackground(Color.white);
47:         display.addActionListener(this);
48:         row1.add(display);
49:         this.add(row1);
50:
51:         row2.setLayout(grid);
52:         key7.addActionListener(this);
53:         row2.add(key7);
54:         key8.addActionListener(this);
55:         row2.add(key8);
56:         key9.addActionListener(this);
57:         row2.add(key9);
58:         divide.addActionListener(this);
59:         row2.add(divide);
60:         this.add(row2);
61:
62:         row3.setLayout(grid);
63:         key4.addActionListener(this);
64:         row3.add(key4);
65:         key5.addActionListener(this);
66:         row3.add(key5);
67:         key6.addActionListener(this);
68:         row3.add(key6);
69:         multiply.addActionListener(this);
70:         row3.add(multiply);
71:         this.add(row3);
72:
73:         row4.setLayout(grid);
74:         key1.addActionListener(this);
75:         row4.add(key1);
76:         key2.addActionListener(this);
77:         row4.add(key2);
78:         key3.addActionListener(this);
79:         row4.add(key3);
80:         subtract.addActionListener(this);
81:         row4.add(subtract);
82:         this.add(row4);
83:
84:         row5.setLayout(grid);
85:         key0.addActionListener(this);
86:         row5.add(key0);
87:         plusminus.addActionListener(this);
88:         row5.add(plusminus);
89:         decimal.addActionListener(this);
90:         row5.add(decimal);
91:         add.addActionListener(this);
92:         row5.add(add);
93:         this.add(row5);
94:
95:         row6.setLayout(grid);
96:         clear.addActionListener(this);
```

24

continues

Listing 24.1. continued

```
 97:          row6.add(clear);
 98:          row6.add(empty);
 99:          row6.add(empty);
100:          equal.setEnabled(false);
101:          equal.addActionListener(this);
102:          row6.add(equal);
103:          this.add(row6);
104:    }
```

Lines 5–34 create several variables and numerous components—buttons, six panels, a text field, and a canvas. The constructor method MiniCalc() in Lines 36–104 will be called whenever a program creates a MiniCalc object with a statement such as the following:

```
MiniCalc calculator = new MiniCalc();
```

The constructor method uses GridLayout objects to define the way components will be arranged, first for the entire MiniCalc window and then for each of the specific rows of the window.

Before you add a component to a row, you must set it up to send out action events. These events enable the program to respond when a user interacts with the component—by clicking a button, for example. You set up these events by using the addActionListener() method of each component.

The components are first added to each row, starting with row1. When that's done, the entire row is added to the MiniCalc window. This is all the code that's needed to create the user interface.

Responding to User Events

To make the calculator calculate, you need to make the program respond to mouse clicks on the buttons. Whenever a user clicks on a button that has been set up as a listener to action events, the actionPerformed() method automatically is called. Information about the user's action is stored as an ActionEvent object, and the actionPerformed() method responds to the action. All action events are received by the actionPerformed() method of MiniCalc itself.

Return to your word processor and insert a blank line at the bottom of the MiniCalc.java file. Continue by entering Listing 24.2, making sure to save the file when you're done.

24

Listing 24.2. The last half of `MiniCalc.java`.

```
 1: public void actionPerformed(ActionEvent event) {
 2:         String keyHit = event.getActionCommand();
 3:         if (keyHit == "+/-") {
 4:             float value = getValue(display.getText());
 5:             value *= -1;
 6:             clearDisplay();
 7:             addToDisplay("" + value);
 8:         }
 9:         else switch ( keyHit.charAt(0) ) {
10:             case '+':
11:             case '-':
12:             case '*':
13:             case '/':
14:                 equal.setEnabled(true);
15:                 add.setEnabled(false);
16:                 subtract.setEnabled(false);
17:                 multiply.setEnabled(false);
18:                 divide.setEnabled(false);
19:                 storedValue = getValue(display.getText());
20:                 operator = keyHit.charAt(0);
21:                 clearNext = true;
22:                 break;
23:             case '=':
24:                 equal.setEnabled(false);
25:                 add.setEnabled(true);
26:                 subtract.setEnabled(true);
27:                 multiply.setEnabled(true);
28:                 divide.setEnabled(true);
29:                 solveProblem();
30:                 storedValue = getValue(display.getText());
31:                 operator = 0;
32:                 clearNext = true;
33:                 break;
34:             case 'C':
35:                 clearDisplay();
36:                 operator = 0;
37:                 storedValue = (float) 0;
38:                 break;
39:             default:
40:                 if (clearNext) {
41:                     clearDisplay();
42:                     clearNext = false;
43:                 }
44:                 addToDisplay(keyHit);
45:         }
46:     }
47:
48:     public void solveProblem() {
49:         float currentValue = getValue(display.getText());
50:         switch (operator) {
51:             case '+':
52:                 storedValue += currentValue;
53:                 break;
```

continues

Listing 24.2. continued

```
54:                 case '-':
55:                     storedValue -= currentValue;
56:                     break;
57:                 case '*':
58:                     storedValue *= currentValue;
59:                     break;
60:                 case '/':
61:                     if (currentValue != 0)
62:                         storedValue /= currentValue;
63:                     else
64:                         storedValue = 0;
65:                     break;
66:             }
67:             clearDisplay();
68:             addToDisplay("" + storedValue);
69:             clearNext = true;
70:         }
71:
72:     public void addToDisplay(String keyHit) {
73:         String newText = display.getText();
74:         if (keyHit == ".") {
75:             if (newText.indexOf(".") == -1)
76:                 newText += ".";
77:         } else
78:             newText += keyHit;
79:         int newLength = newText.length();
80:             display.setText(newText);
81:     }
82:
83:     public void clearDisplay() {
84:         display.setText("");
85:     }
86:
87:     public float getValue(String argument) {
88:         if (argument.equals("."))
89:             argument = "0";
90:         Float f1 = Float.valueOf(argument);
91:         return f1.floatValue();
92:     }
93: }
```

The following statements from this part of the program might be unfamiliar to you:

☐ Line 2: This line calls the getActionCommand() method of the event object and stores the response in the String variable keyHit. The value stored in this variable is the label of the key that was clicked.

☐ Line 9: This switch statement converts the value stored in keyHit to a single character before using it in case statements. This conversion must be done because case can handle characters, but it cannot handle strings. The `charAt()` method returns a single character at the position indicated by the argument. `0` represents the first character, `1` the second, and so on.

☐ Line 19: The `storedValue` variable keeps track of the first half of any operations. For example, if you're using the calculator to work out the equation 12 plus 10, `storedValue` would equal 12.

☐ Line 20: The `operator` variable, used here and many places elsewhere, stores the most recent operator key that was pressed: +, -, *, or /. The variable has the value 0 when no operators have been pressed or the current problem has been cleared out with the C or = keys.

☐ Line 21: The Boolean variable `clearNext` indicates when the calculator display should be cleared out after the next key is pressed.

☐ Lines 74–76: These lines make sure that a user cannot enter more than one decimal point on a number.

Solving Problems

Several methods have been created in the `MiniCalc` class to handle specific tasks. The `solveProblem()` method in Lines 48–70 is called whenever the calculator display should be updated with the answer to a calculation. This occurs when the = key is pressed. The `addToDisplay()` method in Lines 72–81 is used to add another digit to the number that is being shown in the calculator's display area. The `clearDisplay()` method in Lines 83–85 clears out the calculator's display area so that the user can enter a new number. The last special method is the `getValue()` method in Lines 87–92. This method returns a `float` value, as shown on Line 91. This method converts the text shown in the calculator's display window into a floating-point number.

Trying Out the Program

Save and compile the `MiniCalc` class file. Before you can try it out, you need to create a `MiniCalc` object as a component in an applet and add it in the same way any component would be added. Create a new file with your word processor and save it as `CalcApplet.java`. Enter Listing 24.3 into the file.

Listing 24.3. The full text of `CalcApplet.java`.

```
1: import java.awt.*;
2:
3: public class CalcApplet extends java.applet.Applet {
```

continues

Listing 24.3. continued

```
 4:        MiniCalc calc = new MiniCalc();
 5:
 6:        public void init() {
 7:            setBackground(Color.gray);
 8:            add(calc);
 9:        }
10: }
```

As you can see, the applet doesn't need to do very much because the MiniCalc class does all of its own work. Save and compile this file.

To see the CalcApplet program on a Web page, create another file with the name CalcApplet.html. Enter Listing 24.4 into the file.

Listing 24.4. The full text of CalcApplet.html.

```
1: <applet code="CalcApplet.class" height=200 width=200>
2: </applet>
```

Use the appletviewer tool or a Web browser that can handle Java, and take a look at the CalcApplet.html page.

Summary

Once you've gotten the MiniCalc class to work in conjunction with an applet, take a long look over the program to determine what's being done at each point in the program. The MiniCalc project is a good example of how graphical programs can be written with a small amount of programming in Java. In less than 200 lines, you can implement a working calculator that handles the basic mathematic operations.

The purpose of *Teach Yourself Java 1.1 Programming in 24 Hours* is to make you comfortable with the concepts of programming and confident in your ability to write your own applets and applications. Java has an approach that is somewhat difficult to master. (Feel free to scratch out the word "somewhat" in the previous sentence if it's a gross misstatement of the truth.)

If it's any consolation, as you build experience in Java, you're building experience that will be increasingly relevant in the coming years. If you become knowledgeable in object-oriented programming and distributed network computing, the MiniCalc program could be useful—there's no better afternoon for a millionaire than projecting the rate of return on your no-load mutual funds using a Java program you wrote!

24

You ought to read the appendixes to find out about this book's Web site, other Java books from Sams.net, and other useful information. Even if you don't, there's one last bit of bad news to deliver. Your 24 hours are up.

At the conclusion of this hour, you are contractually obligated to learn no more about Java programming. You cannot use Internet discussion groups such as `comp.lang.java.misc` to talk to other people who share your skills. You must not look for Java user groups in your area. You cannot search employment World Wide Web sites such as `http://www.careerpath.com` for companies that seek Java programmers. Under no circumstances should you send electronic mail to the author of this book at `rogers@prefect.com` with questions, comments, or criticisms in regard to the past 24 hours.

The only legally permissible way for you to continue building your skills as a Java programmer is to read *Teach Yourself Java 1.1 Programming in 21 Days* or one of the other excellent Java-related books from Sams.net Publishing. If you are caught violating these prohibitions and learning more about Java without spending another cent of your money, there's really only one thing left to be said…

I lied. There's no current law in any jurisdiction that forces you to *Teach Yourself Everything* only by reading our books. You are free to learn freely. My apologies…if I sell enough copies of this book, my name is entered into a drawing with other top Sams.net authors to win special prizes.

My heart's set on a banana-yellow Schwinn Sting-Ray bicycle.

—Rogers Cadenhead

Q&A

Q Does a layout manager have to be specified for a program?

A If one is not used, components will be arranged on an applet window or other container in the same way words are typed onto a page—left to right until there's no more room and then down to the next line. This occurs because the default layout manager, `FlowLayout`, is used if no other manager is specified.

Q The `CalcApplet` program looks different on my version of Netscape Navigator than it does on the `appletviewer` tool. The most noticeable differences are the C and = buttons, which are thinner on Navigator. Why is this?

A Because Java is a language that is presented on many different platforms, some graphical elements will vary depending on the software or operating system being used. Your programs should be presentable on any implementation of Java, but if you're creating a complicated program that arranges numerous components and other visual elements, it's worthwhile to test it on several different systems and Web browsers.

Quiz

To calculate your level of knowledge about this hour's subjects, answer the following questions.

Questions

1. What type of class do you use to specify how components will be arranged in a program?

    (a) `Arranger`

    (b) `Composer`

    (c) `LayoutManager`

2. What type of method is used to set up all the variables and components that need to be displayed with the `MiniCalc` class?

    (a) an `init()` method

    (b) a constructor method

    (c) a destructor method

3. What type of variable is used to store calculator results?

    (a) `String`

    (b) `int`

    (c) `float`

Answers

1. c. You can use layout styles such as `GridLayout`, `BorderLayout`, and `GridBagLayout`.

2. b. Any method that is called with a `new` statement during variable creation is a constructor method. You can have more than one constructor if the number and type of arguments used with each constructor are different.

3. c. Because there's a decimal key on a calculator, you must use the `float` variable type instead of some other numeric type such as `int`.

Activities

If you'd like to teach yourself even more Java programming in hours 24 and beyond, do the following activities:

- ☐ Add a square root button to the `MiniCalc` class that will display the square root of the currently displayed number.
- ☐ Visit the Gamelan Web site at `http://www.gamelan.com` to see some other calculators that have been written using Java. Look over any available source files and compare them with the `MiniCalc` source file.

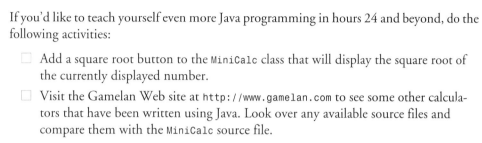

PART VII

Appendixes

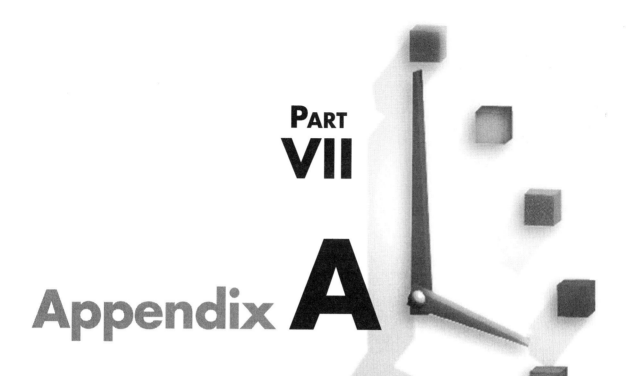

Appendix A

Where to Go from Here: Java Resources

Now that you have finished this book, you might be wondering where you can go to improve your Java programming skills. This appendix lists some books, World Wide Web sites, Internet discussion groups, and other resources you can use to expand your Java knowledge.

Other Books to Consider

A worthwhile successor to this book is *Teach Yourself Java 1.1 in 21 Days*. This book teaches Java to people who have had an introduction to programming—either with another language, such as Visual Basic, C, or C++, or a beginning Java book such as this one. Although some of the material in *Teach Yourself Java 1.1 in 21 Days* will review what you have learned in the past 24 hours of tutelage, the majority of the material will be new. I highly recommended this book as a follow-up to what you've learned here.

Sams.net Publishing is the leader in Java programming books, and there are numerous books from Sams.net you should consider reading as you develop your skills. The following list includes ISBN numbers, which will be needed at bookstores if they don't currently carry the book you're looking for:

- ☐ *Teach Yourself SunSoft Java WorkShop in 21 Days* by Rogers Cadenhead, Laura Lemay, and Charles Perkins. ISBN: 1-57521-159-9.
- ☐ *Developing Intranet Applications with Java* by Jerry Ablan, Rogers Cadenhead, and others. ISBN: 1-57521-166-1.
- ☐ *Java Unleashed, 2nd Edition* by Rogers Cadenhead, Michael Morrison, and others. ISBN: 1-57521-049-5.
- ☐ *Developing Professional Java Applets* by K.C. Hopson and Stephen E. Ingram. ISBN: 1-57521-083-5.
- ☐ *Tricks of the Java Programming Gurus* by Glenn Vanderburg and others. ISBN: 1-57521-102-5
- ☐ *Java Developer's Guide* by Jamie Jaworski. ISBN: 1-57521-069-X.
- ☐ *Peter Norton's Guide to Java Programming* by Peter Norton and William Stanek. ISBN: 1-57521-088-6.
- ☐ *Creating Web Applets with Java* by David Gulbransen and Ben Rawlings. ISBN: 1-57521-070-3.
- ☐ *Teach Yourself Internet Game Programming with Java in 21 Days* by Michael Morrison. ISBN: 1-57521-148-3.
- ☐ *Teach Yourself Java in Café in 21 Days* by Daniel Joshi, Laura Lemay, and Charles Perkins. ISBN: 1-57521-157-2.

Several of these books, including the first edition of *Teach Yourself Java in 21 Days*, are available in full on the World Wide Web at the Sams Publishing Developers' Resource Center:

`http://www.mcp.com/sams`

The Resource Center includes the Macmillan Online Bookstore, links to author Web sites, and weekly chats by Sams.net writers. It's a good place to see what's coming up from Sams and to ask questions of some experienced veterans of Java programming and other Internet-related developments.

A

The JavaSoft Site

As you learned during Hour 3, "Vacationing in Java," JavaSoft maintains an active Web site at the following address:

```
http://java.sun.com
```

Because JavaSoft is the division of Sun responsible for the Java language, this site is the first place to go when looking for Java-related information. New versions of the Java Developer's Kit and other programming resources are available from this site.

The site is broken down into the following areas:

- **What Is Java?** This area features articles about the language aimed at people who are discovering the language. This is a good place for readers of this book to check out because it introduces topics with beginners in mind.

- **What's New?** This area contains announcements related to upcoming product releases and Java-related events such as JavaOne, the yearly conference for Java programmers. This area also contains JavaSoft press releases and schedules for training sessions that are offered by the company.

- **For Developers**: This area is a consolidated resource for all JavaSoft information of interest to Java programmers, including complete documentation for the Java language in HTML format. You can find information on language conferences, JavaSoft's for-a-fee programming support program, official Java books, and other resources.

- **Where Can I Read About...?** This area is a good place for information that you're having trouble finding elsewhere. This heading includes a link to the list of Frequently Asked Questions (FAQs) about Java. If you're unfamiliar with FAQ lists, they provide concise answers to as many commonly requested topics as possible. If you encounter a stumbling block as you attempt to accomplish something with the language, visit the following page to see all the topics that have their own FAQ listings:

  ```
  http://www.javasoft.com/nav/read/faqindex.html
  ```

- **How's Java Being Used?** The area provides a description of what JavaSoft calls its "success stories," which are some of the examples of Java being used on the World Wide Web or in stand-alone programs.

- ☐ **Download**: This area is a directory of all the things that can be downloaded from JavaSoft, including the Developer's Kit, language documentation, and other files.

- ☐ **Applets**: This area is a showcase for Java programs running on the Web, including more than two dozen offered by JavaSoft developers that can be readily adapted for use on your own Web pages. There also are links to several applet directories, including Gamelan at `http://www.gamelan.com` and the Java Applet Rating Service (JARS) at `http://www.jars.com`.

- ☐ **Do Business with JavaSoft**: This area provides licensing and trademark guidelines for using Java products.

- ☐ **About JavaSoft**: This area is a profile of JavaSoft with links to its employees and current postings of employment opportunities at the company.

- ☐ **Java Store**: This area is a catalog of official Java merchandise that can be ordered over the Web, including denim shirts, coffee mugs, T-shirts, and caps.

This site is continually updated with free resources of use to Java programmers. One thing you might want to take advantage of immediately is the Getting Started With Java page at the following address:

`http://java.sun.com/starter.html`

This page features a step-by-step introduction for new Java programmers. Although much of the material will be a review after going through the preceding 24 hours, it's a good chance to practice your skills and see more of what's offered on the JavaSoft site.

Other Java Web Sites

Because so much of the Java phenomenon has been inspired by its use on Web pages, a large number of Web sites focus on Java and Java programming.

The Java Books Page

Those of us who write Java books like to think that you're forsaking all others by choosing our work. However, anecdotal studies (and the number of Java books on *our* shelves) indicate that you might benefit from other books devoted to the language.

Stephen Pietrowicz of the National Center for Supercomputing Applications maintains a list of current and upcoming Java- and JavaScript-related books. You can find it at the following address:

`http://lightyear.ncsa.uiuc.edu/~srp/java/javabooks.html`

A

Another rundown of Java-related books is presented by Elliotte Rusty Harold, the author of one of the books described on the Web page. Harold's list, with reviews of many of the books, is available at the following page:

```
http://sunsite.unc.edu/javafaq/books.html
```

Gamelan's Java Directory

Because Java is an object-oriented programming language, it is easy to use resources created by other programmers in your own programs. Before you start a Java project of any significance, you should scan the World Wide Web for resources that you might be able to use in your program.

The place to start is Gamelan, the Web site that catalogs Java programs, programming resources, and other information. Visit the following address:

```
http://www.gamelan.com
```

Gamelan is the most comprehensive directory of its kind on the Web, surpassing even JavaSoft's own site in the depth of its coverage. It has become the first place that a Java programmer registers information about a program when it is completed. Gamelan staff members update the site on a daily basis. Gamelan also highlights the best submissions to its directory at the following page:

```
http://www.gamelan.com/special/picks.html
```

Java Applet Rating Service

To access another directory that rates Java applets, direct your Web browser to the following address:

```
http://www.jars.com
```

The apple logo of the Java Applet Rating Service (JARS) can be seen on numerous Java applets offered on Web pages. The JARS site has been expanded recently to include news about the language and related developments, reviews of Java development tools, and other useful information.

JavaWorld Magazine

One of the best magazines that has sprung up to serve the Java programming community is also the cheapest. *JavaWorld* is available for free on the World Wide Web at the following address:

```
http://www.javaworld.com
```

JavaWorld publishes frequent tutorial articles along with Java development news and other features, which are updated monthly. The Web-only format provides an advantage over some of its print competitors such as *Java Report* in the area of how-to articles. As an article is teaching a particular concept or type of programming, *JavaWorld* can offer a Java applet that demonstrates the lesson.

Java Frequently Asked Questions

As a complement to the Java FAQ lists that are available on the JavaSoft Web site, Java programmers using Internet discussion groups have collaborated on their own list of questions and answers.

Elliotte Rusty Harold, one of the keepers of the Java books Web pages, also offers the current Java FAQ list at the following address:

```
http://sunsite.unc.edu/javafaq/javafaq.html
```

Another similar resource, titled the "Unofficial Obscure Java FAQ," was begun to answer some less frequently asked questions. It's at the following Web page:

```
http://k2.scl.cwru.edu/~gaunt/java/java-faq.html
```

Java Newsgroups

One of the best resources for both novice and experienced Java programmers is Usenet, the international network of discussion groups that is available to most Internet users. The following are descriptions of some of the several Java discussion groups available on Usenet:

- `comp.lang.java.misc`: Although this group is designated as the Java discussion area for all subjects that don't belong in one of the other groups, it gets more use than any of the others. It replaced `comp.lang.java` in mid-1996. Any Java-related topic is suitable for discussion here.

A

A

☐ `comp.lang.java.advocacy`: This group is devoted to any Java discussions that are likely to inspire heated or comparative debate. If you want to argue the merits of Java against another language, this is the place for it. This group can be a good place to consult if you want to see whether Java is the right choice for a project you're working on.

☐ `comp.lang.java.announce`: This group posts announcements, advertisements, and press releases of interest to the Java development community. It is moderated, so all postings must be submitted for approval before they are posted to the group.

☐ `comp.lang.java.api`: This group discusses the Java language's Application Programming Interface, the full library of class programs that comes with the Java Developer's Kit and other implementations of the language.

☐ `comp.lang.java.programmer`: This group contains questions and answers related to Java programming, which makes it another good place for new programmers to frequent.

☐ `comp.lang.java.security`: This discussion group is devoted to security issues related to Java, especially in regard to running Java programs and other executable content on the World Wide Web.

☐ `comp.lang.java.setup`: This group provides a place to discuss installation problems related to Java programming tools and similar issues.

☐ `comp.lang.java.tech`: The most advanced of the Java discussion groups, this group is devoted to discussing the implementation of the language, issues with porting it to new machines, the specifics of the Java Virtual Machine, and similar subjects.

Job Opportunities

If you're one of those folks who is learning Java as part of your plan to become a captain of industry, you should check out some of the Java-related job openings that become available. Several of the resources listed in this appendix have a section devoted to job opportunities.

If you might be interested in joining JavaSoft itself, visit the following Web page:

`http://www.javasoft.com/aboutJavaSoft/jobs/index.html`

JavaWorld offers a Career Opportunities page that often has several openings for Java developers:

`http://www.javaworld.com/javaworld/common/jw-jobop.html`

One tactic that can make Java employers aware of your skills is to register yourself as a resource for the Gamelan directory. Gamelan will add you to its site, and this listing might result in e-mail about Java-related job assignments. To find out about registering yourself, head to the following address in the Add a Resource section of Gamelan:

```
http://www.gamelan.com/submit/submit_person.shtml
```

Although this Web page isn't specifically a Java employment resource, the World Wide Web site Career Path enables you to search the job classifieds of more than two dozen U.S. newspapers. You have to register to use the site, but it's free, and there are more than 100,000 classifieds that you can search using keywords such as *Java* or *Internet*. Go to the following address:

```
http://www.careerpath.com
```

Appendix B

Java Programming Tools

When the Java programming language was introduced more than a year ago, the Java Developer's Kit was the only development tool that programmers could use. The Kit enables you to write, compile, and debug Java programs, but it is primitive compared to the tools available for programmers using Visual Basic, Borland Delphi, and other languages.

With many languages, programs can be developed with a suite of tools called an integrated development environment (also known as an IDE). An *integrated development environment* combines several development tools into a single package. This package usually contains a program text editor, a compiler, a debugger, and other tools. These tools complement each other as you go through the process of creating programs. Most professional IDEs use drag-and-drop, multiple windows, and other graphical features. If they work well, designing a program should be faster and more efficient than using a more rudimentary tool such as the Java Developer's Kit. Programs also ought to be easier to debug.

Many IDEs use *rapid application development*, also known as RAD, in their approach to programming. RAD is a strategy to speed up program development by using tools such as an interface designer. Product advertisements that promise the capability to "create Java programs without writing a line of code" are referring to a RAD feature. Most Java programming environments to date use RAD tools primarily in the design of a graphical user interface. Some of these IDEs connect interface design directly to programming so that you can create a clickable button, for example, and immediately write statements to handle the button.

More than 40 Java development environments have been released in beta or final form. This appendix focuses on some of the more commonly used environments so that you can decide whether they match your programming needs. You'll be introduced to each IDE with details about the systems it can run on and things to consider when evaluating the development product. This appendix also has capsule descriptions of some other tools, such as Microsoft Visual J++.

JUST A MINUTE

The Gamelan Web directory of Java resources maintains a page with links to IDE Web sites and related information. This page is available by choosing Programming in Java | Development Tools | IDEs from the main Gamelan page at the following address:

```
http://www.gamelan.com
```

You can attempt to go there directly at the following URL:

```
http://www.gamelan.com/pages/Gamelan.programming.tool.ide.html
```

The following development environments are described in this appendix:

- ☐ Rogue Wave JFactory
- ☐ Symantec Café
- ☐ SunSoft Java WorkShop
- ☐ SourceCraft NetCraft
- ☐ Pro-C WinGEN for Java

Choosing Development Software

As you decide whether to choose an IDE and which one you might choose, there are some questions that are helpful to ask about what you need when programming. Issues related to the Java language can make a difference in your choice. Ask yourself each of these questions:

☐ Is graphical interface design important in your programs?

☐ How important is it for your programs to run on more than one type of computer system, instead of being specific to a Microsoft Windows machine, an Apple Macintosh, or other system?

☐ Have you used IDE tools before?

☐ Will you be using other programming languages in addition to Java?

Graphical Interface Design Tools

Thanks to Microsoft Windows and Apple Macintosh machines, windowing systems are the way most users want to operate their computers. Users want their software to use the mouse and offer common windowing features, such as resizable windows. These expectations make user interface design important to consider when you're developing a program. If your software uses a command-line environment in the tradition of the Java Developer's Kit or MS-DOS, your program will be less attractive to people who use it.

In the same vein, interface design is important to consider when selecting an IDE. The available Java IDEs take different approaches to interface design and the other features that should be available as you design an interface. Some tools focus almost entirely on interface development, such as Rogue Wave's JFactory. Many of these interface development tools can automatically create Java code that handles user events. Visual Basic programmers will be familiar with this feature, because that language's IDE enables quick interface design and programming.

Most of the interface builders function similarly to drawing programs. User interface elements are arranged in a palette and can be dropped directly onto a workspace. Most of the components come from the Java Abstract Windowing Toolkit, or AWT. Java WorkShop and other IDEs add a layer between the AWT and your programs that is supposed to make windowing and interface programming easier. For some programmers, this might not be an attractive feature, because they would prefer to do the same kind of AWT programming that was described in this book. Other programmers might like to use these new interface features and avoid AWT programming.

Writing Fully Portable Java Programs

A feature to look for as you evaluate the different IDEs is adherence to Java's promise of platform independence. Some of the development tools are no different than using the Java Developer's Kit—they produce programs that are fully usable on all Java implementations. In fact, many of these IDEs, such as SourceCraft NetCraft, work in conjunction with the JDK, running tools like javac behind the scenes. Java WorkShop, Symantec Café, and other development tools come with their own specialized versions of the JDK.

Almost all IDEs aim to help you to write portable, platform-independent programs. A notable exception is Microsoft Visual J++, which offers features that are specific to Microsoft Windows systems and cannot be handled by other platforms. A Java program designed with Visual J++ can be developed to run on all types of computer systems if it does not use any of the special Windows-specific features.

Many Java programmers believe that all development environments should produce platform-independent programs because this capability is essential to the continuing success of the language. This belief is the subject of contentious discussion on the Internet and elsewhere. Although platform-independent programs are an important part of Java, most IDEs are not completely independent themselves, even when written using Java. These development tools are available only for specific platforms, primarily because they use native code, which consists of parts of Java programs that are written using other languages such as C++ or C.

Experience Using Other IDEs

As you look over the sales pitches for each IDE, one thing that doesn't get enough attention is that many of these tools require a lot of skill and experience to use successfully. It can be difficult for an IDE to improve your programming if you can't figure out how the IDE works.

IDEs are often the most complicated software you will use. They can include multiple-document windows, numerous configuration options, and other sophisticated features. Novice programmers can become confused with many IDEs because of the complexity, especially if they are still learning how to use a new programming language. For this reason, the IDE you choose should be suited to your experience level as a programmer and as an IDE user.

Several Java IDEs are highly suitable for novices. Perhaps the best example of an easy-to-understand interface is SunSoft Java WorkShop, which uses a browser interface that should be well-known to anyone who surfs the World Wide Web. The downside to the easier-to-use IDEs is that they might require more work to get something done than an IDE that has more functions at the programmer's fingertips.

Using an IDE for More than One Language

If you are using more than one language as you program, another thing to consider about an IDE is whether you can use it with multiple languages. The Borland 5.0 C++ IDE, MetroWerks CodeWarrior, and other tools can handle Java and other languages or work identically to other IDEs from the company.

One advantage to using an IDE that works with multiple languages is that you don't have to learn a different IDE when using a different language. (Of course, the IDE isn't any easier to learn the first time around.) Another plus to using a multilanguage tool is that you can write Java statements and non-Java native methods with the same tool. The Borland 5.0 Java environment is an example of this type of IDE; it can compile C and C++ code and Java statements.

Making Sense of IDEs

An IDE should make you a better programmer and make it easier or more enjoyable for you to develop programs. As you evaluate each of the products described in the following sections, you can determine which of the features of a specific IDE you might need. Because so many development tools are available for Java, you should be able to find one that suits your skills and personal preferences. Of course, you can always use the Java Developer's Kit that you learned about during this book and enhance it by using custom interface builders, your preferred word processor, and other software.

CAUTION

If you download trial copies of several different IDEs, as was done for this appendix, you might run into difficulties because of how each IDE configures your system. Many Java development tools use environment variables such as CLASSPATH and JAVAHOME, and these variables could be set up incorrectly if another IDE has already configured them. Before installing a test version of an IDE, you should uninstall any other Java IDEs that are present on your system.

Rogue Wave JFactory

Rogue Wave JFactory is an interface builder instead of an IDE, in contrast to other IDEs that are available for Java programming. It delivers some programming capabilities along with interface design features, enabling interface actions to be handled within JFactory. It also can compile and test programs during development, so it's similar enough to a full IDE to be worth consideration. Though you can use JFactory with any editor and Java compiler, JFactory provides a word processor and can use the JDK compiler. Figure B.1 provides a look at the JFactory environment.

Figure B.1.

Rogue Wave JFactory at work.

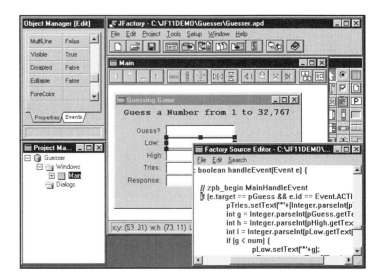

System Requirements

Versions of JFactory are available for the following platforms:

- ☐ Microsoft Windows 95 and Windows NT systems running a 486 or better with 16M of memory, 25M of hard disk space, and the Java Developer's Kit.

- ☐ SPARC Solaris 2.4 or 2.5 running UNIX with 25M of hard disk space, an applet browser, JDK, and X11R5. You must have enough memory to run X11R5, the JDK compiler, and an applet browser at the same time.

- ☐ HP-UX 10.01 systems with 25M of hard disk space, an applet browser, JDK, and X11R5. The memory requirements are the same as for Solaris systems.

- ☐ IBM OS/2 Warp 3.0 systems with 25M of hard disk space, 4M of memory not used by OS/2, a two-button mouse or pointing device, and JDK build os2-19960412.

Overview

JFactory, which is based on a multiplatform C++ programming tool from Rogue Wave, has numerous features that help you to design applications rapidly. Because Rogue Wave has a lot of experience with similar tools, JFactory is different from many Java IDEs that are still

B

in a beta stage of development or are new products. The strength of JFactory is the visual, drag-and-drop editor for interface creation, which is superior to most other visual development tools currently available for the Java language.

As you develop an interface with JFactory, you can test it at any time. Another useful feature is the way that custom components can be added to a program toolbar along with AWT components such as text fields, text labels, and radio buttons. JFactory automatically creates a lot of the Java statements that are needed to offer interface components in a program. If you need to do some of your own programming to customize the interface, you can do it in a way so that you can change the interface later without overwriting the customized portions of your program.

With JFactory, you can use the mouse or the keyboard to place a component. You can set up the height, width, and x and y coordinates of a component from a properties dialog box. This capability makes it easier to align components correctly. When you create a window, menu, or dialog box, you can save it in an object library for use with other programs.

JFactory is not a full-fledged IDE, so it does not include its own compiler, debugger, or other tools. However, the software's visual editor might make up for the loss of some other IDE functionality. Unless the absence of sophisticated tools such as a class browser and integrated debugger slows down your programming, JFactory could be an excellent choice.

Pricing and Additional Information

JFactory retails for $195; a multiplatform package that includes the Microsoft Windows, UNIX, and OS/2 versions is available for $390. For more details and the opportunity to download a demo version or to purchase JFactory online, visit the home page for JFactory at the following URL:

```
http://www.roguewave.com/products/jfactory/jfactory.html
```

The e-mail address for comments and questions regarding JFactory is support@roguewave.com.

Symantec Café

Symantec Café, the first development environment other than the JDK that became widely available for Java programming, is called an *integrated development and debugging environment* (IDDE) by Symantec. (Although other IDEs are missing the extra *D* in their acronyms, most of them contain debuggers as well.) Café is a stand-alone product based on Symantec's C++ environment. Figure B.2 shows an example of Café at work.

Figure B.2.

*A screen capture of
Symantec Café.*

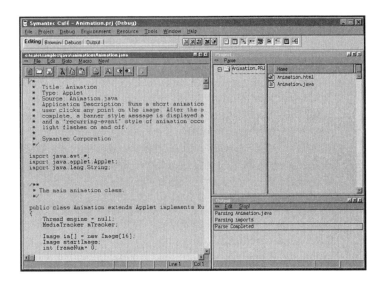

System Requirements

Symantec has released versions of Café for the Microsoft Windows 95, Windows NT 3.5x, and Macintosh systems. Windows users must have at least an Intel 386 processor and 8M memory, but a 486 or better and 16M memory are recommended. You need at least a VGA monitor, but Symantec recommends that you use an SVGA monitor if one is available. The software and all its sample files and Help files require 60M of disk space and a CD-ROM drive. Macintosh owners need a Power Macintosh, 68030, or 68040 Macintosh and 16M memory. The full installation of the software requires 30M of disk space.

Café incorporates the JDK into its release with a full implementation of the Java class libraries and source code samples. You do not have to have the JDK before installing Café. In fact, you should uninstall the JDK if you already have it on your system before implementing Café to avoid configuration conflicts between the two.

Overview

Café is more robust than some other IDEs, and it has been documented more fully than some other IDEs in books such as *Teach Yourself Java in Café in 21 Days,* available now from Sams.net Publishing. The main features of Café are described in the following list:

☐ Café offers an excellent text editor that uses color to highlight different elements of a Java program.

B

- To assist the design of a class hierarchy, Café has a class editor for navigating through classes and editing class methods. It also has a hierarchy editor for viewing and changing class relationships. You can see changes in your programs that would involve the class hierarchy as the program is being written. You also can change a program from within the class editor by selecting a function or method within a class in order to display its source code in a window.

- The AppExpress tool speeds up the process of creating the beginning framework of a Java program. Other *Express Agents*—Café's term for wizards—make it easier to do things within the IDE.

- In the program editor, Java syntax is highlighted, which makes it easier to find errors such as typos and other problems. The editor uses standard Windows cut, copy, and paste commands.

- You can design a graphical user interface for your Java programs in a visual, drag-and-drop manner with Café Studio. It enables programmers to develop the dialog boxes and other visual components visually, and it creates statements to handle these components automatically. There also is a menu editor with an active window that lets you test the menus you create.

- With Café Studio, you can design a form and dictate exactly how it looks. With the Abstract Windowing Toolkit, a graphical user interface might change depending on the computer system the Java program is running on, similar to the way HTML pages can be modified for presentation on the many different platforms that can access the World Wide Web. Programmers can use Café Studio to choose one of these AWT layout managers or to dictate the exact position and size of all interface elements.

- Café offers the choice of using the JDK compiler or a Café compiler, which has been optimized to work faster.

- With the Café debugging tool, there are different ways to halt the execution of code. These include a way to insert a one-time breakpoint that stops the running of a program at a specific line. The debugger also enables you to control multi-threaded programs. During debugging, you can use a watch view to see the value of variables.

- Symantec Café is highly customizable; all toolbars and palettes can be resized and placed where you want them.

- More than four dozen sample Java programs are included with Windows versions of Café, and more than 90 are included with the Macintosh version. Many of these programs are duplicates of the sample applets Sun offers with the JDK or on its Web site at `http://java.sun.com`.

Pricing and Additional Information

The most recent retail price for Café is $129.95 for Windows users. A comparable price is being offered to Macintosh owners. You can purchase Café from Symantec's Web site, as well as from retail and mail-order outlets.

JUST A MINUTE

Some folks might not have to buy Café at all! Customers who bought Symantec C++ between December 1, 1995, and March 1, 1996, are entitled to a free upgrade to Café.

The home page for Symantec Café is the following URL:

```
http://cafe.symantec.com/
```

The customer service number for the company is (800) 441-7234, and its e-mail address for Java-related comments and questions is `javainfo@symantec.com`.

SunSoft Java WorkShop

SunSoft Java WorkShop, the development tool offered by the language's home team, is an IDE written almost entirely in Java. Its development was used at Sun to help improve the Java language by tackling a large-scale software project using Java, but it also is a useful tool for Java programmers to consider. Figure B.3 shows an example of Java WorkShop being used to develop a program.

Figure B.3.

Java WorkShop in use.

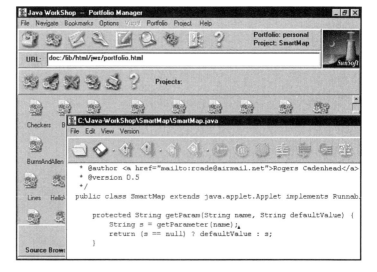

B

System Requirements

Versions of Java WorkShop are available for the following systems: Microsoft Windows 95, Windows NT 3.5.1, SPARC Solaris (2.4 or later), and Intel x86 Solaris systems. Microsoft Windows 95 and NT systems must be running a 90MHz Pentium or better with 16M of memory and 45M of hard disk space. Solaris systems must have 32M of memory, 45M of disk space, and an OSF/Motif 1.2.3-compliant windowing system. The recommended display resolution to use with Java WorkShop is 800 by 600 pixels.

Java WorkShop comes with its own modified version of the JDK, so you cannot use it in conjunction with an existing installation of the Kit. Like Café, Java WorkShop requires that any existing JDK copies be uninstalled before you can install and run WorkShop correctly.

Overview

Java WorkShop, one of the most approachable IDEs for a novice programmer, uses a Web interface to offer a program text editor, class browser, debugger, project management system, and Visual Java. That last tool provides a way to visually design a graphical interface. WorkShop is fully detailed in *Teach Yourself SunSoft Java WorkShop in 21 Days*, available now from Sams.net Publishing.

The most striking difference between Java WorkShop and other IDEs is its interface. Java WorkShop looks more like a Web browser than a programming development environment, because it is a Web browser. Java WorkShop's browser interface is easier to use for programmers who are unfamiliar with more complex IDEs, but the browser interface can be frustrating for developers who are comfortable with these tools. WorkShop has a source browser for viewing variables, a class hierarchy, and public methods. The browser creates HTML pages in the same format as HTML documentation generated by the javadoc utility included with the JDK.

The WorkShop program text editor lacks some of the cut-and-paste functionality of other, more established editors. It works with WorkShop's debugger so that compile errors create links directly into the editor for fixing. The WorkShop debugger provides breakpoints and other methods of debugging.

Visual Java, like Café Studio, provides a way to graphically design an interface. Programmers can develop dialog boxes and other visual elements and automatically create handlers to respond to events generated by these components.

The WorkShop environment is not customizable in the way Café is, but the Web interface makes it easy to integrate other tools and programs into WorkShop. Basically, the program is a group of Web pages with Java programs featured on them. You can go to a different page from within Java WorkShop as easily as you visit a URL in a Web browser. This structure makes it possible for a programmer to create original Java development tools that can be linked to WorkShop pages, an unusual feature. This arrangement is unorthodox in comparison to development environments that are cohesive, unchangeable files. However, it is compatible with the approach to the Java language in general—small, self-contained programs that can reach out to other programs over the Internet or other means.

Pricing and Additional Information

SunSoft Java WorkShop currently sells over the World Wide Web for a retail price of $84.99. The software can be downloaded for a free 30-day evaluation. For more details, visit the following URL:

```
http://www.sun.com/sunsoft/Developer-products/java/index.html
```

The customer service number to use for the company is (800) 786-7638 (SUN-SOFT) in the United States or (512) 434-1511 elsewhere. The company's e-mail address for comments and questions is sunsoft@selectnet.com.

SourceCraft NetCraft

SourceCraft, the developer of the ObjectCraft development environment, is making its Java IDE, NetCraft, available at no cost if you comply with the terms and conditions for use. This makes NetCraft attractive because of the cost, but the IDE still must be useful to you or you will pay in other ways due to lost efficiency. Figure B.4 provides a screen shot of the NetCraft environment.

Figure B.4.

NetCraft at work.

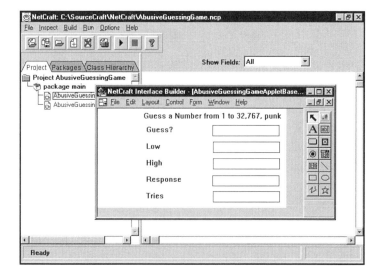

System Requirements

Versions of NetCraft are available for Microsoft Windows 95 and Windows NT 3.5.1 systems running a 486 or better with 8M of memory. NetCraft comes bundled with the current version of the JDK; SourceCraft also makes NetCraft available for download without the JDK if you already have the JDK installed.

Overview

SourceCraft NetCraft does not offer as many features as other IDEs, but it is a comparable replacement for the JDK. It creates Java programs that are usable across Java implementations for all systems. NetCraft has an editor, class inspector, user interface designer, and compiler.

You can use NetCraft for any type of Java applet or application. You can use the Package Inspector, part of NetCraft's system for organizing projects, to browse class methods. The Class Inspector can show you the position of a class in the hierarchy, its methods, and its variables. You can view the source code of the method and how it is used in a program when you are looking at a method with this tool.

Like Café and Java WorkShop, NetCraft includes a way to visually create a graphical user interface. The UI Builder generates Java code that uses the Abstract Windowing Toolkit, so the program does not rely on any new classes introduced with the development environment. When you create an interface component, NetCraft generates Java statements for that component, complete with a TODO comment line where the action event handling statements for that component are placed. The approach is simpler than some of the alternatives, so a programmer familiar with the AWT should be comfortable with it.

NetCraft's program editor uses cut-and-paste commands and is similar to other small word processors. Though the components in the currently available release have the odd habit of moving around a little after they are clicked, a nice feature of the builder is the capability to set a component's height and width coordinates by entering numbers into text fields. This feature enables you to easily align wandering components with each other.

The NetCraft environment is simpler to use than other IDEs, but this simplicity might be a problem when you need to create programs that have numerous windows and interactive components. Some of the tools that can make complex software more manageable to design are not available in NetCraft. NetCraft appears to be a good substitute for JDK users who want to use a graphical interface as they write simple programs and applets. Because it is free, this IDE can be a good place for novices to start when they're deciding which IDE to use.

Pricing and Additional Information

For more details and the opportunity to download NetCraft at no cost, visit the home page for NetCraft at the following URL:

```
http://www.sourcecraft.com:4800/about/netcraft/
```

The customer service number for the company is (617) 221-5665; the company's e-mail address for comments and questions is edc@sourcecraft.com.

Pro-C WinGEN for Java

Pro-C WinGEN for Java is an IDE designed for people who do not write programs. The focus is on automatically generating code so that HTML designers and other programming novices can develop Java programs. You can develop the graphical interface of an applet or application using drag-and-drop and introduce elements such as animation without writing a single Java statement. The IDE calls the JDK from within WinGEN to run and compile programs. Figure B.5 shows the WinGEN environment.

Figure B.5.

WinGEN for Java in use.

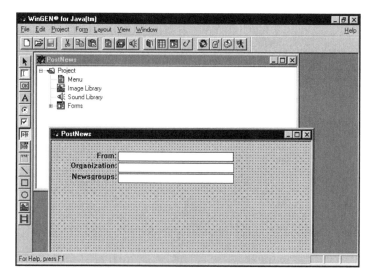

B

System Requirements

Versions of WinGEN are available for Microsoft Windows 95 and Windows NT 3.5.1 systems running a 486 or better with 8M of memory and 10M of hard disk space. To unpack WinGEN Lite, the evaluation edition of the software, you must have a program that can unpack ZIP files into long file names. (For users of Windows systems, the Windows 95 operating system introduced file names longer than eight characters and a three-character extension.) If you use a ZIP unpack program that does not support long file names, files will not be named correctly, and the setup will fail. WinGEN includes the current version of the JDK, which must be installed before WinGEN is installed so that the IDE will function.

B

Overview

WinGEN supports the JDK rather than replacing it and can run the Kit's compiler and interpreter from within the IDE. Because of WinGEN's focus on beginners, WinGEN emphasizes a point-and-click approach to graphical user interface creation. You can create many user events through WinGEN without any programming.

The arrangement of WinGEN's user interface should be familiar to programmers who have used other GUI design tools, especially for those who have used Visual Basic. The current WinGEN version can be difficult to use when aligning components, but laying out text fields, labels, and other things is easier than it can be with other programming tools.

The IDE takes a resource-centric view of development. What this means is that you start with the menus and dialog boxes and then create programming functions rather than using programming to create those components. One thing that WinGEN does not offer is the capability to preview a program's interface before any Java statements have been generated.

A system called CodeHooks enables you to add Java statements that handle circumstances WinGEN can't handle. These hooks, which accomplish specific tasks like a special event handler, are separated from the statements that WinGEN automatically generates. This separation of statements enables programmers to change the GUI and use CodeHooks without reentering anything.

WinGEN can be useful for the programming of simple applets and applications or as a tool for Java novices. Though it lacks a debugger, source browser, and other IDE features, later versions of the software might implement some of these tools.

Pricing and Additional Information

You can purchase WinGEN online for $79.95. For more details, the opportunity to download WinGEN Lite at no cost, or to purchase the full version online, visit the home page for WinGEN at the following URL:

```
http://www.pro-c.com/products/wfj/java.html
```

The phone number at Pro-C for inquiries related to the software is (813) 227-7762; the company's e-mail address for comments and questions regarding WinGEN is `support@pro-c.com`.

Other Offerings

The following products for Java development are profiled to provide a more complete picture of the programming tools that are available.

Borland C++ 5.0 with Java Enhancements

Borland C++ 5.0 with Java Enhancements is a C++ development environment that has been extended to include Java programming tools. The advantages of this approach are multilanguage development within the same environment for native method use, the capability to program in three languages (C, C++, and Java) without learning three IDEs, and the use of software that has become robust from several years of use by the C and C++ development community. The home page for Borland's Internet development tools is as follows:

```
http://www.borland.com/internet/.
```

MetroWerks CodeWarrior

CodeWarrior is one of several IDEs that are available for Apple Macintosh or Microsoft Windows Java development. CodeWarrior is a multilanguage development environment with an introductory version called Discover Programming with Java that is intended for novices. You can use CodeWarrior to develop programs in C, C++, ObjectPascal, and Java. One interesting feature of this development environment is that you can compile Windows versions of a Java program using a Macintosh and vice versa. The main page for MetroWerks is the following URL:

```
http://www.metrowerks.com
```

B

Kalimantan

Before being christened Kalimantan, this IDE was one of several Java-related products that staked a claim to the name *Espresso*. The developers have been kind enough to offer links to the other Espressos, so the Kalimantan Web page is a good place to sort out any Espresso confusion you may have.

Kalimantan is another cross-platform IDE. It has been tested for use with Solaris 2.4 and up, as well as Windows 95 systems. Kalimantan's current beta release includes only an inspector to look at the values of internal variables and a debugger, but it is bundled with the `teikade` suite of utilities from PFU Limited. This suite includes a class browser that is familiar to those who have used class browsers with the Smalltalk programming language. The home page for Kalimantan is the following URL:

```
http://www.real-time.com/java/kalimantan/index.html
```

Natural Intelligence Roaster

Roaster was made available to developers in January 1996, making it the first Java IDE for the Macintosh. The Roaster Professional Edition includes a visual interface builder, the ability to compile programs that can be targeted for Macintosh or Microsoft Windows systems, and an extended class library. The Sams.net book *Teach Yourself Java for the Macintosh in 21 Days* was written for the Roaster environment. Details on Roaster are available from the following URL:

```
http://www.natural.com/pages/products/roaster/index.html
```

Microsoft Visual J++

Microsoft Visual J++ is Microsoft's machine-proprietary answer to Java development. It features extensions to the Java class library that are specific to Microsoft's operating system and integrates Java with the component object model (COM) through Microsoft ActiveX. Visual J++ is integrated with the Internet Explorer browser that implemented Java with its 3.0 release. The home page for Visual J++ is the following URL:

```
http://www.microsoft.com/visualj/
```

Summary

The integrated development environment that you choose depends on many factors: your programming experience, the tasks you must accomplish, and personal preference. Java Usenet newsgroups such as comp.lang.java.misc and comp.lang.java.programmer are a way to get a range of user opinions on the IDEs you are considering. Many IDE developers also participate in these forums, including Symantec representatives and the developers of Java WorkShop.

Most Java IDEs that are not in final release can be downloaded over the World Wide Web. It can be troublesome to download and install these trial versions, especially if you must first uninstall something else, but the approaches taken in each IDE are worth examining in detail. Of course, if you have grown comfortable with the Java Developer's Kit from your use of it during this book, no one says you have to use one of the more complex IDEs.

Appendix C

This Book's Web Site

One of the advantages of a 24-hour course of study is that it gets you quickly up to speed on a subject. However, because programming is a technical, jargon-packed field, there might be things you're still unclear about. There also might be things I was unclear about—errors and other confusing information that could benefit from a clarification.

If you have questions about any of the subjects covered in this book or suggestions on ways this and other books could be improved, please visit the official Web site for *Teach Yourself Java 1.1 Programming in 24 Hours*:

```
http://www.prefect.com/java24
```

This Web site will feature several different types of information, updated by the author:

☐ Error corrections and clarifications: When errors are brought to my attention, they will be described on the site with the corrected text and any other material that will help.

☐ Answers to reader questions: If readers have questions that aren't covered in this book's Q&A sections, they might be presented on the site.

☐ Links to other Sams.net book pages: These links will provide a quick way to see what else is available from Sams, including the other books of the *24 Hours* series.

☐ Sample Java programs: Working versions of some programs that were featured in this book will be available on the site.

☐ Updated links to the sites mentioned in this book: Since the Web changes faster than Roseanne changes surnames, you might try some of the URLs mentioned in this book and find that they no longer work. If the site has moved elsewhere and I know about the new URL, I'll offer it here.

☐ An AOL-style chat page implemented with Java: Using EarthWeb's chat applet, a Java programming chat room will be offered on the site for informal gatherings about the subjects covered in the book.

☐ An expanded version of the `Craps` applet from Hours 21 and 22: If you're still feeling a little depressed about the craps skills you didn't develop while growing up, come to the site for an adaptation of this book's `Craps` applet that displays some other advanced programming.

☐ At least one link related to the Dallas Stars: This link is offered for no other reason than the author's newfound love of professional hockey.

As you might know, the *24 Hours* books represent a new line from Sams.net. Your suggestions, comments, and questions are welcome at any time. In addition to visiting the site, you can contact author Rogers Cadenhead at the following e-mail address:

`rogers@prefect.com`

Please feel free to voice all opinions, positive or negative. The author has been a user of the Internet and online services long enough to have his parentage questioned in seven languages. Any criticism that you send will be interpreted as "toughlove," and nothing you say could be rougher than what my music teacher said after my audition for the lead in the Yale Elementary School production of *Jesus Christ Superstar*.

Rogers Cadenhead

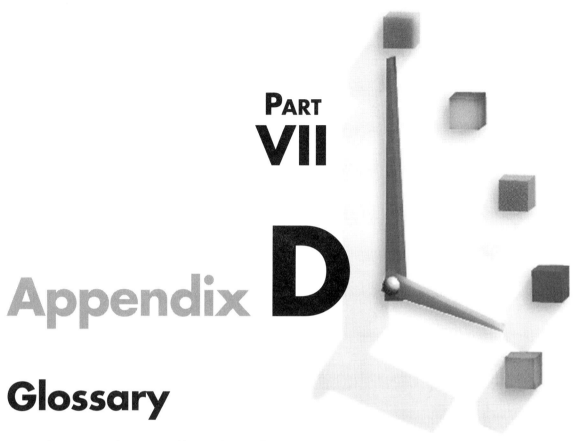

Appendix D

Glossary

Abstract Windowing Toolkit   The set of Java classes that are used to display and control a graphical user interface. Also called the AWT.

ActiveX   A way to run programs on World Wide Web pages that was developed by Microsoft. ActiveX is an extension of the Component Object Model, and it is a rival of sorts to Java.

applet   A Java program that runs as part of a World Wide Web page.

`appletviewer`   The Java Developer's Kit tool that can display applets that are included on a World Wide Web page.

application   A Java program that runs locally on your computer rather than as part of a World Wide Web page.

argument   Extra information that is sent to a program when it is run or information that is sent to a method in a program when it begins.

array   A group of variables that share the same name and store the same kind of information. Each variable in the group is called an element, and elements are numbered so that they can be distinguished from each other.

ASCII text file   A text file that does not contain any special character or formatting commands such as centering, boldfaced text, and different point sizes.

attribute   Part of an HTML tag that affects what the tag does. Also, in object-oriented programming, it is a thing that describes an object and distinguishes it from other objects. These attributes are stored in variables.

autodialer   Software that uses a modem to dial a series of phone numbers in sequence.

BASIC   A language designed for use by beginning programmers. Dozens of different versions of BASIC are available.

behavior   The things that an object does, as conducted by the methods of the object.

bit   An integer that can equal 0 or 1. Each byte is made up of 8 bits.

block   A group of statements in a Java program. Blocks begin with a { mark and end with a } mark.

block statement   Another term for a block.

Boolean   A value that can be either true or false.

browser   Software that can be used to view World Wide Web pages on the Internet.

bug   An error in a program that must be fixed in order for the program to operate correctly.

byte   A number that can store 256 integer values—either 0 to 255 or, in the case of Java, -127 to 128. A byte consists of 8 bits.

bytecode   The compiled form of a Java source file that is run by a Java interpreter.

C++   An extension of the C programming language developed by Bjarne Stroustrop that includes features such as object-oriented programming, multiple inheritance, and the use of pointers.

character   A single letter, number, punctuation mark, or other symbol.

check box   A user interface component that presents a box next to a line of text. The box can be checked or unchecked by the user.

choice list   A user interface component that presents a pop-up list of choices from which a single choice can be made. Only one of the selections is visible unless the pop-up list is being displayed.

class   A master copy of an object that determines what behavior and attributes an object should have. Because every Java program is also a class, programs also are called classes.

class method   A method that is associated with a class of objects instead of a specific object.

class variable   A variable that is associated with a class of objects instead of an object and has a value specific to the class.

D

command line   A way to operate a computer entirely with the keyboard by typing commands at a prompt. MS-DOS is the most popular operating system to use a command line.

comments   Lines in a source file that are provided strictly for the benefit of humans trying to understand the program.

compiler   A program that turns a source file into a computer program by interpreting the whole file beforehand and creating a compiled file that can be run. This program is more efficient than an interpreter but is slower to debug.

component   An item such as a clickable button or scrollbar that can be manipulated by a user in a program.

concatenate   To link two things together. This term is often used to describe the process of attaching two strings to each other so they can be displayed together.

conditional   A statement that causes something to happen only if a specific condition is met.

constant   A variable that cannot change in value throughout a program.

constructor   A special method that only is handled when an object is being created.

container   A component that can contain other components in a graphical user interface.

decrement   To subtract one from something.

debug   The process of fixing bugs in a computer program.

double-buffering   Drawing graphics to an off-screen work area first in order to improve the quality of animation.

element   A specific variable of an array.

event-handling   Responding to a user's mouse and keyboard use in a program's graphical user interface.

expressions   Statements that involve a mathematic equation or that change the value of something.

floating-point numbers   Numbers that might include a decimal point.

GIF file   An image file format that was developed by CompuServe.

GIF 89a file   A version of the GIF format that includes support for transparent colors.

graphical user interface   The buttons, text fields, and other components of a program that enable a user to interact with the program using a mouse and keyboard. Also called a GUI.

hierarchy   A pyramid-shaped grouping of classes in which the topmost class is the superclass of all classes below it.

HSB values   A way of defining a color by determining the percentage of hue, saturation, and brightness that exist in the color.

hypertext markup language   HTML, the simple programming language used to present information on World Wide Web pages.

increment   To add one to something.

inheritance   The capability of a class of objects to automatically have the attributes and behavior of another object. The extent of this capability is determined by the class' position in the class hierarchy.

integer   A whole number.

interface   A special type of class that enables a class to inherit methods it would not be able to use through inheritance alone.

Internet Explorer   Web browser software from Microsoft that can run Java programs.

interpreter   A program that turns a source file into a computer program by interpreting each line one at a time. An interpreted language runs programs more slowly than a compiled language does, but it is easier to debug.

initialization   The process of setting something up for the first time in a program. This term is used often in reference to variables.

Java   An object-oriented programming language developed by Sun Microsystems that was first released to the public in 1995. Java programs are compiled into class files that can run on any computer platform that has a Java interpreter.

java   The interpreter that is part of the Java Developer's Kit.

Java Developer's Kit   A free set of tools from Sun Microsystems that makes it possible to write and test Java programs in a command-line environment.

Java WorkShop   Software from Sun Microsystems that enables Java programs to be written in a graphical, point-and-click environment.

javac   The compiler that is included with the Java Developer's Kit.

JavaScript   An interpreted programming language unrelated to Java that offers limited programming capabilities on a Web page. The source code of JavaScript programs is included as text on Web pages.

JPG file   An image file format developed by the Joint Photographic Expert Groups, also called a JPEG file. This format is considered the best for presenting photographic images without taking up a lot of disk space.

layout manager   An object that controls how components will be arranged in a graphical user interface.

logic error   A bug that causes a program to do something it isn't supposed to do but doesn't prevent the program from running. These errors must be found during testing, but they can be hard to find.

long integers   Integers that are larger than 2.14 billion or smaller than -2.14 billion.

loop   A statement or set of statements that will be repeated in a program.

method   A way to accomplish a task in a Java program. Methods begin with a { and end with a }.

multiple inheritance   The capability of a class of objects to inherit attributes and behavior from more than one superclass.

multithreading   The capability of a program or operating system to run more than one program at the same time. Also known as multitasking.

Navigator   Web browser software from Netscape that includes the capability to run Java programs in its current versions.

newline   A special character represented by '\N' that causes the display of text to continue at the leftmost column of the next line.

object variable   A variable that is associated with an object and has a value that is specific to that object.

object-oriented programming   A way of thinking of computer programs as a group of objects that work together, each object containing everything it needs to handle a specific task.

operator   The part of an expression that causes a mathematical operation to occur, such as addition or multiplication, or tests a condition such as equality.

overriding   Creating a method or variable in a subclass that replaces something it inherited from its superclass.

parameters   Extra information sent to a Java applet when it runs that is included using an HTML tag on a World Wide Web page.

platform   A computer operating system and central processing unit.

platform-independence   The ability of software to run without modification on several different platforms.

point and click   The ability to control a program by using a mouse device and clicking its buttons.

pointer   A variable in a program that points to where another value is stored. Java does not include pointers.

program   A set of instructions that tell a computer what to do. Also called software.

pull-down menus   Menus in a program that you use by clicking a menu title, holding down the mouse, and releasing it over the item you want.

RGB values   A way of defining the color of something by specifying the percentage of red, green, and blue that exist in the color.

scope   The area of a program in which a variable exists, defined by the nearest { and } marks that surround the variable. A variable's scope is the block in which the variable was created, and it cannot be used outside of that scope.

short integers   Integers that can range from -32,768 to 32,767.

software   A computer program or group of computer programs designed to work together.

source file   The text file created by a programmer that will be turned into a computer program by an interpreter or a compiler. Also called source code.

statement   One of the instructions that is handled by the computer when it runs a program.

string   A group of characters that represent one or more lines of text.

subclass   A class that is below another class in a hierarchy, inheriting attributes and behavior from the classes that are above it.

superclass   A class that is above another class in a hierarchy, giving its attributes and behavior to any classes that are below it.

syntax error   A bug in a program that is caused by using a statement or other part of the language incorrectly. Syntax errors are easier to find than other errors because they cause error messages.

tab   A special character represented by ' \t ' that causes text to continue at the next column, based on how wide columns have been defined. This character is used to format text for display.

tag   An HTML command used on a World Wide Web page to format text, present images, run Java applets, or accomplish similar things. Tags are enclosed within < and > marks.

D

ternary operator   An operator represented by ? that uses a conditional test to set a value. If the test is true, the first value is used, and if the test is false, the second value is used.

text area   A user interface component that presents a text field where a user can enter more than one line of text.

text editor   Another term for word processor.

text field   A user interface component that presents an area where a user can enter a single line of text.

thread   A single program that can run as part of a multithreaded system.

variables   Special storage places where a computer program can store information.

VBScript   An interpreted programming language from Microsoft that offers limited programming capabilities on a Web page. VBScript is based on Visual Basic, and its source code is included as text on Web pages.

Visual Basic   A programming language from Microsoft that speeds up the process of developing windowing software for Microsoft systems.

Visual C++   An object-oriented programming language from Microsoft with extensive support for windowing and many other Windows-specific technologies.

word processor   A computer program used for the editing and presentation of text documents.

PART
VII

Appendix E

What's on the CD-ROM?

On the *Teach Yourself Java 1.1 Programming in 24 Hours* CD-ROM, you will find all the sample files that have been presented in this book, along with a wealth of other applications and utilities.

JUST A MINUTE

Please refer to the `readme.wri` file on the CD-ROM (Windows) or the `Guide to the CD-ROM` (Macintosh) for the latest listing of software.

Windows Software

Java

- ☐ Sun's Java Developer's Kit for Windows 95/NT
- ☐ JPad IDE

- ☐ JPad Pro IDE
- ☐ Kawa IDE
- ☐ Jamba IDE

HTML Tools

- ☐ Hot Dog 32-bit HTML editor
- ☐ HoTMetaL HTML editor
- ☐ HTMLed HTML editor

Graphics, Video, and Sound Applications

- ☐ Paint Shop Pro 3.12 graphics editor and graphic file format converter for Windows
- ☐ SnagIt screen capture utility
- ☐ ThumbsPlus image viewer and browser

Utilities

- ☐ Adobe Acrobat viewer
- ☐ WinZip for Windows NT/95
- ☐ WinZip Self-Extractor

Macintosh Software

Java

- ☐ Sun's Java Developer's Kit for Macintosh

HTML Tools

- ☐ BBEdit 3.5.1
- ☐ BBEdit 4 demo

Graphics, Video, and Sound Applications

- [ ] Graphic Converter v2.1.4
- [ ] GIFConverter v2.3.7
- [ ] Fast Player v1.1
- [ ] Sparkle 2.4.5
- [ ] SoundApp v1.5.1

Utilities

- [ ] ZipIt for Macintosh
- [ ] ScrapIt Pro
- [ ] Adobe Acrobat

About Third-Party Software

Please read all documentation associated with a third-party product (usually contained with files named `readme.txt` or `license.txt`) and follow all guidelines.

INDEX

W-X-Y-Z

MACMILLAN COMPUTER PUBLISHING USA
A VIACOM COMPANY

 **Technical** ---- **Support:**

If you need assistance with the information in this book or with a CD/Disk accompanying the book, please access the Knowledge Base on our Web site at **http://www.superlibrary.com/general/support**. Our most Frequently Asked Questions are answered there. If you do not find the answer to your questions on our Web site, you may contact Macmillan Technical Support **(317) 581-3833** or e-mail us at **support@mcp.com**.

Java Developer's Guide

—Jamie Jaworski & Carie Jardean

Java is one of the major growth areas for developers on the World Wide Web. With Java, you can download and run small applications, called *applets*, from a Web server. *Java Developer's Guide* teaches developers everything they need to know to effectively develop Java applications.

The CD-ROM includes source code from the book and valuable utilities. *Java Developer's Guide* covers Java 1.1 and explains the Java interface, VRML extensions, security, and more. It also explores new technology and future trends of Java development.

$49.99 USA, $67.99 CDN,
ISBN 1-57521-069-x, 768 pp.

Laura Lemay's Web Workshop: 3D Graphics and VRML 2

—Laura Lemay, Kelly Murdock, & Justin Couch

This book is the easiest way for readers to learn how to add three-dimensional virtual worlds to Web pages. It describes the new VRML 2.0 specifications, explores the wide arrray of existing VRML sites on the Web, and steps the readers through the process of creating their own 3D Web environments.

The CD-ROM contains the book in HTML format, a hand-picked selection of the best VRML and 3D graphics tools, plus a collection of ready-to-use virtual worlds.

$39.99 USA, $56.95 CDN,
ISBN 1-57521-143-2, 504 pp.

Laura Lemay's Web Workshop: Graphics and Web Page Design

—Laura Lemay, Jon Duff, & James Mohler

With the number of Web pages increasing daily, only the well-designed will stand out and grab the attention of those browsing the Web. This book illustrates, in classic Laura Lemay style, how to design attractive Web pages that will be visited over and over again.

The CD-ROM contains HTML editors, graphics software, and royalty-free graphics and sound files.

$55.00 USA, $77.95 CDN,
ISBN 1-57521-125-4, 408 pp.

Laura Lemay's Web Workshop: JavaScript

—Laura Lemay & Michael Moncur

Readers will explore various aspects of Web publishing—whether CGI scripting and interactivity or graphics design or Netscape Gold—in greater depth than the *Teach Yourself* books.

CD-ROM includes the complete book in HTML format, publishing tools, templates, graphics, backgrounds, and more. *Laura Lemay's Web Workshop: JavaScript* provides a clear, hands-on guide to creating sophisticated Web pages.

$39.99 USA, $56.95 CDN,
ISBN 1-57521-141-6, 432 pp.

Laura Lemay's Web Workshop: Microsoft FrontPage

—Laura Lemay & Denise Tyler

This book is a clear, hands-on guide to maintaining Web pages with Microsoft's FrontPage. Written in the clear, conversational style of Laura Lemay, it is packed with many interesting, colorful examples that demonstrate specific tasks of interest to the reader.

The included CD-ROM contains all the templates, backgrounds, and materials needed.

$39.99 USA, $56.95 CDN,
ISBN 1-57521-149-1, 672 pp.

Developing Professional Java Applets

—Casey Hopson, Stephen E. Ingram

Developing Professional Java Applets is a reference for the professional programmer who needs to develop real-world, business-oriented Java applets, not just animations and games. The book assumes a basic familiarity with Java and gets right down to the business of applying Java to professional development. This comprehensive guide to developing professional Java applets teaches how to create new Java applets for business, research, and education and is filled with extensive examples of real-world Java applets.

$49.99 USA, $67.99 CDN,
ISBN 1-57521-083-5, 560 pp.

Teach Yourself Web Publishing with HTML 3.2 in 14 Days, Professional Reference Edition

—Laura Lemay

This book is the updated edition of Lemay's previous bestseller, *Teach Yourself Web Publishing with HTML in 14 Days, Premier Edition*. In it, readers will find all the advanced topics and updates—including adding audio, video, and animation—to Web page creation.

This book includes a CD-ROM and explores the use of CGI scripts, tables, HTML 3.0, the Netscape and Internet Explorer extensions, Java applets and JavaScript, and VRML.

$59.99 USA, $81.95 CDN,
ISBN 1-57521-096-7, 1,104 pp.

Add to Your Sams.net Library Today
with the Best Books for Internet Technologies

ISBN	Quantity	Description of Item	Unit Cost	Total Cost
1-57521-069-X		Java Developer's Guide (Book/CD-ROM)	$49.99	
1-57521-030-4		Teach Yourself Java in 21 Days (Book/CD-ROM)	$39.99	
1-57521-143-2		Laura Lemay's Web Workshop: 3D Graphics and VRML 2 (Book/CD-ROM)	$39.99	
1-57521-125-4		Laura Lemay's Web Workshop: Graphics and Web Page Design (Book/CD-ROM)	$55.00	
1-57521-141-6		Laura Lemay's Web Workshop: JavaScript (Book/CD-ROM)	$39.99	
1-57521-149-1		Laura Lemay's Web Workshop: Microsoft FrontPage (Book/CD-ROM)	$39.99	
1-57521-083-5		Developing Professional Java Applets (Book/CD-ROM)	$49.99	
1-57521-096-7		Teach Yourself Web Publishing with HTML 3.2 in 14 Days, Professional Reference Edition (Book/CD-ROM)	$59.99	
		Shipping and Handling: See information below.		
		TOTAL		

Shipping and Handling: $4.00 for the first book, and $1.75 for each additional book. If you need to have it NOW, we can ship product to you in 24 hours for an additional charge of approximately $18.00, and you will receive your item overnight or in two days. Overseas shipping and handling adds $2.00. Prices subject to change. Call between 9:00 a.m. and 5:00 p.m. EST for availability and pricing information on latest editions.

201 W. 103rd Street, Indianapolis, Indiana 46290

1-800-428-5331 — Orders   1-800-835-3202 — FAX   1-800-858-7674 — Customer Service

Book ISBN 1-57521-270-6

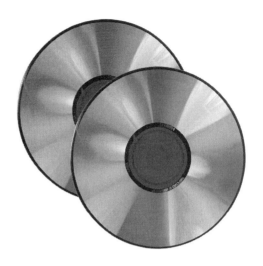

Installing the CD-ROM

The companion CD-ROM contains all the source code and project files developed by the author, plus an assortment of evaluation versions of third-party products. To install this software, please follow the steps appropriate to your system.

Windows 95 / NT 4 Installation Instructions

1. Insert the CD-ROM into your CD-ROM drive.
2. From the Windows 95 desktop, double-click on the My Computer icon.
3. Double-click on the icon representing your CD-ROM drive.
4. Double-click on the icon titled `setup.exe` to run the CD-ROM installation program.

Windows NT 3.51 Installation Instructions

1. Insert the CD-ROM into your CD-ROM drive.
2. From File Manager or Program Manager, choose Run from the File menu.
3. Type `<drive>:\SETUP` and press Enter, where `<drive>` corresponds to the drive letter of your CD-ROM drive. For example, if your CD-ROM drive is drive D:, type `D:\SETUP` and press Enter.
4. Follow the on-screen instructions.

Macintosh Installation Instructions

1. Insert the CD-ROM into your CD-ROM drive.
2. When an icon for the CD appears on your desktop, open the disc by double-clicking on its icon.
3. Double-click on the icon named `Guide to the CD-ROM` and follow the directions that appear on-screen.